2

TOEFL Writing 만점 수강생
다수 배출한 만점 강사의
노트테이킹, 패러프레이징,
템플릿 완벽 공개

3

기출 반영 실전 문제
집중 연습을 통해
실전 응용력이 상승하여
고득점 달성!

토플 정복을 위한 확실한 왕도!

입문 및 초급 [40~65점]

TOEFL Basic

한 권으로 토플 시험을 체계적으로 완벽히 이해하는
입문자들의 필독서

기본 및 중급 [60~85점]

TOEFL Intermediate (80+)

한 권으로 시원스쿨 토플 스타 강사진의
과목별 노하우 습득 및 80+ 달성

정규 및 고급 [80~115점]

TOEFL Reading   TOEFL Listening   TOEFL Speaking   TOEFL Writing

토플 기출 족보를 낱낱이 분석해 정리한 최빈출 주제 학습 + 스피킹/라이팅 만점 수강생 다수 배출한 만점 강사의 템플릿 완벽 공개

실전 및 심화 [90~120점]

TOEFL Actual Tests

실제 시험 진행과 동일한 TOEFL 고득점용
최종 마무리 실전 모의고사

어휘 정복

TOEFL Vocabulary

정답과 연관된 토플 기출 단어만을 수록한
진정한 토플 전문 보카 학습서

고득점을 위한 **토플 라이팅 기본서**

SIWONSCHOOL
TOEFL
Writing

시원스쿨어학연구소 · 박주영

시원스쿨 **LAB**

SIWONSCHOOL
TOEFL Writing

초판 1쇄 발행 2023년 1월 2일
개정 2쇄 발행 2023년 9월 15일

지은이 시원스쿨어학연구소, 박주영
펴낸곳 (주)에스제이더블유인터내셔널
펴낸이 양홍걸 이시원

홈페이지 www.siwonschool.com
주소 서울시 영등포구 국회대로74길 12 시원스쿨
교재 구입 문의 02)2014-8151
고객센터 02)6409-0878

ISBN 979-11-6150-733-0 13740
Number 1-110505-18180400-09

머리말

토플 시험 개정 반영,
시원스쿨 토플 TOEFL Writing!

시원스쿨어학연구소가 토플 왕초보를 위한 [시원스쿨 처음토플]과 토플 전용 어휘집인
[시원스쿨 토플 기출 보카]를 출간하고 나서, 독자분들로부터 다음 학습 단계에 대해 많은 문의가
쇄도했습니다. 이 문의에 대한 응답으로 중급 학습자를 위한 [TOEFL 80+], 시험을 앞둔 실전 학생들을 위한
[TOEFL Actual Tests]를 출간하였습니다. 또한 최신 토플 트렌드를 학습자들에게 제공하고자 [처음토플]
을 [TOEFL Basic]으로, [TOEFL 80+]를 [TOEFL Intermediate]으로 개정하였습니다.

그리고 이제, 시원스쿨 토플 라인업을 완성하는 과목별 토플 정규서가 세상에 나오게 되었습니다. 그동안
시원스쿨어학연구소는 학습자의 학습 편의와 효율성을 위해 한 권에 4과목을 다 아우르는 교재를 출간하여
왔습니다. 하지만 이번 정규라인은 가장 넓은 점수대(80~115점)를 대상으로 하고 있으며, 많은 문제 양을
풀어보며 점수를 올리는 것이 중요하기에, 기존과 달리 과목별 분권으로 나오게 되었습니다.

시원스쿨어학연구소는 과목별 전문성을 최대한 높이기 위해 오프라인 학원에서 인정받은 선생님들과 함께
도서 작업을 하였습니다. 선생님들은 본인들이 과목별 만점을 받은 것은 물론, 다수의 수강생들을 해당 과목
만점으로 이끈 전문가들로, 오프라인 강의에서 소수의 학생들에게만 공개하던 토플 학습 비법들을 이번 도서
에서 전격 공개하였습니다.

「시원스쿨 토플 TOEFL Writing」은

① 검증받은 만점 답안 템플릿을 제공합니다.
　　라이팅 만점 수강생을 다수 배출한 만점 강사의 노트테이킹, 브레인스토밍, 템플릿을 충실히 반영한 도서
　　로, 시중의 다른 토플 도서들과 달리, 선생님이 자신의 이름을 걸고 공개하는 신뢰성 높은 컨텐츠를 제공
　　합니다.

② 기출 반영 실전 문제를 집중 연습하도록 합니다.
　　토플 기출 족보를 낱낱이 분석해 정리한 다량의 기출 반영 실전 문제를 집중적으로 풀어봄으로써, 수험생
　　들은 실전 응용력이 상승하여 고득점 달성을 이룰 수 있습니다.

③ 다수의 전문가가 컨텐츠 제작에 참여하였습니다.
　　국내 유명 토플 선생님, 다수의 원어민 연구원들과 토플 고득점 연구원들이 도서 집필과 검수에 참여하여
　　대한민국 최고의 토플 컨텐츠를 제작하기 위해 심혈을 쏟았습니다.

아무쪼록 이 도서를 통해 영어 실력이 상승하고 토플 목표 점수를 달성하여 성공적인 유학의 길로 나아갈 수
있기를 진심으로 바랍니다.

시원스쿨어학연구소·박주영 드림

목차

| Chapter 01 Integrated Writing: Question 1

01 Introduction to Question 1

02 Strategies for Question 1

03 Practice Test

Chapter 02 Writing for an Academic Discussion: Question 2

01   Introduction to Question 2

02   Strategies for Question 2

03   Practice Test

Actual Tests

▪ **별책** 해설집: 해설, 모범 답안, 어휘 정리

이 책의 구성과 특징

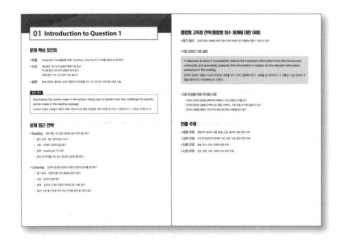

한눈에 핵심 파악

각 문제 유형의 핵심 정보를 일목요연하게 정리하여 최대한 빠르게 문제 유형을 이해할 수 있도록 한다.

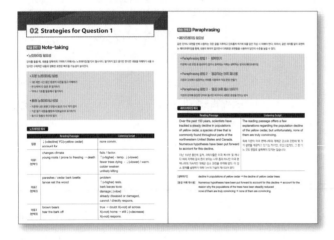

고득점 전략

라이팅 만점 수강생들을 다수 배출한 만점 강사의 노트테이킹, 브레인스토밍, 템플릿을 통해 고득점 답안을 작성하는 방법을 익힌다.

실전문제 집중 연습

토플 기출 족보를 낱낱이 분석해 정리한 다량의 기출 반영 실전 문제를 집중적으로 풀어보면, 실전 응용력이 상승하여 고득점 달성을 이룰 수 있다.

실전 모의고사

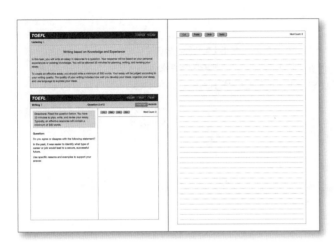

최신 개정 출제 경향이 반영된 실전 모의고사 2세트를 풀어보면서, 자신의 실력을 점검해 보고 앞에서 학습한 내용을 다시 한번 복습한다.

해설집

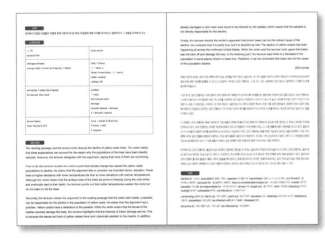

별책으로 제공하는 해설집에는 영문 해석과 노트테이킹 또는 브레인스토밍, 모범답안과 어휘 정리가 나와 있어서, 학습자들의 독학을 최대한 돕고 있다.

MP3 다운로드

토플 실제 시험과 동일한 스피드로 원어민 전문 성우들이 녹음한 음원을 시원스쿨 토플 홈페이지에서 무료로 다운받아 학습할 수 있다.

toefl.siwonschool.com ▶ 교재/MP3 ▶ 과목명 탭에서 『토플』 클릭 후 『TOEFL Writing』 찾기

토플 시험 소개

▪토플 시험

TOEFL(Test of English as a Foreign Language)은 미국 대학에서 수학할 비영어권 학생을 선별하기 위해 미국 ETS(Educational Testing Service)가 개발한 영어 능력 평가 시험이다. 즉, 미국을 비롯한 영어권 국가 대학에서 수학할 능력의 영어 수준이 되는지를 측정하는 시험인데, 보통 토플 시험이라고 하면 컴퓨터 인터넷 연결로 시험을 보는 iBT(internet-based test) TOEFL을 말한다.

▪시험 영역

영역	지문 및 문제 수	시간	배점
Reading	총 2개 지문 (한 지문에 10문제씩 출제)	약 35분	0~30점
Listening	총 2개 대화 + 강의 3개 (대화 하나에 5문제, 강의 하나에 6문제씩 출제)	약 36분	0~30점
Speaking	총 4문제 (독립형 1번, 통합형 2, 3, 4번)	약 16분	0~30점
Writing	총 2문제 (통합형 1번, 토론형 2번)	약 30분	0~30점
합계		약 2시간, 120점 만점	

▪2023년 7월 26일 이후 시험 변경 내용

1. Reading 또는 Listening에 나오던 더미 문제(점수에 포함되지 않는 연습 문제)가 사라짐
2. Reading 지문 세트가 3개에서 2개로 변경
3. Writing 독립형(Independent) 대신 토론형(Academic Discussion) 출제
4. 전체 시험 시간이 약 3시간에서 2시간으로 단축

▪시험 접수

접수 방법	▹ 시험일로부터 최소 7일 전 ETS 토플 홈페이지에서 접수
접수 비용	▹ 시험 접수 비용: US $220(2023년 7월 기준) ▹ 추가 접수 비용: US $260 　└ 시험일로부터 7일~2일 사이 접수 시 연체료(late fee) US $40 추가 ▹ 날짜 변경 비용: US $60 ▹ 재채점 비용: US $80 (Speaking/Writing 각각, Reading/Listening 불가) ▹ 추가 리포팅 비용: US $20 (건당) 　└ 시험 접수 시, 무료로 4개까지 성적 리포팅 받을 기관 선택 가능 ▹ 취소 성적 복원 비용: US $20
등록 취소	▹ ETS 토플 홈페이지에서 취소 가능 ▹ 응시료 환불은 시험 접수 후 7일 이내 100%, 응시 4일 전까지는 50%, 응시일로부터 3일 이내는 환불 불가
시험일	▹ 1년에 50회 정도로 보통 주말마다 실시되며, 실시 국가마다 차이가 있음
시험 장소	▹ 다수의 컴퓨터를 비치하고 있는 전국/전세계 교육기관 또는 ETS Test Center에서 시행 ▹ 집에서 Home Edition으로도 응시 가능

▪시험 당일 준비물

공인된 신분증(여권, 주민등록증, 운전면허증, 군인신분증 중 하나)의 원본을 반드시 지참한다. 참고로 필기도구 및 노트는 시험장에서 제공되는 것만 사용할 수 있기에 따로 준비할 필요는 없다.

▪성적 확인

시험 응시일로부터 약 6일 후에 온라인으로 성적이 공개된다. PDF 형식의 성적표는 온라인 성적 공개 2일 후부터 다운로드 가능하다. 성적표 유효기간은 시험 응시일로부터 2년이다.

TOEFL Writing 정복
학습 플랜

- 반드시 직접 답안을 작성하면서 학습한다. 자신이 직접 답안을 쓰지 않으면 문제를 풀어보지 않은 것과 같기에 그날 Writing 공부를 하지 않은 것이다.
- 교재를 끝까지 한 번 보고 나면 2회독에 도전한다. 같은 교재를 여러 번 읽을수록 훨씬 효과가 좋으니 다독하도록 한다.
- 혼자서 학습하기 어렵다면, 시원스쿨 토플 홈페이지(toefl.siwonschool.com)에서 토플 스타 강사진의 강의를 들으면 보다 쉽고 재미 있게 공부할 수 있다.

▪ 초고속 23일 완성 학습 플랜

[Integrated Writing과 Writing for an Academic Discussion 진도 함께 나가기]

1일	2일	3일	4일	5일
통합형 & 토론형 이론 학습 (실전문제 전)	통합형 & 토론형 실전문제 1	통합형 & 토론형 실전문제 2	통합형 & 토론형 실전문제 3	통합형 & 토론형 실전문제 4
6일	**7일**	**8일**	**9일**	**10일**
통합형 & 토론형 실전문제 5	통합형 & 토론형 실전문제 6	통합형 & 토론형 실전문제 7	통합형 & 토론형 실전문제 8	통합형 & 토론형 실전문제 9
11일	**12일**	**13일**	**14일**	**15일**
통합형 & 토론형 실전문제 10	통합형 & 토론형 실전문제 11	통합형 & 토론형 실전문제 12	통합형 & 토론형 실전문제 13	통합형 & 토론형 실전문제 14
16일	**17일**	**18일**	**19일**	**20일**
통합형 & 토론형 실전문제 15	통합형 & 토론형 실전문제 16	통합형 & 토론형 실전문제 17	통합형 & 토론형 실전문제 18	통합형 & 토론형 실전문제 19
21일	**22일**	**23일**		
통합형 & 토론형 실전문제 20	Actual Test 1	Actual Test 2		

▪45일 완성 학습 플랜

1일	2일	3일	4일	5일
통합형 이론 학습 (실전문제 전)	통합형 실전문제 1	통합형 실전문제 2	통합형 실전문제 3	통합형 실전문제 4

6일	7일	8일	9일	10일
통합형 실전문제 5	통합형 실전문제 6	통합형 실전문제 7	통합형 실전문제 8	통합형 실전문제 9

11일	12일	13일	14일	15일
통합형 실전문제 10	통합형 실전문제 11	통합형 실전문제 12	통합형 실전문제 13	통합형 실전문제 14

16일	17일	18일	19일	20일
동합형 실진문제 15	통합형 실전문제 16	통합형 실전문제 17	통합형 실전문제 18	통합형 실전문제 19

21일	22일	23일	24일	25일
통합형 실전문제 20	토론형 이론 학습 (실전문제 전)	토론형 실전문제 1	토론형 실전문제 2	토론형 실전문제 3

26일	27일	28일	29일	30일
토론형 실전문제 4	토론형 실전문제 5	토론형 실전문제 6	토론형 실전문제 7	토론형 실전문제 8

31일	32일	33일	34일	35일
토론형 실전문제 9	토론형 실전문제 10	토론형 실전문제 11	토론형 실전문제 12	토론형 실전문제 13

36일	37일	38일	39일	40일
토론형 실전문제 14	토론형 실전문제 15	토론형 실전문제 16	토론형 실전문제 17	토론형 실전문제 18

41일	42일	43일	44일	45일
토론형 실전문제 19	토론형 실전문제 20	Actual Test 1	Actual Test 2	총복습

toefl.siwonschool.com

Chapter

01

Integrated Writing:
Question 1

01 Introduction to Question 1

문제 핵심 포인트

- **유형**   Integrated Task(통합형 과제): Reading, Listening 추가 자료를 바탕으로 영작하기

- **시간**   3분 동안 250 단어 분량의 독해 지문 읽기
  약 2분 동안 250 단어 분량의 강의 듣기
  20분 동안 150~225 단어 이상 글쓰기

- **질문**   독해 지문과 대비되는 강의 진행자의 포인트를 150~225 단어로 20분 동안 글로 기술

질문 예시

Summarize the points made in the lecture, being sure to explain how they challenge the specific points made in the reading passage.

강의에서 언급된 요점들이 어떻게 독해 지문에 제시된 특정 주장들에 대해 의문을 제기하는지 설명하면서 그 내용을 요약해 보시오.

문제 접근 전략

- **Reading**   3분 제한 시간 동안 중요한 정보 찾아 필기하기

  ▷ 필기 준비 - 필기 종이 8칸 나누기

  ▷ 서론 - 주제와 지문의 입장 찾기

  ▷ 본론 - Reading의 근거 찾기

  ▷ 중요! 한 단락을 모두 읽고 중요한 정보만 필기하기

- **Listening**   강의의 중요한 정보와 지문과 연관된 정보를 필기하기

  ▷ 필기 준비 - 지문의 필기 칸 내용을 보면서 필기

  ▷ 서론 - 강의의 입장 찾기

  ▷ 본론 - 강의의 근거와 지문과 연관성 있는 부분 필기

  ▷ 중요! 지문 필기 칸에 이미 적은 단어를 중복 필기하지 않기

통합형 고득점 전략(통합형 점수 체계에 대한 이해)

■ **평가 원리**   강의의 중요 내용을 독해 지문의 관련 부분과 잘 연결했는지를 0~5점으로 평가

■ 5점 만점 평가 기준

A response at score 5 successfully selects the important information from the lecture and coherently and accurately presents this information in relation to the relevant information presented in the reading.

강의의 중요한 내용과 리딩과 연관된 내용을 조리 있게 연결해야 한다. 내용을 잘 정리하고 그 내용은 사실 정보의 내용을 왜곡하거나 부정확해서는 안된다.

■ 5점 만점을 위해 주의할 사항

- 지문과 강의의 입장을 정확하게 이해하고 그와 관련된 근거를 찾기
- 강의의 중요한 내용을 요약한다는 점을 기억하고, 지문 내용 추가에 공들이지 않기
- 강의의 내용을 재해석, 의미 부여 혹은 평가하는 내용을 담지 않기

빈출 주제

■ **생명 주제**   생명과학 분야로 식물, 동물, 곤충, 생리학, 영양 관련 주제

■ **과학 주제**   자연 및 환경과학 분야로 기상, 천문, 지질, 환경 관련 주제

■ **인류 주제**   예술, 역사, 건축, 인류학 관련 주제

■ **사회 주제**   경영, 경제, 규제, 사회적 이슈 관련 주제

02 Strategies for Question 1

학습 전략 1 Note-taking

▪노트테이킹 필요성

강의를 들을 때, 내용을 정확하게 기억하기 위해서는 노트테이킹(필기)이 필수이다. 필기하지 않고 듣기만 한다면 내용을 이해하기 쉬울 수 있지만 구체적인 내용과 정확한 표현은 빠뜨릴 가능성이 높아진다.

▪**지문 노트테이킹 방법**
- 3분 제한 시간 동안 충분히 지문을 읽고 이해하기
- 한 단락씩 다 읽은 후 필기하기
- 약어나 기호를 활용해서 필기하기

▪**음원 노트테이킹 방법**
- 지문에 나온 표현(고유명사 등)은 다시 적지 않기
- 지문 필기 내용을 활용하기(화살표로 표기하기)
- 동사나 형용사 위주의 필기

노트테이킹 예시

	Reading Passage	Listening Script
입장	↓ (=decline) YC(=yellow cedar) account for	none convin.
이유1 (반박1)	changes climate young roots / prone to freezing → death	fails / factor. ↑ (=higher) - temp. ↓ (=lower) fewer trees dying - ↓ (=lower) / warm. colder weaken unlikely killing
이유2 (반박2)	parasites / cedar bark beetle larvae eat the wood	problem ↑ (=higher) resis. bark leaves toxic damage ↓ (=low) already diseased or damaged, cannot / directly respons.
이유3 (반박3)	brown bears tear the bark off	true → doubt X(=not) all across X(=not) home → still ↓ (=decrease) X(=not) respons.

학습 전략 2 Paraphrasing

▪ 패러프레이징 필요성

같은 단어나 표현을 반복 사용하는 것은 글을 지루하고 단조롭게 하기에 토플 답안 작성 시 피해야 한다. 따라서, 같은 의미를 달리 표현하는 패러프레이징을 통해, 내용의 왜곡이 없으면서 다채로운 표현들을 사용하여 답안의 수준을 높일 수 있다.

> ### ▪ Paraphrasing 방법 1 – 생략하기
> 지문에 나온 문장 중 중요하지 않거나 중복되는 어휘는 생략하는 방식의 패러프레이징
>
> ### ▪ Paraphrasing 방법 2 – 등장하는 어휘 재사용
> 지문과 강의에서 등장하는 어휘를 사용하여 직접 문장 만들기
>
> ### ▪ Paraphrasing 방법 3 – 등장 어휘 품사 바꾸기
> 지문과 강의에 등장한 단어의 품사만 바꾸어서 새로운 문장을 만드는 방식

패러프레이징 예시

Reading Passage	Listening Script
Over the past 150 years, scientists have tracked a steady decline in populations of yellow cedar, a species of tree that is commonly found throughout parts of the northwestern United States and Canada. Numerous hypotheses have been put forward to account for this decline.	The reading passage offers a few explanations regarding the population decline of the yellow cedar, but unfortunately, none of them are truly convincing.
지난 150년 동안에 걸쳐, 과학자들은 미국 북서부 및 캐나다 여러 지역에 걸쳐 흔히 보이는 나무 종의 하나인 미국 편백나무의 지속적인 개체군 감소 과정을 추적해 왔다. 이 감소 문제를 설명하기 위해 다수의 가설이 제시되어 왔다.	독해 지문이 미국 편백나무의 개체군 감소와 관련해 몇 가지 설명을 제공하고 있기는 하지만, 유감스럽게도, 그 중 어느 것도 정말로 설득력이 있지는 않습니다.

[생략하기]   decline in populations of yellow cedar → the decline of yellow cedar trees

[등장 어휘 재사용]   Numerous hypotheses have been put forward to account for this decline → account for the reason why the populations of the trees have been steadily reduced
none of them are truly convincing → none of them are convincing.

Reading Passage	Listening Script
The first hypothesis centers on changes in climate as the main cause of the decline in yellow cedar populations. Seasonal temperatures have been changing in the regions where yellow cedars grow. As a result, the growth of the surface roots of the trees no longer begins in the early spring, but in the late winter. This change has a considerable impact on overall tree health. Because the young roots are sensitive to temperature change, they are prone to freezing during cold winter nights, and such root damage may eventually lead to the death of many trees.	First, there is the hypothesis about roots being damaged by cold temperatures. Well, the passage fails to point out one very important factor. At higher elevations, where the temperature is lower, there are far fewer trees dying than at lower elevations, where it is relatively warm. So, if the decline were due to freezing temperatures, we would see a larger number of trees dying at higher elevations. With that in mind, even if colder temperatures weaken the roots of the trees, it seems unlikely that this is what is killing the trees.
첫 번째 가설은 미국 편백나무 개체군의 감소에 대한 주된 원인으로서 기후 변화를 중심으로 한다. 미국 편백나무가 자라는 지역에서 계절적 기온이 변화하고 있다. 그 결과, 이 나무의 지표면 뿌리 성장이 더 이상 이른 봄에 시작되지 않고 늦은 겨울에 시작되고 있다. 이러한 변화는 나무의 전반적인 건강에 상당한 영향을 미치고 있다. 어린 뿌리가 기온 변화에 민감하기 때문에, 추운 겨울 밤에는 얼어붙기 쉬우며, 그러한 뿌리 손상은 결국 많은 나무의 죽음으로 이어질 수 있다.	첫 번째로, 추운 기온으로 인해 손상되는 뿌리에 관한 가설이 있습니다. 음, 독해 지문은 한 가지 아주 중요한 요인을 지적하지 못하고 있습니다. 기온이 더 낮은, 높은 고도에서는, 상대적으로 따뜻한, 더 낮은 고도에 비해 죽는 나무가 훨씬 더 적습니다. 따라서, 감소 문제가 차가운 기온 때문이라면, 고도가 더 높은 곳에서 더 많은 나무가 죽는 것을 보게 될 겁니다. 이를 감안하면, 설사 더 추운 기온이 나무의 뿌리를 약화시킨다 하더라도, 이것이 나무를 죽이고 있을 가능성은 없어 보입니다.

[등장 어휘 품사 바꾸기]   changes in climate as the main cause of the decline in yellow cedar populations
→ climate changes mainly cause yellow cedar populations to decline.

[등장 어휘 재사용]   fail, factor → fails to consider one important factor, an elevation
higher elevations, temperature. lower / fewer trees dying than at lower, warm. → Fewer trees at higher elevations with lower temperature die than at lower elevations with warmer temperature.

[생략하기]   Because the young roots are sensitive to temperature change,they are prone to freezing during cold winter nights, and such root damage may eventually lead to the death of many trees.
→ the surface roots of the trees are prone to freezing during the cold winter and eventually lead to the death

[등장 어휘 재사용]   colder, weaken / unlikely, killing
→ colder temperatures weaken the roots but it does not seem to kill the trees

아래는 통합형 에세이를 위한 기본틀(template)로, 글의 흐름에 따라 내용의 순서를 바꿀 수 있다.

입장	The reading passage and the lecture both discuss 토픽(공통주제). + The writer states that 지문의 입장. + However, the lecturer disagrees with the argument, saying that 강의의 입장.
이유1 [반박1]	First of all, the lecturer doubts the writer's point that 지문의 이유1. + He/She argues/claims that 강의의 반박1. + 강의의 내용 중 근거가 되는 내용 제시. + 지문과 강의의 내용 중 구체적으로 비교가 되는 부분. → Although the writer states that 지문의 구체적인 내용, the lecturer points out that 지문 내용과 관련된 강의의 구체적인 내용.
이유2 [반박2]	Secondly, the lecturer refutes the argument in the reading passage that 지문의 이유2. He/She states that 강의의 반박2. + 강의의 내용 중 근거가 되는 내용 제시. + 지문과 강의의 내용 중 구체적으로 비교가 되는 부분. → While the writer states that 지문의 구체적인 내용, the lecturer highlights that 지문 내용과 관련된 강의의 구체적인 내용. + In addition, 추가적으로 들어가야 할 강의의 구체적인 내용.
이유3 [반박3]	Finally, the lecturer doubts the writer's argument that 지문의 이유3. + He/She contends that 강의의 반박3. + 강의의 내용 중 근거가 되는 내용 제시. + 지문과 강의의 내용 중 구체적으로 비교가 되는 부분. → While the writer and the lecturer both agree that 지문의 구체적인 내용, in the listening part, the lecturer says 지문 내용과 관련된 강의의 구체적인 내용.

03 Practice Test

실전문제 1 – 생물 주제 (1)

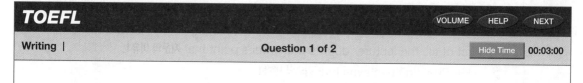

Over the past 150 years, scientists have tracked a steady decline in populations of yellow cedar, a species of tree that is commonly found throughout parts of the northwestern United States and Canada. Numerous hypotheses have been put forward to account for this decline.

The first hypothesis centers on changes in climate as the main cause of the decline in yellow cedar populations. Seasonal temperatures have been changing in the regions where yellow cedars grow. As a result, the growth of the surface roots of the trees no longer begins in the early spring, but in the late winter. This change has a considerable impact on overall tree health. Because the young roots are sensitive to temperature change, they are prone to freezing during cold winter nights, and such root damage may eventually lead to the death of many trees.

A second hypothesis is that parasites such as the cedar bark beetle are largely responsible for the decline. The larvae of cedar bark beetles are known to eat the wood of the trees, damaging them severely. Several cases have been documented where the beetles attacked yellow cedars so extensively that hundreds of trees died, so these parasites are certainly capable of causing a decrease in tree population.

A third hypothesis singles out brown bears as the cause of the decline. The bark of the yellow cedar is high in sugar and bears often tear the bark off with their claws to eat it. In fact, the sugar content of the yellow cedar bark is even higher than that of the forest berries that the bears regularly consume. While the stripping of the bark is unlikely to kill the trees outright, the feeding habits of the bears leave the trees in a vulnerable state, indirectly contributing to their decline.

Directions: You have 20 minutes to plan and write your response. Your response will be judged on the basis of the quality of your writing and on how well your response presents the points in the lecture and their relationship to the reading passage. Typically, an effective response will be 150 to 225 words.

Question: Summarize the points made in the lecture, being sure to explain how they challenge the specific points made in the reading passage.

Over the past 150 years, scientists have tracked a steady decline in populations of yellow cedar, a species of tree that is commonly found throughout parts of the northwestern United States and Canada. Numerous hypotheses have been put forward to account for this decline.

The first hypothesis centers on changes in climate as the main cause of the decline in yellow cedar populations. Seasonal temperatures have been changing in the regions where yellow cedars grow. As a result, the growth of the surface roots of the trees no longer begins in the early spring, but in the late winter. This change has a considerable impact on overall tree health. Because the young roots are sensitive to temperature change, they are prone to freezing during cold winter nights, and such root damage may eventually lead to the death of many trees.

A second hypothesis is that parasites such as the cedar bark beetle are largely responsible for the decline. The larvae of cedar bark beetles are known to eat the wood of the trees, damaging them severely. Several cases have been documented where the beetles attacked yellow cedars so extensively that hundreds of trees died, so these parasites are certainly capable of causing a decrease in tree population.

A third hypothesis singles out brown bears as the cause of the decline. The bark of the yellow cedar is high in sugar and bears often tear the bark off with their claws to eat it. In fact, the sugar content of the yellow cedar bark is even higher than that of the forest berries that the bears regularly consume. While the stripping of the bark is unlikely to kill the trees outright, the feeding habits of the bears leave the trees in a vulnerable state, indirectly contributing to their decline.

Cut   Paste   Undo   Redo   Word Count: 0

실전문제 2 - 생물 주제 (2)

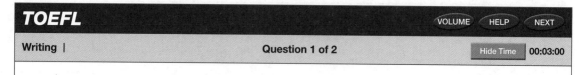

Genetically modified (GM) crops are produced using recombinant DNA technology that allows favorable genes to be transferred from one organism to another. The successful expression of transferred genes may have a variety of advantages in GM crops, such as increased growth rate or an ability to grow in harsh conditions. As such, this technology has several far-reaching benefits on a global scale.

First, GM crops can improve human health as they contain fewer potential allergens and higher levels of essential amino acids, essential fatty acids, vitamins, and minerals. They can also play a potential role in fighting malnutrition in developing countries where poor people rely heavily on single food sources such as rice for their diet. Typically, rice does not contain sufficient quantities of essential nutrients required to prevent malnutrition, but GM rice has a much higher nutritional value, making it more beneficial to human health.

Moreover, a direct benefit of GM crops is the reduction of pesticide applications. This means that farmers have less exposure to harmful chemicals, and there will be lower amounts of pesticide residues in food and feed crops. For example, insect resistance in GM maize has been achieved by transferring the gene for toxin creation from the bacterium, *Bacillus thuringiensis* (Bt). This toxin is commonly used as an insecticide in agriculture and is considered safe to use on food and feed crops. GM crops that have the ability to produce this toxin themselves require no additional pesticide application.

Lastly, due to the higher yield and lower production cost of GM crops, farmers who purchase GM seeds will benefit economically and produce more food at affordable prices. With more and more multinational GM seed companies emerging, it is getting easier for farmers in developing nations to purchase GM seeds and enjoy the financial benefits of GM crop cultivation.

TOEFL VOLUME

Writing | Question 1 of 2

Directions: You have 20 minutes to plan and write your response. Your response will be judged on the basis of the quality of your writing and on how well your response presents the points in the lecture and their relationship to the reading passage. Typically, an effective response will be 150 to 225 words.

Question: Summarize the points made in the lecture, being sure to explain how they challenge the specific points made in the reading passage.

Genetically modified (GM) crops are produced using recombinant DNA technology that allows favorable genes to be transferred from one organism to another. The successful expression of transferred genes may have a variety of advantages in GM crops, such as increased growth rate or an ability to grow in harsh conditions. As such, this technology has several far-reaching benefits on a global scale.

First, GM crops can improve human health as they contain fewer potential allergens and higher levels of essential amino acids, essential fatty acids, vitamins, and minerals. They can also play a potential role in fighting malnutrition in developing countries where poor people rely heavily on single food sources such as rice for their diet. Typically, rice does not contain sufficient quantities of essential nutrients required to prevent malnutrition, but GM rice has a much higher nutritional value, making it more beneficial to human health.

Moreover, a direct benefit of GM crops is the reduction of pesticide applications. This means that farmers have less exposure to harmful chemicals, and there will be lower amounts of pesticide residues in food and feed crops. For example, insect resistance in GM maize has been achieved by transferring the gene for toxin creation from the bacterium, *Bacillus thuringiensis* (Bt). This toxin is commonly used as an insecticide in agriculture and is considered safe to use on food and feed crops. GM crops that have the ability to produce this toxin themselves require no additional pesticide application.

Lastly, due to the higher yield and lower production cost of GM crops, farmers who purchase GM seeds will benefit economically and produce more food at affordable prices. With more and more multinational GM seed companies emerging, it is getting easier for farmers in developing nations to purchase GM seeds and enjoy the financial benefits of GM crop cultivation.

Cut   Paste   Undo   Redo   Word Count: 0

실전문제 3 – 생물 주제 (3)

Paleontologists recently uncovered 66-million-year-old fossilized remains of a Tyrannosaurus rex and were surprised to discover that the specimen still contained some actual living tissues. The find is virtually unprecedented, as fossils typically contain only minerals that have replaced an animal's tissues. The paleontologists made their groundbreaking discovery when they cracked open one of the fossilized bones and found what appeared to be the remains of collagen, red blood cells, and blood vessels inside the exposed cavity.

First, upon analyzing the inside of the broken bone, the scientists observed numerous hollow grooves that branched off in various directions. They concluded that these were likely the channels where blood vessels were once located in the bone. Closer inspection revealed a soft organic substance within the grooves. This caused much excitement among the scientists, as they believed it could be the remnants of the Tyrannosaurus rex's actual blood vessels.

Second, the scientists examined the interior structures of the bone using powerful microscopes, and they detected rounded particles that may once have been red blood cells. Further analysis showed the presence of iron within the spherical particles. Iron is critical to the transportation of oxygen by red blood cells. Furthermore, the center of each particle was dark red in color, and each particle was of comparable size to a red blood cell.

Third, another test indicated that collagen - a key component of living bone tissue - was still contained within the bone. This fibrous protein combines with other proteins to form a matrix that basically acts as a strong scaffolding inside living bones. So, its presence supported the notion that actual bone tissue still existed in the bone.

Directions: You have 20 minutes to plan and write your response. Your response will be judged on the basis of the quality of your writing and on how well your response presents the points in the lecture and their relationship to the reading passage. Typically, an effective response will be 150 to 225 words.

Question: Summarize the points made in the lecture, being sure to explain how they respond to the specific points made in the reading passage.

Paleontologists recently uncovered 66-million-year-old fossilized remains of a Tyrannosaurus rex and were surprised to discover that the specimen still contained some actual living tissues. The find is virtually unprecedented, as fossils typically contain only minerals that have replaced an animal's tissues. The paleontologists made their groundbreaking discovery when they cracked open one of the fossilized bones and found what appeared to be the remains of collagen, red blood cells, and blood vessels inside the exposed cavity.

First, upon analyzing the inside of the broken bone, the scientists observed numerous hollow grooves that branched off in various directions. They concluded that these were likely the channels where blood vessels were once located in the bone. Closer inspection revealed a soft organic substance within the grooves. This caused much excitement among the scientists, as they believed it could be the remnants of the Tyrannosaurus rex's actual blood vessels.

Second, the scientists examined the interior structures of the bone using powerful microscopes, and they detected rounded particles that may once have been red blood cells. Further analysis showed the presence of iron within the spherical particles. Iron is critical to the transportation of oxygen by red blood cells. Furthermore, the center of each particle was dark red in color, and each particle was of comparable size to a red blood cell.

Third, another test indicated that collagen - a key component of living bone tissue - was still contained within the bone. This fibrous protein combines with other proteins to form a matrix that basically acts as a strong scaffolding inside living bones. So, its presence supported the notion that actual bone tissue still existed in the bone.

Cut   Paste   Undo   Redo   Word Count: 0

실전문제 4 – 생물 주제 (4)

Among all of the marine species endangered by the fishing industry, sea turtles face the gravest threat. When turtles get tangled up in nets used by commercial shrimp-fishing boats, they are unable to swim to the surface for air. An invention called a turtle excluder device (TED) has been proposed as a solution to this problem. A TED is incorporated into the nets and functions by letting captured turtles escape through a door in the net. However, many people are opposed to the use of TEDs for a variety of reasons.

First, TEDs may not be as effective as other strategies when it comes to limiting the threat to sea turtles. One strategy that has been suggested is enforcing a law that restricts the amount of time that nets can be kept underwater. Before a set time limit, the shrimp boats must raise their nets so that any turtles tangled up in them can have a chance to breathe and subsequently be set free by the shrimp boat crew.

Second, certain species of threatened sea turtles grow to such large sizes that TEDs would be ineffective in saving them. For instance, adult leatherbacks and loggerheads - two of the largest species of sea turtles - would be unable to pass through the relatively narrow escape passages that are installed in TEDs. So, for these species, even nets equipped with TEDs would still pose a threat to adult turtles.

Third, many shrimp boat captains report that turtles rarely ever get tangled up in nets. Fishing industry data indicate that a shrimp boat may accidentally catch only around ten turtles per year. Moreover, TEDs will reduce the amount of shrimp that the boats can catch, and the profitability of each catch, because a significant number of them will escape through the turtle passage. Shrimpers argue that this is a disproportionately high cost to pay just to save ten turtles per year.

TOEFL

Writing | **Question 1 of 2**

Directions: You have 20 minutes to plan and write your response. Your response will be judged on the basis of the quality of your writing and on how well your response presents the points in the lecture and their relationship to the reading passage. Typically, an effective response will be 150 to 225 words.

Question: Summarize the points made in the lecture, being sure to explain how they respond to the specific points made in the reading passage.

Among all of the marine species endangered by the fishing industry, sea turtles face the gravest threat. When turtles get tangled up in nets used by commercial shrimp-fishing boats, they are unable to swim to the surface for air. An invention called a turtle excluder device (TED) has been proposed as a solution to this problem. A TED is incorporated into the nets and functions by letting captured turtles escape through a door in the net. However, many people are opposed to the use of TEDs for a variety of reasons.

First, TEDs may not be as effective as other strategies when it comes to limiting the threat to sea turtles. One strategy that has been suggested is enforcing a law that restricts the amount of time that nets can be kept underwater. Before a set time limit, the shrimp boats must raise their nets so that any turtles tangled up in them can have a chance to breathe and subsequently be set free by the shrimp boat crew.

Second, certain species of threatened sea turtles grow to such large sizes that TEDs would be ineffective in saving them. For instance, adult leatherbacks and loggerheads - two of the largest species of sea turtles - would be unable to pass through the relatively narrow escape passages that are installed in TEDs. So, for these species, even nets equipped with TEDs would still pose a threat to adult turtles.

Third, many shrimp boat captains report that turtles rarely ever get tangled up in nets. Fishing industry data indicate that a shrimp boat may accidentally catch only around ten turtles per year. Moreover, TEDs will reduce the amount of shrimp that the boats can catch, and the profitability of each catch, because a significant number of them will escape through the turtle passage. Shrimpers argue that this is a disproportionately high cost to pay just to save ten turtles per year.

Cut   Paste   Undo   Redo   Word Count: 0

실전문제 5 - 생물 주제 (5)

The underwater noises, or songs, produced by whales can be useful for tracking the migration routes of whale populations. Scientists studying whale song recently discovered one unique whale who makes noises like no other whale. To be specific, the song of this whale is unique in that it is sung at 52 hertz, which is an unusually high pitch or frequency. The 52-hertz whale's distinctive ability confused scientists when they first detected the animal, but they have now put forward a few theories to explain the phenomenon.

The first theory is that the 52-hertz whale may simply be a highly uncommon species of whale - a species that has so few members that scientists have never encountered one before. The species may have been more abundant in the past, but its population may have significantly declined. The 52-hertz whale may even be the only surviving member of the species.

A second theory is that two different species of whales mated and gave birth to the 52-hertz whale, making it a hybrid. It is known that when different species of whales mate, it is common for the offspring to carry species-specific traits from both parents. The 52-hertz whale may sing in such a distinctive way because its song is a unique combination of its parents' songs, rather than being the same as either parent's song.

A third theory is that the hearing of the 52-hertz whale is impaired in some way. Whales learn to make sounds in the same way that humans do - by mimicking the sounds they hear. When humans are born with hearing deficiencies, their speech develops very differently from that of someone with perfect hearing. So, the 52-hertz whale may sing uniquely because it has been unable to hear the songs produced by other whales.

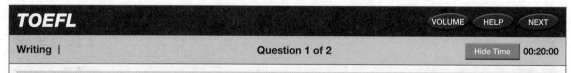

Directions: You have 20 minutes to plan and write your response. Your response will be judged on the basis of the quality of your writing and on how well your response presents the points in the lecture and their relationship to the reading passage. Typically, an effective response will be 150 to 225 words.

Question: Summarize the points made in the lecture, being sure to explain how they challenge the specific points made in the reading passage.

The underwater noises, or songs, produced by whales can be useful for tracking the migration routes of whale populations. Scientists studying whale song recently discovered one unique whale who makes noises like no other whale. To be specific, the song of this whale is unique in that it is sung at 52 hertz, which is an unusually high pitch or frequency. The 52-hertz whale's distinctive ability confused scientists when they first detected the animal, but they have now put forward a few theories to explain the phenomenon.

The first theory is that the 52-hertz whale may simply be a highly uncommon species of whale - a species that has so few members that scientists have never encountered one before. The species may have been more abundant in the past, but its population may have significantly declined. The 52-hertz whale may even be the only surviving member of the species.

A second theory is that two different species of whales mated and gave birth to the 52-hertz whale, making it a hybrid. It is known that when different species of whales mate, it is common for the offspring to carry species-specific traits from both parents. The 52-hertz whale may sing in such a distinctive way because its song is a unique combination of its parents' songs, rather than being the same as either parent's song.

A third theory is that the hearing of the 52-hertz whale is impaired in some way. Whales learn to make sounds in the same way that humans do - by mimicking the sounds they hear. When humans are born with hearing deficiencies, their speech develops very differently from that of someone with perfect hearing. So, the 52-hertz whale may sing uniquely because it has been unable to hear the songs produced by other whales.

Cut   Paste   Undo   Redo   Word Count: 0

실전문제 6 – 과학 주제 (1)

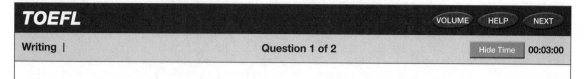

These days, many people in the United States are pushing the idea that ethanol fuel, which is made from feedstocks such as potatoes and barley, should be used instead of gasoline. However, opponents of the idea say that ethanol is not a suitable alternative to gasoline for the following reasons.

First, when it comes to price, ethanol fuel simply cannot compete with gasoline. You see, to the average consumer, it might appear that the current prices of ethanol and gasoline are almost identical, but you have to take tax subsidies into account. Over the past 25 years, the US government has been helping ethanol producers by providing them with over $10 million in tax subsidies. If this assistance were ever to end, which seems likely, we would see a significant rise in the price of ethanol.

Second, gasoline-related environmental issues such as global warming will not be solved by an increase in ethanol fuel use. When it is burned as a fuel, ethanol releases carbon dioxide - a greenhouse gas that traps heat in the atmosphere - in the same way that traditional gasoline does. So, in the end, there are no environmental benefits from using ethanol fuel as opposed to gasoline.

Third, if the production of ethanol fuel were to rise, it would result in a significant decrease in the number of plants available for food. In particular, a large proportion of the feedstocks that farm animals rely on would likely be diverted for use in the ethanol fuel industry. Even if ethanol fuel were to make up just 15 percent of motor fuel in the US, its production could require up to 65 percent of feedstocks such as corn or grain. This would drastically reduce the availability of animal feedstocks, leading to a decline in the agricultural industry.

◀» Writing_6

TOEFL

VOLUME

Writing | Question 1 of 2

Directions: You have 20 minutes to plan and write your response. Your response will be judged on the basis of the quality of your writing and on how well your response presents the points in the lecture and their relationship to the reading passage. Typically, an effective response will be 150 to 225 words.

Question: Summarize the points made in the lecture, being sure to explain how they cast doubt on the specific points made in the reading passage.

These days, many people in the United States are pushing the idea that ethanol fuel, which is made from feedstocks such as potatoes and barley, should be used instead of gasoline. However, opponents of the idea say that ethanol is not a suitable alternative to gasoline for the following reasons.

First, when it comes to price, ethanol fuel simply cannot compete with gasoline. You see, to the average consumer, it might appear that the current prices of ethanol and gasoline are almost identical, but you have to take tax subsidies into account. Over the past 25 years, the US government has been helping ethanol producers by providing them with over $10 million in tax subsidies. If this assistance were ever to end, which seems likely, we would see a significant rise in the price of ethanol.

Second, gasoline-related environmental issues such as global warming will not be solved by an increase in ethanol fuel use. When it is burned as a fuel, ethanol releases carbon dioxide - a greenhouse gas that traps heat in the atmosphere - in the same way that traditional gasoline does. So, in the end, there are no environmental benefits from using ethanol fuel as opposed to gasoline.

Third, if the production of ethanol fuel were to rise, it would result in a significant decrease in the number of plants available for food. In particular, a large proportion of the feedstocks that farm animals rely on would likely be diverted for use in the ethanol fuel industry. Even if ethanol fuel were to make up just 15 percent of motor fuel in the US, its production could require up to 65 percent of feedstocks such as corn or grain. This would drastically reduce the availability of animal feedstocks, leading to a decline in the agricultural industry.

Cut   Paste   Undo   Redo   Word Count: 0

실전문제 7 - 과학 주제 (2)

Many parts of the Earth underwent a period of extremely low temperature from approximately 1350 to 1900 CE, and this time period is often referred to as the Little Ice Age. During that time, glaciers expanded significantly, and many regions experienced very harsh winter weather. Scientists have debated the possible causes of the Little Ice Age, and several theories have been proposed.

First, a disruption of ocean currents may have been responsible for the temperature decrease. Just before the beginning of the Little Ice Age, many of the planet's glaciers melted during a period of uncharacteristically warm weather. This resulted in a large volume of cold fresh water being released into the Gulf Stream, a vast ocean current that directly influences the climate of the Earth. Some scientists think that the Gulf Stream was temporarily disrupted by this rapid influx of fresh water, triggering the Little Ice Age.

Second, the cooling of the climate may have indirectly resulted from a decline in human populations. Prior to the Little Ice Age, and in its earliest stage, the human population shrunk due to various factors such as disease and war. Land that was once used for agriculture was abandoned, and new forests began to grow in the fields. These trees removed large amounts of carbon dioxide from the atmosphere, and this had a cooling effect on the Earth.

Third, some scientists think that the Little Ice Age may have been caused by the eruption of numerous volcanoes at the beginning of that time period. Volcanic eruptions involve the emission of massive, thick clouds of ash and gas into the atmosphere, and these can form a barrier that sunlight cannot pass through. If sunlight was unable to penetrate the ash cloud and reach the Earth's surface, global temperatures would have gone down.

TOEFL VOLUME

Writing | Question 1 of 2

Directions: You have 20 minutes to plan and write your response. Your response will be judged on the basis of the quality of your writing and on how well your response presents the points in the lecture and their relationship to the reading passage. Typically, an effective response will be 150 to 225 words.

Question: Summarize the points made in the lecture, being sure to explain how they cast doubt on the specific points made in the reading passage.

Cut   Paste   Undo   Redo   Word Count: 0

Many parts of the Earth underwent a period of extremely low temperature from approximately 1350 to 1900 CE, and this time period is often referred to as the Little Ice Age. During that time, glaciers expanded significantly, and many regions experienced very harsh winter weather. Scientists have debated the possible causes of the Little Ice Age, and several theories have been proposed.

First, a disruption of ocean currents may have been responsible for the temperature decrease. Just before the beginning of the Little Ice Age, many of the planet's glaciers melted during a period of uncharacteristically warm weather. This resulted in a large volume of cold fresh water being released into the Gulf Stream, a vast ocean current that directly influences the climate of the Earth. Some scientists think that the Gulf Stream was temporarily disrupted by this rapid influx of fresh water, triggering the Little Ice Age.

Second, the cooling of the climate may have indirectly resulted from a decline in human populations. Prior to the Little Ice Age, and in its earliest stage, the human population shrunk due to various factors such as disease and war. Land that was once used for agriculture was abandoned, and new forests began to grow in the fields. These trees removed large amounts of carbon dioxide from the atmosphere, and this had a cooling effect on the Earth.

Third, some scientists think that the Little Ice Age may have been caused by the eruption of numerous volcanoes at the beginning of that time period. Volcanic eruptions involve the emission of massive, thick clouds of ash and gas into the atmosphere, and these can form a barrier that sunlight cannot pass through. If sunlight was unable to penetrate the ash cloud and reach the Earth's surface, global temperatures would have gone down.

실전문제 8 - 과학 주제 (3)

Hail can cause serious damage to fields of crops, and this is becoming an increasing problem for farmers throughout the United States. These small pellets of ice form in clouds instead of rain and snow and can fall from the sky with great force, destroying plants and even buildings. A method called cloud seeding has been developed in an effort to make clouds produce harmless rain or snow instead of hail. To do this, airplanes fly over storm clouds and spray them with silver iodide. Several sources indicate that cloud seeding is an effective way to protect crops from hail.

First, several countries in Asia have provided evidence that confirms the effectiveness of cloud seeding. For example, in some large cities, the method has been successfully used to regulate precipitation. The success seen in these urban areas suggests that it would be equally successful when used in the rural United States to protect crops and farming facilities.

Second, some local reports also show that cloud seeding is highly beneficial. An extensive research study was recently carried out in the Midwest of the United States. The researchers kept track of crop damage due to hail in various agricultural regions and compared the differences. They found that there was a significant reduction in hail damage in the areas that use the cloud seeding method compared with those that do not.

Third, laboratory experiments have also strongly indicated that cloud seeding is effective. Scientists have consistently shown that by adding silver iodide to cold water vapor, they can create light snow rather than hail pellets, which would typically form when water vapor reaches the freezing point.

Directions: You have 20 minutes to plan and write your response. Your response will be judged on the basis of the quality of your writing and on how well your response presents the points in the lecture and their relationship to the reading passage. Typically, an effective response will be 150 to 225 words.

Question: Summarize the points made in the lecture, being sure to explain how they respond to the specific points made in the reading passage.

Hail can cause serious damage to fields of crops, and this is becoming an increasing problem for farmers throughout the United States. These small pellets of ice form in clouds instead of rain and snow and can fall from the sky with great force, destroying plants and even buildings. A method called cloud seeding has been developed in an effort to make clouds produce harmless rain or snow instead of hail. To do this, airplanes fly over storm clouds and spray them with silver iodide. Several sources indicate that cloud seeding is an effective way to protect crops from hail.

First, several countries in Asia have provided evidence that confirms the effectiveness of cloud seeding. For example, in some large cities, the method has been successfully used to regulate precipitation. The success seen in these urban areas suggests that it would be equally successful when used in the rural United States to protect crops and farming facilities.

Second, some local reports also show that cloud seeding is highly beneficial. An extensive research study was recently carried out in the Midwest of the United States. The researchers kept track of crop damage due to hail in various agricultural regions and compared the differences. They found that there was a significant reduction in hail damage in the areas that use the cloud seeding method compared with those that do not.

Third, laboratory experiments have also strongly indicated that cloud seeding is effective. Scientists have consistently shown that by adding silver iodide to cold water vapor, they can create light snow rather than hail pellets, which would typically form when water vapor reaches the freezing point.

Cut   Paste   Undo   Redo   Word Count: 0

실전문제 9 - 과학 주제 (4)

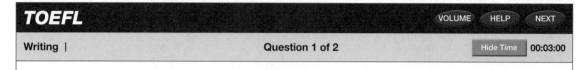

Natural reefs are found throughout the world's oceans, and these sturdy structures serve as perfect habitats for a wide variety of marine organisms. Plants and sponges cling to the rigid reefs, providing shelter and food for countless fish. In order to increase the amount of habitat available to fish, companies involved in the fishing industry are building artificial reefs in coastal waters. Such reefs - built from various metal objects and concrete - offer many advantages.

The world is filled with unwanted objects and materials, and artificial reefs are an excellent way to recycle them. Some reefs are constructed from old vehicle tires and appliances which would typically be hard to dispose of safely. The objects are thoroughly cleaned to ensure that they pose no harm to marine life or the environment once they are placed in the ocean. So, artificial reefs help us to reuse old materials in an environmentally friendly and affordable manner.

Next, small-scale fishing companies can benefit financially from private artificial reefs. When such companies construct their own artificial reefs in locations that are unknown to larger companies, they improve their economic competitiveness. At the moment, smaller companies struggle to have a presence in fertile fishing grounds that are overrun by the larger companies. By building new fishing areas, smaller firms can improve their catch sizes and help their local communities to prosper.

Finally, artificial reefs may help fish populations to grow by offering a safe habitat. Several reports from fishing companies have indicated that fish populations are showing steady growth around artificial reefs, and this benefits not only the ecosystem but also the local economy in places where fishing is prevalent.

TOEFL   VOLUME

Writing | **Question 1 of 2**

Directions: You have 20 minutes to plan and write your response. Your response will be judged on the basis of the quality of your writing and on how well your response presents the points in the lecture and their relationship to the reading passage. Typically, an effective response will be 150 to 225 words.

Question: Summarize the points made in the lecture, being sure to explain how they challenge the specific points made in the reading passage.

Natural reefs are found throughout the world's oceans, and these sturdy structures serve as perfect habitats for a wide variety of marine organisms. Plants and sponges cling to the rigid reefs, providing shelter and food for countless fish. In order to increase the amount of habitat available to fish, companies involved in the fishing industry are building artificial reefs in coastal waters. Such reefs - built from various metal objects and concrete - offer many advantages.

The world is filled with unwanted objects and materials, and artificial reefs are an excellent way to recycle them. Some reefs are constructed from old vehicle tires and appliances which would typically be hard to dispose of safely. The objects are thoroughly cleaned to ensure that they pose no harm to marine life or the environment once they are placed in the ocean. So, artificial reefs help us to reuse old materials in an environmentally friendly and affordable manner.

Next, small-scale fishing companies can benefit financially from private artificial reefs. When such companies construct their own artificial reefs in locations that are unknown to larger companies, they improve their economic competitiveness. At the moment, smaller companies struggle to have a presence in fertile fishing grounds that are overrun by the larger companies. By building new fishing areas, smaller firms can improve their catch sizes and help their local communities to prosper.

Finally, artificial reefs may help fish populations to grow by offering a safe habitat. Several reports from fishing companies have indicated that fish populations are showing steady growth around artificial reefs, and this benefits not only the ecosystem but also the local economy in places where fishing is prevalent.

Cut   Paste   Undo   Redo   Word Count: 0

실전문제 10 - 과학 주제 (5)

These days, it is common for people to discuss the possibility of sending humans to colonize Earth's Moon, or even Mars, but there may be a better option. Our solar system is home to hundreds of thousands of massive asteroids, and they may be more suitable targets for human colonization for a variety of reasons.

For a start, asteroids are often abundant sources of rare metals and elements that would fetch a high price back on Earth due to their scarcity here. By colonizing an asteroid, we would gain access to huge deposits of gold and platinum among other materials, and these could be mined and transported back to Earth. The profits gained through asteroid mining could greatly offset the costs of the colonization expedition.

Another reason that asteroids are prime targets for colonization is that they are relatively close to Earth. Every year, many of them briefly enter Earth's orbit, and some of them even come closer to our planet than the Moon! So, it would be fairly easy and affordable to reach these particular asteroids, especially compared with the dangerous and expensive 4-year round-trip that would be required to take colonists to Mars and back.

Last, due to their relatively small size compared to moons and planets, asteroids have lower gravity. This makes it a lot easier to land a spacecraft on an asteroid than on the Moon or Mars, where the gravity would strongly pull the spacecraft down toward the surface. The same is true when it comes to leaving the asteroid - lower gravity facilitates take-off. So, a spacecraft visiting and returning from an asteroid would require less fuel, and would be able to carry more equipment for the colonization operation.

TOEFL

VOLUME

Writing | Question 1 of 2

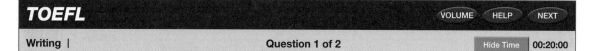

Directions: You have 20 minutes to plan and write your response. Your response will be judged on the basis of the quality of your writing and on how well your response presents the points in the lecture and their relationship to the reading passage. Typically, an effective response will be 150 to 225 words.

Question: Summarize the points made in the lecture, being sure to explain how they cast doubt on the specific points made in the reading passage.

These days, it is common for people to discuss the possibility of sending humans to colonize Earth's Moon, or even Mars, but there may be a better option. Our solar system is home to hundreds of thousands of massive asteroids, and they may be more suitable targets for human colonization for a variety of reasons.

For a start, asteroids are often abundant sources of rare metals and elements that would fetch a high price back on Earth due to their scarcity here. By colonizing an asteroid, we would gain access to huge deposits of gold and platinum among other materials, and these could be mined and transported back to Earth. The profits gained through asteroid mining could greatly offset the costs of the colonization expedition.

Another reason that asteroids are prime targets for colonization is that they are relatively close to Earth. Every year, many of them briefly enter Earth's orbit, and some of them even come closer to our planet than the Moon! So, it would be fairly easy and affordable to reach these particular asteroids, especially compared with the dangerous and expensive 4-year round-trip that would be required to take colonists to Mars and back.

Last, due to their relatively small size compared to moons and planets, asteroids have lower gravity. This makes it a lot easier to land a spacecraft on an asteroid than on the Moon or Mars, where the gravity would strongly pull the spacecraft down toward the surface. The same is true when it comes to leaving the asteroid - lower gravity facilitates take-off. So, a spacecraft visiting and returning from an asteroid would require less fuel, and would be able to carry more equipment for the colonization operation.

Cut   Paste   Undo   Redo   Word Count: 0

실전문제 11 - 인류 주제 (1)

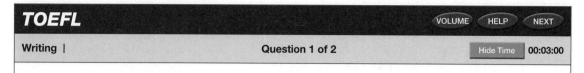

In 1936, during the construction of a railway line in Iraq, workers unearthed a set of distinctive clay jars. These artifacts were passed on to an archaeologist, who determined that they were approximately 2,200 years old and proposed that they were used as ancient batteries. Inside each jar was an iron rod surrounded by copper wire. As demonstrated by the archaeologist, when the jars were filled with certain liquids, they produced an electric current. However, it is unlikely that these jars actually functioned as electric batteries when they were created.

First of all, virtually identical clay jars were also discovered at an archaeological site nearby, where the city of Seleucia once stood. These jars also contained the copper wire, but testing determined that the jars were used for storing religious scrolls, not for any electrical purpose. Since the jars believed to be batteries have the same design as those found at Seleucia, it is likely that they were also used for storing scrolls, which would naturally have degraded and vanished over the past 2,200 years.

Second, if the jars were used to generate electricity, we would expect them to be connected to additional metal wires or some other means of conducting electricity. However, nothing was found in the vicinity of the jars that could be used to transfer an electrical current.

Finally, why would people who lived 2,200 years ago require electricity in the first place? They had no objects or machines that were powered by electricity. So, the clay jars that people believe are batteries would have been useless to the ancient people who built them.

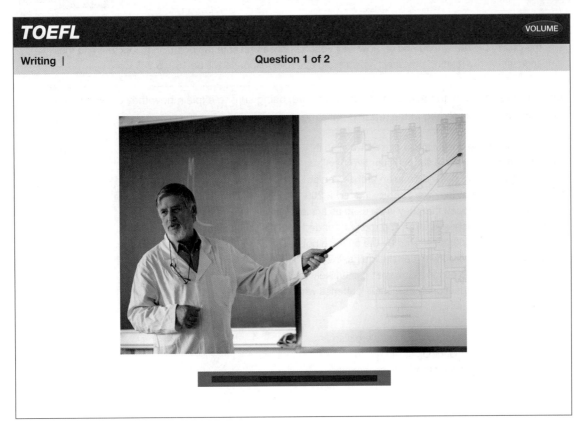

Directions: You have 20 minutes to plan and write your response. Your response will be judged on the basis of the quality of your writing and on how well your response presents the points in the lecture and their relationship to the reading passage. Typically, an effective response will be 150 to 225 words.

Question: Summarize the points made in the lecture, being sure to explain how they challenge the specific theories presented in the reading passage.

In 1936, during the construction of a railway line in Iraq, workers unearthed a set of distinctive clay jars. These artifacts were passed on to an archaeologist, who determined that they were approximately 2,200 years old and proposed that they were used as ancient batteries. Inside each jar was an iron rod surrounded by copper wire. As demonstrated by the archaeologist, when the jars were filled with certain liquids, they produced an electric current. However, it is unlikely that these jars actually functioned as electric batteries when they were created.

First of all, virtually identical clay jars were also discovered at an archaeological site nearby, where the city of Seleucia once stood. These jars also contained the copper wire, but testing determined that the jars were used for storing religious scrolls, not for any electrical purpose. Since the jars believed to be batteries have the same design as those found at Seleucia, it is likely that they were also used for storing scrolls, which would naturally have degraded and vanished over the past 2,200 years.

Second, if the jars were used to generate electricity, we would expect them to be connected to additional metal wires or some other means of conducting electricity. However, nothing was found in the vicinity of the jars that could be used to transfer an electrical current.

Finally, why would people who lived 2,200 years ago require electricity in the first place? They had no objects or machines that were powered by electricity. So, the clay jars that people believe are batteries would have been useless to the ancient people who built them.

Cut   Paste   Undo   Redo   Word Count: 0

실전문제 12 – 인류 주제 (2)

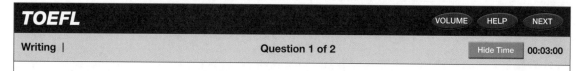

The "Voynich manuscript" is a handwritten book that was acquired by Wilfrid Voynich, a Polish book dealer, in 1912. The book contains text and beautiful drawings that were produced on vellum, a material used for manuscripts before the use of paper became common. It has similarities with manuscripts produced in the 15th and 16th centuries, but it is written in a mysterious text that no one has ever been able to decipher. The true origin of the Voynich manuscript has been the subject of several theories.

One theory is that Voynich himself wrote the manuscript in an effort to create a modern fake of a potentially valuable book. Through his work as an antiquarian and book dealer, Voynich certainly knew how to produce a very convincing centuries-old manuscript. So, many people have theorized that he intended to sell his modern fake to a collector of old manuscripts for a large sum of money.

Another theory is that the strange text in the manuscript has no real meaning and was devised by Edward Kelley in order to trick wealthy book collectors. Kelley was notorious in the sixteenth century for traveling around Europe and conning rich people out of their money, normally by making them believe he possessed magical powers. He may have written the book as part of another scam to take somebody's money. He likely would have convinced that person that the random letters that make up the text were actually the words of a spell or incantation.

Finally, according to some other theories, the manuscript may be a legitimate book that was written in a complex code to keep the true meaning of the text hidden from those who did not have the key to decipher it. Some have speculated that it was written in the 16th century by Anthony Ascham, a botanist and physician, because many of the illustrations contained within it bear similarities with those in one of Ascham's published works, *A Little Herbal*.

TOEFL

VOLUME

Writing | **Question 1 of 2**

Directions: You have 20 minutes to plan and write your response. Your response will be judged on the basis of the quality of your writing and on how well your response presents the points in the lecture and their relationship to the reading passage. Typically, an effective response will be 150 to 225 words.

Question: Summarize the points made in the lecture, being sure to explain how they respond to the specific points made in the reading passage.

Cut   Paste   Undo   Redo   Word Count: 0

The "Voynich manuscript" is a handwritten book that was acquired by Wilfrid Voynich, a Polish book dealer, in 1912. The book contains text and beautiful drawings that were produced on vellum, a material used for manuscripts before the use of paper became common. It has similarities with manuscripts produced in the 15th and 16th centuries, but it is written in a mysterious text that no one has ever been able to decipher. The true origin of the Voynich manuscript has been the subject of several theories.

One theory is that Voynich himself wrote the manuscript in an effort to create a modern fake of a potentially valuable book. Through his work as an antiquarian and book dealer, Voynich certainly knew how to produce a very convincing centuries-old manuscript. So, many people have theorized that he intended to sell his modern fake to a collector of old manuscripts for a large sum of money.

Another theory is that the strange text in the manuscript has no real meaning and was devised by Edward Kelley in order to trick wealthy book collectors. Kelley was notorious in the sixteenth century for traveling around Europe and conning rich people out of their money, normally by making them believe he possessed magical powers. He may have written the book as part of another scam to take somebody's money. He likely would have convinced that person that the random letters that make up the text were actually the words of a spell or incantation.

Finally, according to some other theories, the manuscript may be a legitimate book that was written in a complex code to keep the true meaning of the text hidden from those who did not have the key to decipher it. Some have speculated that it was written in the 16th century by Anthony Ascham, a botanist and physician, because many of the illustrations contained within it bear similarities with those in one of Ascham's published works, *A Little Herbal*.

실전문제 13 – 인류 주제 (3)

In 1909, an experienced explorer named Robert E. Peary embarked on an expedition in an attempt to be the first person to visit the North Pole. Upon his return, Peary claimed that he did in fact reach the North Pole on April 7th, and his apparent success brought him international fame. While the truth of his claim has been disputed by many historians over the years, there are three arguments that support Peary's assertion that he successfully made it to the North Pole.

First, according to Peary, he and his party set off from Ellesmere Island and arrived at the North Pole in just 37 days. Many people have disputed this claim, noting that even expedition teams using modern technology take longer than that to traverse the same route. In 2005, however, a British explorer named Tom Avery traveled from Ellesmere Island to the North Pole in four hours less than Peary. Moreover, Avery made sure to replicate the conditions of Peary's journey, using the same number of dogs and the same type of dogsled, so his success indicates that Peary's claim may well have been truthful.

Second, Peary took several photographs during his expedition, and some of these pictures help to support his claim. Scientists analyzed Peary's photos and determined the Sun's position in each photo based on the length of shadows. By cross-referencing the positional data with historical charts of the Sun's position, they determined that the photos were very likely taken at the North Pole on April 7th.

Third, a committee was assembled by the National Geographic Society to investigate all of Peary's expedition documentation and equipment. The committee members concluded that Peary's field notes and equipment usage seemed legitimate and that he had indeed been successful in his efforts to reach the North Pole.

Directions: You have 20 minutes to plan and write your response. Your response will be judged on the basis of the quality of your writing and on how well your response presents the points in the lecture and their relationship to the reading passage. Typically, an effective response will be 150 to 225 words.

Question: Summarize the points made in the lecture, being sure to explain how they cast doubt on the specific points made in the reading passage.

In 1909, an experienced explorer named Robert E. Peary embarked on an expedition in an attempt to be the first person to visit the North Pole. Upon his return, Peary claimed that he did in fact reach the North Pole on April 7th, and his apparent success brought him international fame. While the truth of his claim has been disputed by many historians over the years, there are three arguments that support Peary's assertion that he successfully made it to the North Pole.

First, according to Peary, he and his party set off from Ellesmere Island and arrived at the North Pole in just 37 days. Many people have disputed this claim, noting that even expedition teams using modern technology take longer than that to traverse the same route. In 2005, however, a British explorer named Tom Avery traveled from Ellesmere Island to the North Pole in four hours less than Peary. Moreover, Avery made sure to replicate the conditions of Peary's journey, using the same number of dogs and the same type of dogsled, so his success indicates that Peary's claim may well have been truthful.

Second, Peary took several photographs during his expedition, and some of these pictures help to support his claim. Scientists analyzed Peary's photos and determined the Sun's position in each photo based on the length of shadows. By cross-referencing the positional data with historical charts of the Sun's position, they determined that the photos were very likely taken at the North Pole on April 7th.

Third, a committee was assembled by the National Geographic Society to investigate all of Peary's expedition documentation and equipment. The committee members concluded that Peary's field notes and equipment usage seemed legitimate and that he had indeed been successful in his efforts to reach the North Pole.

Cut   Paste   Undo   Redo   Word Count: 0

실전문제 14 - 인류 주제 (4)

Before Giacomo Casanova died in 1798, he wrote an extensive memoir that included many amazing tales from his life. Casanova was known for socializing with a wide range of high-profile people during the 18th century, so his memoir has become an important document that gives an insight into European society at the time. However, many critics have argued that the events, adventures, and relationships described in the memoir were fabricated by Casanova in an effort to make his life seem more interesting than it actually was.

One aspect of the memoir that has been highly doubted by critics is Casanova's account of his escape from prison in Venice, Italy. According to Casanova, he managed to break through the ceiling of his cell and climb onto the roof, before fleeing into the night. While it is an entertaining anecdote, critics believe that it is very far-fetched. They point out that Casanova was friends with very powerful people in Venice, including politicians, so it is more likely that he had someone offer a bribe to the prison warden to secure his freedom.

Another part of Casanova's memoir that has been disputed is the way he describes his lifestyle while living in Switzerland. According to Casanova, he was extraordinarily wealthy at that time, throwing lavish parties and betting huge sums of money while gambling. But, recent evidence has emerged that indicates he had to take out numerous loans from a local moneylender. So, critics argue that Casanova would never have needed to borrow money if he had been as rich as he claimed to be in his memoir.

Finally, there is a lot of skepticism regarding the conversations with the famous writer Voltaire that Casanova describes in his memoir. There is evidence that Voltaire and Casanova were indeed acquaintances, but critics doubt that Casanova could have remembered their conversations in such vivid detail and written about them decades after they occurred. They suspect that Casanova greatly embellished his simple conversations with Voltaire in his memoir, because the level of detail seems highly suspicious.

Directions: You have 20 minutes to plan and write your response. Your response will be judged on the basis of the quality of your writing and on how well your response presents the points in the lecture and their relationship to the reading passage. Typically, an effective response will be 150 to 225 words.

Question: Summarize the points made in the lecture, being sure to explain how they respond to the specific points made in the reading passage.

Before Giacomo Casanova died in 1798, he wrote an extensive memoir that included many amazing tales from his life. Casanova was known for socializing with a wide range of high-profile people during the 18th century, so his memoir has become an important document that gives an insight into European society at the time. However, many critics have argued that the events, adventures, and relationships described in the memoir were fabricated by Casanova in an effort to make his life seem more interesting than it actually was.

One aspect of the memoir that has been highly doubted by critics is Casanova's account of his escape from prison in Venice, Italy. According to Casanova, he managed to break through the ceiling of his cell and climb onto the roof, before fleeing into the night. While it is an entertaining anecdote, critics believe that it is very far-fetched. They point out that Casanova was friends with very powerful people in Venice, including politicians, so it is more likely that he had someone offer a bribe to the prison warden to secure his freedom.

Another part of Casanova's memoir that has been disputed is the way he describes his lifestyle while living in Switzerland. According to Casanova, he was extraordinarily wealthy at that time, throwing lavish parties and betting huge sums of money while gambling. But, recent evidence has emerged that indicates he had to take out numerous loans from a local moneylender. So, critics argue that Casanova would never have needed to borrow money if he had been as rich as he claimed to be in his memoir.

Finally, there is a lot of skepticism regarding the conversations with the famous writer Voltaire that Casanova describes in his memoir. There is evidence that Voltaire and Casanova were indeed acquaintances, but critics doubt that Casanova could have remembered their conversations in such vivid detail and written about them decades after they occurred. They suspect that Casanova greatly embellished his simple conversations with Voltaire in his memoir, because the level of detail seems highly suspicious.

Cut   Paste   Undo   Redo   Word Count: 0

실전문제 15 – 인류 주제 (5)

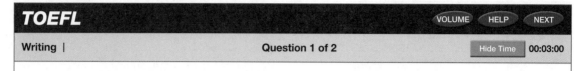

Sometime during the 12th century, massive stone buildings were constructed in the settlements of Chaco Canyon in the US state of New Mexico. These "great houses," as they have become known, stand up to four stories tall and include hundreds of rooms. Although there is still no consensus on the purpose of such buildings, three main theories have been put forward.

The first theory is that the buildings were used as venues for special ceremonies. Archaeologists unearthed a large number of fractured pots that had been buried near one of the buildings, known as Pueblo Alto. They concluded that the pots were evidence that Pueblo Alto served as an important site for ceremonial gatherings. It is known that Native American cultures did engage in such ceremonies, so it is assumed that the Chaco people ate meals together at these events and then discarded the empty food pots afterwards.

Another theory contends that the buildings were simply housing for hundreds of the Chaco people. Proponents of this theory argue that architecture in the Southwest regions of the US has obviously evolved directly from the great houses of the Chaco. For instance, people have been living in large "apartment-style" buildings in Taos, New Mexico for centuries, and these bear an uncanny resemblance to the large structures in Chaco Canyon.

A third theory argues that the Chaco "great houses" were used to store important crops such as maize. Maize was a staple food for the Chaco people, who would store the grain for several months and use it to prepare a wide variety of foods. All of this grain needed to be stored somewhere suitable to ensure that it didn't spoil, and the great houses would have been ideal storage buildings for that purpose.

Directions: You have 20 minutes to plan and write your response. Your response will be judged on the basis of the quality of your writing and on how well your response presents the points in the lecture and their relationship to the reading passage. Typically, an effective response will be 150 to 225 words.

Question: Summarize the points made in the lecture, being sure to explain how they cast doubt on the specific points made in the reading passage.

Cut   Paste   Undo   Redo   Word Count: 0

Sometime during the 12th century, massive stone buildings were constructed in the settlements of Chaco Canyon in the US state of New Mexico. These "great houses," as they have become known, stand up to four stories tall and include hundreds of rooms. Although there is still no consensus on the purpose of such buildings, three main theories have been put forward.

The first theory is that the buildings were used as venues for special ceremonies. Archaeologists unearthed a large number of fractured pots that had been buried near one of the buildings, known as Pueblo Alto. They concluded that the pots were evidence that Pueblo Alto served as an important site for ceremonial gatherings. It is known that Native American cultures did engage in such ceremonies, so it is assumed that the Chaco people ate meals together at these events and then discarded the empty food pots afterwards.

Another theory contends that the buildings were simply housing for hundreds of the Chaco people. Proponents of this theory argue that architecture in the Southwest regions of the US has obviously evolved directly from the great houses of the Chaco. For instance, people have been living in large "apartment-style" buildings in Taos, New Mexico for centuries, and these bear an uncanny resemblance to the large structures in Chaco Canyon.

A third theory argues that the Chaco "great houses" were used to store important crops such as maize. Maize was a staple food for the Chaco people, who would store the grain for several months and use it to prepare a wide variety of foods. All of this grain needed to be stored somewhere suitable to ensure that it didn't spoil, and the great houses would have been ideal storage buildings for that purpose.

실전문제 16 - 사회 주제 (1)

These days, there is a push to make forestry practices more ecologically sustainable. In an effort to encourage wood companies to recycle materials and use fewer resources, a committee has been set up to issue certification to companies that meet specific ecological standards. By receiving this certification, companies can label their products as "eco-certified," which can give them an edge over their uncertified competitors. Although many companies around the world have improved their practices in order to receive the certification, American companies are reluctant to do the same, for several reasons.

First off, if a company wishes to receive certification, it must pay to have the certification committee investigate its business practices. As a result, it will probably need to raise the prices of its wood products to offset this expense. This puts the company at a disadvantage, because consumers in the United States are highly influenced by price and are unlikely to pay more for certified wood products instead of cheaper uncertified options. Therefore, maintaining low prices is more important to American wood companies than receiving eco-certification.

Second, some people argue that, in order to remain competitive, American wood companies must keep up with foreign wood companies by adopting the same new ecological practices, but this claim is inaccurate. American wood companies market and sell the vast majority of their products in the domestic market, so pursuing certification in order to compete with foreign companies makes little sense. Moreover, the huge American consumer base is more interested in the quality of the products rather than how they were made.

Third, in America, consumers are constantly inundated with advertising and industry buzzwords, so there is a high chance that they will not be impressed by the "eco-certified" label. Almost all products are labeled as being "eco-friendly" or "new and improved" in some way - even low-quality products - so American consumers have lost trust in this type of marketing claim. As a result, they are increasingly wary of purchasing products that bear such labels.

■) Writing_16

TOEFL VOLUME

Writing | **Question 1 of 2**

Directions: You have 20 minutes to plan and write your response. Your response will be judged on the basis of the quality of your writing and on how well your response presents the points in the lecture and their relationship to the reading passage. Typically, an effective response will be 150 to 225 words.

Question: Summarize the points made in the lecture, being sure to explain how they cast doubt on the specific points made in the reading passage.

Cut   Paste   Undo   Redo   Word Count: 0

These days, there is a push to make forestry practices more ecologically sustainable. In an effort to encourage wood companies to recycle materials and use fewer resources, a committee has been set up to issue certification to companies that meet specific ecological standards. By receiving this certification, companies can label their products as "eco-certified," which can give them an edge over their uncertified competitors. Although many companies around the world have improved their practices in order to receive the certification, American companies are reluctant to do the same, for several reasons.

First off, if a company wishes to receive certification, it must pay to have the certification committee investigate its business practices. As a result, it will probably need to raise the prices of its wood products to offset this expense. This puts the company at a disadvantage, because consumers in the United States are highly influenced by price and are unlikely to pay more for certified wood products instead of cheaper uncertified options. Therefore, maintaining low prices is more important to American wood companies than receiving eco-certification.

Second, some people argue that, in order to remain competitive, American wood companies must keep up with foreign wood companies by adopting the same new ecological practices, but this claim is inaccurate. American wood companies market and sell the vast majority of their products in the domestic market, so pursuing certification in order to compete with foreign companies makes little sense. Moreover, the huge American consumer base is more interested in the quality of the products rather than how they were made.

Third, in America, consumers are constantly inundated with advertising and industry buzzwords, so there is a high chance that they will not be impressed by the "eco-certified" label. Almost all products are labeled as being "eco-friendly" or "new and improved" in some way - even low-quality products - so American consumers have lost trust in this type of marketing claim. As a result, they are increasingly wary of purchasing products that bear such labels.

실전문제 17 – 사회 주제 (2)

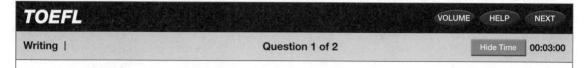

In the United States, particularly in the northwestern region, forests suffer tremendous damage each year due to storms and forest fires. Salvage logging is a practice that is used to deal with the destruction left behind by these natural disasters. The dead trees are removed from the destroyed areas and used for lumber and various wood products. The practice of salvage logging is beneficial both environmentally and economically for several reasons.

First, if dead trees are left alone after a natural disaster, they can have a negative impact on the environment. The decaying wood serves as an ideal habitat for insects like the spruce bark beetle. If populations of such insects are allowed to thrive, they will eventually infest nearby healthy trees, causing further damage to forests. Salvage logging ensures that this rotten wood is cleared, preventing unchecked insect infestation and maintaining the health of the undamaged trees in the forest.

Second, the local economy can be boosted by salvage logging. Forests are vital to a wide range of industries, so forest fires and severe storms can cause major economic problems for a large number of businesses. In some cases, however, even trees that have been damaged by natural disasters can still provide enough wood to meet the production needs of many companies. Moreover, more workers are required for salvage logging than for standard logging practices, so it has the added advantage of creating more employment opportunities for local workers.

Third, there is the issue of wasted space. When a natural disaster decimates a forest, the area is left littered with dead trees. These trees, if they are left alone, take several years to decompose, and this severely limits the space available for new trees. By removing the dead trees through salvage logging, space immediately becomes available for new vegetation, and this allows the affected area to regrow and recover from the disaster at a much quicker rate.

Directions: You have 20 minutes to plan and write your response. Your response will be judged on the basis of the quality of your writing and on how well your response presents the points in the lecture and their relationship to the reading passage. Typically, an effective response will be 150 to 225 words.

Question: Summarize the points made in the lecture, being sure to explain how they cast doubt on the specific points made in the reading passage.

Cut   Paste   Undo   Redo   Word Count: 0

In the United States, particularly in the northwestern region, forests suffer tremendous damage each year due to storms and forest fires. Salvage logging is a practice that is used to deal with the destruction left behind by these natural disasters. The dead trees are removed from the destroyed areas and used for lumber and various wood products. The practice of salvage logging is beneficial both environmentally and economically for several reasons.

First, if dead trees are left alone after a natural disaster, they can have a negative impact on the environment. The decaying wood serves as an ideal habitat for insects like the spruce bark beetle. If populations of such insects are allowed to thrive, they will eventually infest nearby healthy trees, causing further damage to forests. Salvage logging ensures that this rotten wood is cleared, preventing unchecked insect infestation and maintaining the health of the undamaged trees in the forest.

Second, the local economy can be boosted by salvage logging. Forests are vital to a wide range of industries, so forest fires and severe storms can cause major economic problems for a large number of businesses. In some cases, however, even trees that have been damaged by natural disasters can still provide enough wood to meet the production needs of many companies. Moreover, more workers are required for salvage logging than for standard logging practices, so it has the added advantage of creating more employment opportunities for local workers.

Third, there is the issue of wasted space. When a natural disaster decimates a forest, the area is left littered with dead trees. These trees, if they are left alone, take several years to decompose, and this severely limits the space available for new trees. By removing the dead trees through salvage logging, space immediately becomes available for new vegetation, and this allows the affected area to regrow and recover from the disaster at a much quicker rate.

실전문제 18 - 사회 주제 (3)

Great Britain has been intermittently occupied by settlers for hundreds of thousands of years. Countless ruins and ancient artifacts, ranging from tools to decorative art, have been unearthed and dated back to the Stone Age, the Bronze Age, the Iron Age, and later time periods. However, throughout the 20th century, archaeology was a science that failed to reach its true potential in Great Britain, because it faced many obstacles.

First, pursuing a career in archaeology was an incredibly difficult thing to do. Employment opportunities for budding archaeologists were occasionally offered through universities and the government, but these were in short supply. As a result, many people who had hoped to make a living as archaeologists were forced to branch off onto different career paths, while some worked as part-time amateurs on archaeological projects for little or no pay.

Second, the large number of construction projects that took place in the 20th century resulted in the loss of many historical artifacts. Starting in the 1950s, Britain experienced a population boom, so many of its cities and towns underwent rapid development and expansion. Construction workers often accidentally uncovered archaeologically significant ruins and artifacts. Unfortunately, in most cases, these were either discarded or destroyed in order to proceed with construction as quickly as possible.

Third, there was not enough funding available for archaeological expeditions. During the twentieth century, archaeology was financially supported primarily through grants issued by government agencies. These grants only allowed archaeologists to investigate a few key sites of interest, while thousands of other potentially significant archaeological projects were left unfunded. Moreover, as government priorities shifted, funding for archaeologists decreased even further.

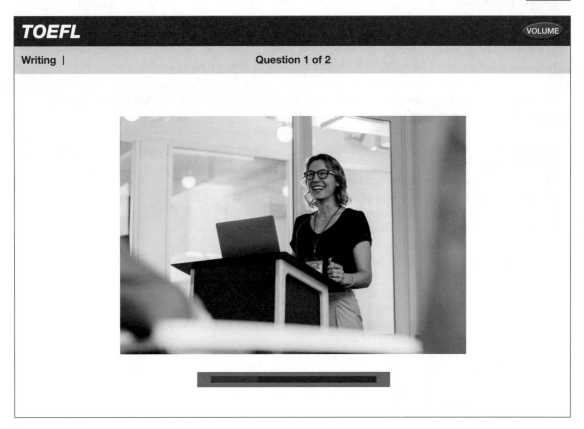

Directions: You have 20 minutes to plan and write your response. Your response will be judged on the basis of the quality of your writing and on how well your response presents the points in the lecture and their relationship to the reading passage. Typically, an effective response will be 150 to 250 words.

Question: Summarize the points made in the lecture, being sure to explain how the new guidelines helped to address the specific problems discussed in the reading passage.

Great Britain has been intermittently occupied by settlers for hundreds of thousands of years. Countless ruins and ancient artifacts, ranging from tools to decorative art, have been unearthed and dated back to the Stone Age, the Bronze Age, the Iron Age, and later time periods. However, throughout the 20th century, archaeology was a science that failed to reach its true potential in Great Britain, because it faced many obstacles.

First, pursuing a career in archaeology was an incredibly difficult thing to do. Employment opportunities for budding archaeologists were occasionally offered through universities and the government, but these were in short supply. As a result, many people who had hoped to make a living as archaeologists were forced to branch off onto different career paths, while some worked as part-time amateurs on archaeological projects for little or no pay.

Second, the large number of construction projects that took place in the 20th century resulted in the loss of many historical artifacts. Starting in the 1950s, Britain experienced a population boom, so many of its cities and towns underwent rapid development and expansion. Construction workers often accidentally uncovered archaeologically significant ruins and artifacts. Unfortunately, in most cases, these were either discarded or destroyed in order to proceed with construction as quickly as possible.

Third, there was not enough funding available for archaeological expeditions. During the twentieth century, archaeology was financially supported primarily through grants issued by government agencies. These grants only allowed archaeologists to investigate a few key sites of interest, while thousands of other potentially significant archaeological projects were left unfunded. Moreover, as government priorities shifted, funding for archaeologists decreased even further.

Cut   Paste   Undo   Redo   Word Count: 0

실전문제 19 – 사회 주제 (4)

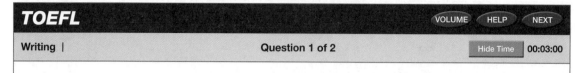

It is a sad fact that rhinoceroses are still being hunted illegally for their horns, even though the sale of rhinoceros horns is illegal all over the world. Rhino horns remain extremely valuable on the black market, often being sold for tens of thousands of dollars per kilogram, and rising demand for them has already led to one species of rhino becoming extinct due to poaching. If nothing is done to protect rhinos, many more species will eventually go extinct. People have suggested several ways to address this issue.

The first way is to make government sales of rhinoceros horns legal. In some countries, governments arrest hundreds of poachers and confiscate the horns they took from rhinos. If governments were allowed to legally sell the huge number of horns they accumulate, they would do so at reasonable prices. This would drive down the market price of rhino horns and make poaching less profitable. This in turn would result in a decline in poaching, giving endangered rhino populations a chance to recover.

The second way is for rhinos to be "dehorned" by trained professionals. By removing the horns of rhinos living in the wild, we could greatly reduce the chance of them being targeted by poachers. Assuming that proper medical equipment and drugs are used, the dehorning procedure can be carried out quickly and painlessly. This approach was attempted on a limited basis in the early 1990s, and none of the rhinos who had their horns removed were hunted by poachers.

The third way is to educate the public. Rhino horn is very commonly used as a medicinal ingredient, as many consumers believe it to have various health benefits. However, there is no scientific evidence that this is true. In fact, rhino horns are primarily composed of keratin, the same material that is found in human fingernails and hair. If we could educate consumers so that they understand keratin has no medicinal value and offers no health benefits, the demand for rhino horn products would drastically decrease.

TOEFL

VOLUME

Writing | 　　　　　　　　　　　　　Question 1 of 2

Directions: You have 20 minutes to plan and write your response. Your response will be judged on the basis of the quality of your writing and on how well your response presents the points in the lecture and their relationship to the reading passage. Typically, an effective response will be 150 to 225 words.

Question: Summarize the points made in the lecture, being sure to explain how they challenge the specific points made in the reading passage.

It is a sad fact that rhinoceroses are still being hunted illegally for their horns, even though the sale of rhinoceros horns is illegal all over the world. Rhino horns remain extremely valuable on the black market, often being sold for tens of thousands of dollars per kilogram, and rising demand for them has already led to one species of rhino becoming extinct due to poaching. If nothing is done to protect rhinos, many more species will eventually go extinct. People have suggested several ways to address this issue.

The first way is to make government sales of rhinoceros horns legal. In some countries, governments arrest hundreds of poachers and confiscate the horns they took from rhinos. If governments were allowed to legally sell the huge number of horns they accumulate, they would do so at reasonable prices. This would drive down the market price of rhino horns and make poaching less profitable. This in turn would result in a decline in poaching, giving endangered rhino populations a chance to recover.

The second way is for rhinos to be "dehorned" by trained professionals. By removing the horns of rhinos living in the wild, we could greatly reduce the chance of them being targeted by poachers. Assuming that proper medical equipment and drugs are used, the dehorning procedure can be carried out quickly and painlessly. This approach was attempted on a limited basis in the early 1990s, and none of the rhinos who had their horns removed were hunted by poachers.

The third way is to educate the public. Rhino horn is very commonly used as a medicinal ingredient, as many consumers believe it to have various health benefits. However, there is no scientific evidence that this is true. In fact, rhino horns are primarily composed of keratin, the same material that is found in human fingernails and hair. If we could educate consumers so that they understand keratin has no medicinal value and offers no health benefits, the demand for rhino horn products would drastically decrease.

Cut   Paste   Undo   Redo   Word Count: 0

실전문제 20 - 사회 주제 (5)

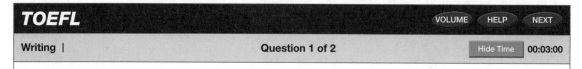

In Canada, most workers normally spend 8 hours a day for 5 days a week at their jobs. However, many of them are pushing for a 4-day week and are even willing to get paid less in order to do so. A national policy requiring companies to give their employees the option of working a 4-day workweek for 4/5 (80%) of their normal salary would be beneficial to the economy overall as well as the individual companies and the employees who choose to take advantage of that option.

A shortened workweek would increase profits for companies because workers would be more rested and focused, and as a result, they would be less likely to make errors while they work. Recruiting more staff to ensure that the same amount of work gets done would not lead to additional payroll costs because the 4-day staff would only be paid at 4/5 of the normal rate. In the end, companies would have less staff who are overworked and prone to making errors, for the same total sum of money, which would increase company profits.

For the country in general, one of the primary benefits of this option being made available would be reduced unemployment rates. If large numbers of full-time employees reduced their working hours, the remainder of their workload would have to be covered by others. Therefore, for every 4 employees who choose the 80% week, a new employee could be hired at the same reduced 4/5 rate.

Finally, having the option of a 4-day workweek would be more beneficial for individual employees. Those who could afford to accept the lower salary in exchange for more personal time throughout the week could improve their quality of life by spending more time with family and friends, pursuing private interests, or just simply enjoying hobbies.

Directions: You have 20 minutes to plan and write your response. Your response will be judged on the basis of the quality of your writing and on how well your response presents the points in the lecture and their relationship to the reading passage. Typically, an effective response will be 150 to 225 words.

Question: Summarize the points made in the lecture, being sure to explain how they challenge the specific points presented in the reading passage.

In Canada, most workers normally spend 8 hours a day for 5 days a week at their jobs. However, many of them are pushing for a 4-day week and are even willing to get paid less in order to do so. A national policy requiring companies to give their employees the option of working a 4-day workweek for 4/5 (80%) of their normal salary would be beneficial to the economy overall as well as the individual companies and the employees who choose to take advantage of that option.

A shortened workweek would increase profits for companies because workers would be more rested and focused, and as a result, they would be less likely to make errors while they work. Recruiting more staff to ensure that the same amount of work gets done would not lead to additional payroll costs because the 4-day staff would only be paid at 4/5 of the normal rate. In the end, companies would have less staff who are overworked and prone to making errors, for the same total sum of money, which would increase company profits.

For the country in general, one of the primary benefits of this option being made available would be reduced unemployment rates. If large numbers of full-time employees reduced their working hours, the remainder of their workload would have to be covered by others. Therefore, for every 4 employees who choose the 80% week, a new employee could be hired at the same reduced 4/5 rate.

Finally, having the option of a 4-day workweek would be more beneficial for individual employees. Those who could afford to accept the lower salary in exchange for more personal time throughout the week could improve their quality of life by spending more time with family and friends, pursuing private interests, or just simply enjoying hobbies.

Cut   Paste   Undo   Redo   Word Count: 0

toefl.siwonschool.com

Chapter

02

Writing for an Academic Discussion: Question 2

01 Introduction to Question 2

문제 핵심 포인트

- **유형**   Writing for an Academic Discussion(토론형 과제): 온라인 토론 주제에 참여하여, 자신의 주장을 논리적으로 영작하기
- **시간**   10분 동안 100단어 이상 글쓰기
- **질문**   다양한 아카데믹 주제의 토론에 자신의 의견 작성하기

질문 예시

지시사항

Your professor is teaching a class on sociology. Write a post responding to the professor's question.

In your response, you should do the following.
- Express and support your opinion.
- Make a contribution to the discussion in your own words.

An effective response will contain at least 100 words.

Dr. Brown

질문 배경

In next week's class, we are going to read some materials on how watching television programs affect people's lives. Afterwards, you will engage in a short class discussion. To prepare, I would like for you to think and write about the following topic:

In your opinion, in what ways – whether positive or negative – does watching television affect people?   **질문**

두 학생의 의견 댓글

Julie

I think the main effect that watching television can have on people is reducing physical activity. Most people sit still or lie down instead of being active when they watch television. For example, if children spend their free time watching television instead of playing outside, they are at great risk of becoming overweight.

Peter

In my opinion, a positive effect television has on people is that it helps them to experience more things. There are many great travel shows and nature documentaries on television. Through these programs, people can experience things they otherwise couldn't. I recently watched a documentary about wildlife in Costa Rica, and I thought it was very informative.

| Cut | Paste | Undo | Redo | | Word Count: 0 |

나의 의견 댓글 적는 공간

문제 접근 전략

- **생략하기**   시험 화면 속 Directions(지시사항) 부분은 고정된 내용이기 때문에 실제 시험 상황에서는 수업 이름만 확인 후 읽기 생략

- **논제 포인트 잡기**   토론 주제와 학생들의 의견들을 빠르게 읽어내려가며, 주제에서 논하고자 하는 포인트 기억하기

- **나의 의견 생각하기**   제시된 학생들의 의견을 반복하는 것이 아니라 언급되지 않은 나만의 이유 1가지 생각하기

- **참고하면 좋은 아이디어 키워드**

아이디어가 바로 떠오르지 않을 때는 아래 키워드와 연관지어 생각해보기!

- easy(convenient, accessible)   예 smartphones – easy access to information
- money(finance)   예 working from home – saving money
- health
- safety(a social security system)
- danger
- a better work and life balance
- good memories
- education

토론형 고득점 전략(토론형 점수 체계에 대한 이해)

- **평가원리**   온라인 토론에 완벽하게 기여하며, 적절하고 구체적인 근거와 예시, 다양한 문장 구조와 어휘를 정확하게 사용

- **5점 만점 평가 기준**

- The response is a relevant and very clearly expressed contribution to the online discussion
  답변이 온라인 토론에 대한 관련성이 높고 매우 명확하게 표현되어 토론에 기여

- Relevant and well-elaborated explanations, exemplifications, and/or details
  관련성 있고 정교한 근거, 예시 및/또는 세부 사항

- Effective use of a variety of syntactic structures and precise, idiomatic word choice
  다양한 구문 구조의 효과적인 사용과 정확한 관용어 선택

- Almost no lexical or grammatical errors
  어휘 또는 문법 오류가 거의 완벽

02 Strategies for Question 2

학습전략 1 표현 반복 피하기

▪ 표현 반복 피하기 필요성

100단어 조금 넘는 짧은 글에서 표현을 반복하면 좋은 점수를 받기 어렵다. 예시를 작성할 때 구체적인 묘사를 하려고 노력하면, 표현 반복을 피할 수 있다.

표현 반복 피하기 예시

[질문] What are your thoughts on remote work? Do you think it's beneficial or not?

　여러분은 원격 근무에 대해 어떻게 생각하나요? 원격 근무가 유익하다고 생각하나요, 그렇지 않다고 생각하나요?

[나의 의견] remote work의 장점

　　　이유: save money

　　　예시: London – countryside, saving transportation and housing costs.

여기서 주의할 점은 '돈'을 표현하기 위해 money를 반복하여 사용해서는 안 된다는 점이다. money를 구체화하면 living costs, housing cost, transportation costs 등으로 바꾸어 표현할 수 있다.

[답변] Clara made a good point that working from home increases productivity. In addition, working at home does not have the distraction of workplace gossip. However, she did not mention another important effect of remote work. In my opinion, the biggest benefit of working from home is that it can save workers money. This is because they can live away from a metropolis, where housing and living costs are very high. For example, my sister used to live in London to be close to her company. Fortunately, her company implemented a remote work policy, and she was able to return to her hometown in the countryside, saving transportation and housing costs. Therefore, remote work must be seriously considered.

　클라라는 재택근무가 생산성을 높인다는 좋은 지적을 했습니다. 또한 재택근무는 직장 내 소문으로 인한 심란함도 없습니다. 그러나 그녀는 원격 근무의 또 다른 중요한 효과에 대해서는 언급하지 않았습니다. 내 생각에는, 재택근무의 가장 큰 장점은 근로자가 비용을 절감할 수 있다는 점입니다. 이는 주거비와 생활비가 매우 높은 대도시에서 멀리 떨어져 살 수 있기 때문입니다. 예를 들어, 내 여동생은 회사 근처에 있기 위해 런던에 살곤 했습니다. 다행히, 회사에서 원격 근무 정책을 시행하면서, 시골에 있는 고향으로 돌아와 교통비와 주거비를 절약할 수 있었습니다. 그러므로, 원격 근무는 진지하게 고려되어야 합니다.

- 토론형 에세이는 7~8 문장으로 된 한 문단으로 작성
- 첫 번째 문장: 토론에 참가한 다른 학생을 존중하는 모습을 보임
- 두 번째 문장: 그 학생의 의견을 보충해 줌
- 세 번째 문장: 나의 의견으로 전환함
- 네 번째 문장: 나의 의견 기술
- 다섯 번째 문장: 나의 의견을 뒷받침하는 근거
- 여섯~일곱 번째 문장: 구체적 예시
- 마지막 문장: 결론으로 나의 의견 강조

첫 번째 문장	학생의 이름 made a good point that 학생의 의견.	학생1 and 학생2 gave good examples of 주제 키워드.	
두 번째 문장	In addition, 학생의 의견에 추가할 나만의 예시.	Certainly, 예시 1 and 예시 2.	
세 번째 문장	However, he/she/they did not mention another important effect/factor/reason/benefit/method of 주제 키워드.		
네 번째 문장	In my opinion, 나의 의견.		
다섯 번째 문장	This is because 나의 이유(장점).		
여섯~일곱 번째 문장	For example(To explain), 짧은 1~2문장의 예시.		
마지막 문장	Therefore, 나의 의견.	Therefore, 주제 키워드 must be seriously considered.	Therefore, 주제 키워드 must be given high priority.

※ 본 템플릿은 ETS에서 공개한 여러 만점답안을 분석하여 추출한 템플릿으로 여러 원어민 전문가와 토플 전문 강사들의 검증을 거침

03 Practice Test

실전문제 1 - 표적 광고

Your professor is teaching a class on marketing. Write a post responding to the professor's question.
In your response, you should do the following.
• Express and support your opinion.
• Make a contribution to the discussion in your own words.
An effective response will contain at least 100 words.

Doctor Jones

Businesses have developed a new advertising strategy called targeted advertising. Instead of creating advertisements for a general audience, businesses are now directing their advertisements to consumers with certain traits or interests. Write your answer to the following question on the discussion board: is targeted advertising ethical, or is it a violation of privacy?

Justin

I don't think there are any problems with targeted advertising. If we don't want to receive targeted ads, we can just change our privacy settings. Also, businesses can save money by reaching people who have interests that are relevant to their services or products. By saving money on marketing, businesses can lower their prices for their customers.

Hailey

I disagree with Justin. I think targeted advertising violates people's privacy. Websites should not be allowed to keep track of people's personal information and use it for their own purpose. Instead of invading people's lives, companies should make advertisements that would appeal to a large audience.

Cut Paste Undo Redo   Word Count: 0

실전문제 2 - 경제 성장 vs 환경 보호

Your professor is teaching a class on political science. Write a post responding to the professor's question.

In your response, you should do the following.

- Express and support your opinion.
- Make a contribution to the discussion in your own words.

An effective response will contain at least 100 words.

Doctor Reed

Some people say that the government should prioritize economic growth since it provides people with jobs and money to spend. Others say that protecting the environment is more urgent. I would like to know your opinion on this topic. Before our next class, please discuss the following: if you were a policy-maker, would you prioritize economic growth or environmental protections? Why?

Mark

Personally, I would choose economic growth. Many social problems can be solved only through economic growth. There are so many people who are poor and jobless. A strong economy would create more jobs, which would reduce poverty and provide higher standards of living for everyone.

Kelly

We only have one planet Earth. If we do not take care of it, future generations would suffer. Although economic growth is important, it should not negatively affect the environment. We need to invest in environmentally friendly practices, such as green energy, so that we can have a clean environment.

Cut Paste Undo Redo   Word Count: 0

실전문제 3 - 전공 선택 기준

Your professor is teaching a class on education. Write a post responding to the professor's question.

In your response, you should do the following.

• Express and support your opinion.
• Make a contribution to the discussion in your own words.

An effective response will contain at least 100 words.

Doctor Chavez

Students who apply for universities face the difficult task of choosing which field of study to pursue. As this choice may influence their future careers, students need to take many factors into careful consideration. Before our discussion in class, I want to hear what you think about the question: what do you think is the most important factor when choosing a major in college? Why do you think it is important?

Lucy

I think choosing a major based on your academic skills is the most important. For instance, if you struggle with calculating numbers but are good at creative writing, an English major would be more suitable than a degree in physics. Otherwise, you might not be able to understand the lectures and handle the workload.

Peter

While your aptitude may be important, I think your passion should be the deciding factor for your major. If you are not passionate about the subject you are studying, you might find the classes very boring. You might lose interest in the major you're studying and even end up dropping out!

Cut   Paste   Undo   Redo   Word Count: 0

실전문제 4 – 우주 탐사 vs 빈곤 퇴치

Your professor is teaching a class on political science. Write a post responding to the professor's question.

In your response, you should do the following.

• Express and support your opinion.
• Make a contribution to the discussion in your own words.

An effective response will contain at least 100 words.

Doctor Yang

Many countries spend billions of dollars to fund space organizations every year. These organizations aim to find life on other planets, discover new galaxies, and understand space. Before our class next week, I want to know what you think about this topic. Discuss the following question on the class discussion board: should governments spend money on space exploration, or should the money be spent on combating poverty?

Tom

I think the government should focus on problems on Earth first. There are so many people in poverty who need help from the government. I read that over ten percent of citizens currently live under the poverty line, and this number is even bigger in the global population.

Katie

I disagree. I think space programs can benefit people by creating jobs. Thanks to space programs and space research facilities, thousands of jobs are being created. These include skilled jobs such as scientists, researchers, and computer programmers. Others are hired to maintain the research buildings.

Cut   Paste   Undo   Redo   Word Count: 0

실전문제 5 - 프리랜서 vs 회사 고용

Writing | Question 2 of 2

Your professor is teaching a class on business management. Write a post responding to the professor's question.

In your response, you should do the following.

- Express and support your opinion.
- Make a contribution to the discussion in your own words.

An effective response will contain at least 100 words.

Doctor Singh

Many university graduates apply for jobs at companies after graduation. However, others choose the path of being a freelancer or starting their own business. Before next class, I would like you to write about this question in the class discussion board: is it better to work for yourself or be employed at a company?

Grace

One of the biggest benefits of being a freelancer is the high income. I read an article that freelance jobs such as editors, tutors, and web designers have salaries over $50,000 per year, which is quite high. I have to go to another class right now, but I will post more examples later.

Joseph

I disagree with Grace. Being a freelancer means that your income can vary vastly from month to month. However, if you work for a company, you get a steady monthly income. Instead of worrying about whether you will receive work tomorrow, you can focus on saving and spending on your hobbies.

     Word Count: 0

실전문제 6 - 스마트폰

Your professor is teaching a class on sociology. Write a post responding to the professor's question.

In your response, you should do the following.

• Express and support your opinion.
• Make a contribution to the discussion in your own words.

An effective response will contain at least 100 words.

Doctor Hall

It would not be an overstatement to say that most people own or use a smartphone. With this prevalence, it is important to explore the impact smartphones have on people's lives. But first, I want to know what you think about this topic. Please discuss the following question: do smartphones have a positive or negative effect on how people communicate?

Dylan

Smartphones are a great technological advancement with many benefits. Thanks to smartphones, we can stay in touch with friends and family who are far away. We can use instant messaging applications and video calls to connect with our loved ones. Just last night, I went on a video call with my friend who was in Sweden!

Joy

I think smartphones can lead to miscommunications that could have been avoided. Too often, people use text messages or social media platforms to communicate. Although they are convenient, this method of communication lacks facial expressions, body language, and tone of voice. Accordingly, it is easy to misunderstand messages.

Cut   Paste   Undo   Redo   Word Count: 0

실전문제 7 – 기업의 긍정적 영향

Your professor is teaching a class on business management. Write a post responding to the professor's question.

In your response, you should do the following.
- Express and support your opinion.
- Make a contribution to the discussion in your own words.

An effective response will contain at least 100 words.

Doctor Price

Whether good or bad, it is undeniable that companies have a huge impact on society. Some even say companies have a social responsibility to contribute for the good of all. I want to know your opinion on this topic. Here's a question for the class discussion board: what do you think is the most effective way for a company to positively impact society?

Diana

The best way for businesses to have a meaningful impact is to give back to the community. This can have an immediate impact to those in need. Some ways companies can do this is by funding schools, donating money to homeless shelters, and providing the company's products for free. These donations will be beneficial, especially if given out locally.

Charles

I think by following environmentally friendly business practices, companies can have a significant impact on society. Companies can use renewable energy to produce products that use less plastic or are biodegradable. If these practices become the business standard, other companies will follow suit, leading to a greener society.

Cut   Paste   Undo   Redo   Word Count: 0

실전문제 8 - 세금 부과

Your professor is teaching a class on political science. Write a post responding to the professor's question.

In your response, you should do the following.

- Express and support your opinion.
- Make a contribution to the discussion in your own words.

An effective response will contain at least 100 words.

Doctor Robinson

The government often taxes goods and services, which in turn influences the consumer market. In our next class, we are going to discuss government taxation on unhealthy products. I would like to know your opinion on this topic. Please answer this question before class: would you support or oppose a policy that would tax unhealthy products? Why?

Julie

I think taxing unhealthy products is a good idea. Consuming sugary drinks and junk food is a cause of many serious diseases, including diabetes and obesity. If the government taxes these products, people will be discouraged from buying them and fewer people will suffer from these health issues.

Paul

I oppose putting taxes on such products. Such taxes unfairly target families that do not have a lot of income. Although affluent people will not be affected, lower-income families who can only afford these products as a reliable source of food will buy even unhealthier products to save money. Thus, taxing these products will not solve health problems.

Cut   Paste   Undo   Redo   Word Count: 0

실전문제 9 - 동아리 활동

Your professor is teaching a class on education. Write a post responding to the professor's question.

In your response, you should do the following.

- Express and support your opinion.
- Make a contribution to the discussion in your own words.

An effective response will contain at least 100 words.

Doctor Stewart

While universities are known primarily as a place of learning, students also form organizations and clubs. Some examples include sports teams, student government, and religious organizations. Before next class, I would like you to write about this question on the class discussion board: are student organizations and club activities beneficial or distracting for university students?

Brad

Oftentimes, club activities distract students from their studies. I strongly believe that academic achievement is the most important aspect of attending university. However, some student organizations require a large amount of time and commitment. This can take away precious study time, resulting in lower grades.

Jennifer

I think extracurricular activities are a great way to relieve stress. University students experience a lot of pressure from their classes, which can lead to anxiety and depression. Club activities like sports and art can help students lighten some of the academic pressure.

Cut   Paste   Undo   Redo   Word Count: 0

실전문제 10 – 스마트폰

Your professor is teaching a class on sociology. Write a post responding to the professor's question.

In your response, you should do the following.

- Express and support your opinion.
- Make a contribution to the discussion in your own words.

An effective response will contain at least 100 words.

Doctor Santos

It would not be an overstatement to say that most people own a smartphone. Today, smartphones occupy a significant place in people's lives. I want you to think about this topic before our next class. Please answer the following question on the class discussion board: what do you think is the most significant effect using smartphones has on people? Why do you think smartphones have this effect?

Calvin

I think smartphones have made people less sociable. People are constantly on their phones whether on the subway, bus, or even while walking down the street. They prefer to be on social media or watch videos instead of interacting with the real people around them.

Jane

I disagree with Calvin. I think smartphones have helped people stay connected. Thanks to the smartphone, distance is not an issue when communicating with others. We can always send text messages, make phone calls, or write emails anywhere, anytime with our smartphones.

Cut   Paste   Undo   Redo   Word Count: 0

실전문제 11 – 대학 자원 투자

Your professor is teaching a class on education. Write a post responding to the professor's question.

In your response, you should do the following.

• Express and support your opinion.
• Make a contribution to the discussion in your own words.

An effective response will contain at least 100 words.

Doctor Patel

Because universities have limited funds, they have to prioritize different areas to give more attention and resources. Before our next class, I want you to think about this topic. Please answer the following question on the class discussion board: which area would you argue universities should prioritize funding for – athletic programs or libraries?

Ryan

I don't think sports programs should be prioritized over libraries. The main focus of universities should be to provide an environment where people can study and conduct academic research, and libraries are an essential resource for information. If universities invest more money in libraries, students will have better access to a higher quality of education.

Emma

I think athletic programs are more important. Sports can unite the university community. Students and faculty alike can attend their university's games and cheer for their school to win. Think of all the friends you can make at these events! Last night, I went to our university's basketball game, and it was a memorable experience!

Cut   Paste   Undo   Redo   Word Count: 0

실전문제 12 – 대형 슈퍼마켓 vs 지역 시장

Your professor is teaching a class on economics. Write a post responding to the professor's question.

In your response, you should do the following.

• Express and support your opinion.
• Make a contribution to the discussion in your own words.

An effective response will contain at least 100 words.

Doctor Gray

Shopping has evolved over the last few decades. With the rise of large supermarket chains, many small stores are struggling to compete. I want to know your thoughts before you come to class. Here's a question to answer on the discussion board: is it better to shop in large supermarkets or in local markets?

Thomas

I think people choose to shop at supermarkets because it is convenient. Supermarkets have different sections, such as produce, meat, and dairy, all on one floor. Supermarkets even sell non-food items like clothes, soap, and TVs. We can find everything we need on our shopping list under one roof.

Nora

I know that local markets have fresher produce. Supermarkets sell produce that has been grown commercially, harvested early, then transported a long distance to their stores. However, local markets sell fruits and vegetables grown by local farmers and picked when ripe. These are not only fresher but also tastier.

Cut Paste Undo Redo   Word Count: 0

실전문제 13 – 삶의 질 향상 정책

Writing | Question 2 of 2

Your professor is teaching a class on political science. Write a post responding to the professor's question.

In your response, you should do the following.

• Express and support your opinion.
• Make a contribution to the discussion in your own words.

An effective response will contain at least 100 words.

Doctor Myers

Over the next few weeks, we are going to look at how different local governments improve the quality of life of their residents. But first, I would like to know your thoughts on this topic. Please discuss the following question on the discussion board: if you were a policy-maker, what strategy would you use to improve the overall quality of life of local citizens?

Harry

In my opinion, local governments should invest in education. Many of the social issues citizens face, such as poverty and discrimination, can be solved with better education. Studies show that educated people earn more money and are more socially aware. Thus, investing in better education is a great strategy to improve people's lives.

Luna

Building better infrastructure should be every local government's priority. This includes things like repairing roads, building bridges, and creating a better public transportation system. These types of projects will make it easier for people to travel within the city, which will save time and make moving around safer for citizens.

Cut   Paste   Undo   Redo   Word Count: 0

실전문제 14 - 원격 근무

Your professor is teaching a class on business management. Write a post responding to the professor's question.

In your response, you should do the following.

• Express and support your opinion.
• Make a contribution to the discussion in your own words.

An effective response will contain at least 100 words.

Doctor Evans

Over the last few years, many companies have introduced remote work policies. Employees are now working at home instead of going to offices, and other companies are considering doing the same. Before our class next week, I want to know your opinion about this topic. Please write on the discussion board about this question: what are your thoughts on remote work? Do you think it's beneficial or not?

Clara

In my opinion, remote work is largely positive. Employees reported that they were more productive when they were working from home. This might be because there are many distractions that take away work time at a company, such as engaging in meaningless conversations with coworkers and having noisy coworkers.

Kevin

While there are some benefits to remote work, I think it makes it harder to communicate effectively with others. In my experience, having a meeting in person is more productive than having one online. A face-to-face meeting makes it much easier to concentrate on the discussion.

Cut Paste Undo Redo   Word Count: 0

Cut　　Paste　　Undo　　Redo

Word Count: 0

실전문제 15 - 온라인 수업

Your professor is teaching a class on education. Write a post responding to the professor's question.

In your response, you should do the following.

• Express and support your opinion.
• Make a contribution to the discussion in your own words.

An effective response will contain at least 100 words.

Doctor Nelson

Recently, many universities are implementing more online courses. Students can now take classes at home instead of going on campus, and other universities are considering following this trend. Before our class session next week, I would like to know your opinion on this issue. Please discuss the following question: do you think online classes are overall a positive trend in universities or not? Why?

Karen

I think online classes make education more accessible by lowering costs. In the past, students who were from low-income families struggled with tuition fees, housing, and commuting costs. However, as online courses allow students to take classes from home, a lot of the financial burden is lifted.

Chad

I see Karen's point. However, I think online classes lower the quality of education. When the professor and our classmates are just faces on a screen, it is natural that we engage less in class and lose concentration. Also, it is hard to communicate and work together constructively. I think universities should bring back offline classes.

 Cut   Paste   Undo   Redo   Word Count: 0

실전문제 16 - 리더십

Writing | Question 2 of 2

Your professor is teaching a class on sociology. Write a post responding to the professor's question.

In your response, you should do the following.

- Express and support your opinion.
- Make a contribution to the discussion in your own words.

An effective response will contain at least 100 words.

Doctor Harris

While some say a leader is simply someone who leads, others argue that there is more to being a good leader. With more universities and businesses looking for people with leadership, it is important to consider the following question: what do you think is the most important quality of a good leader?

Anna

I would say patience is the most important quality of a leader. It is normal for there to be small miscommunications, conflicts, and other difficulties when working with a group of people. Instead of being frustrated, a good leader should be patient and guide the team through these obstacles.

Christopher

I believe that a good leader should be an active listener. Active listening means trying to understand the meaning and intention behind the words. This is especially important for leaders because they should be able to listen to feedback from their team members and make them feel like their opinions matter.

Cut   Paste   Undo   Redo   Word Count: 0

실전문제 17 - 도시화

Your professor is teaching a class on sociology. Write a post responding to the professor's question.

In your response, you should do the following.

- Express and support your opinion.
- Make a contribution to the discussion in your own words.

An effective response will contain at least 100 words.

Doctor Garcia

Over the next few weeks, we are going to look at different effects of urbanization. As more people are leaving the countryside to live in the city than ever before, the population of cities has grown worldwide. Before next class, I want you to consider the following question: is the rapid growth of cities mostly positive or negative for society?

Bella

I think more people coming to live in cities is a good thing. Cities are known to have greater opportunities for work and education. When people come to the city, they can send their children to schools with better teachers. Also, there are far more job opportunities in the city than in the country.

Jacob

Cities have a greater chance of spreading diseases. Because cities are densely populated, people are always at close proximity to each other, especially in places such as buses and subways. Thus, diseases are easily transmitted since people breathe in the same air in an enclosed space.

Cut   Paste   Undo   Redo   Word Count: 0

실전문제 18 – 토론 수업 vs 강의 수업

Your professor is teaching a class on education. Write a post responding to the professor's question.

In your response, you should do the following.

- Express and support your opinion.
- Make a contribution to the discussion in your own words.

An effective response will contain at least 100 words.

Doctor Alvarez

As teachers aim to provide the best education for their students, there has always been a debate on what are the best teaching methods. Over the next few weeks, we are going to look at different teaching methods practiced in the classroom. Before class, I would like you to prepare an answer to this question: which do you prefer – a discussion-oriented class or a lecture-oriented class?

James

Personally, I am an auditory learner. What this means is that I understand information better when a teacher explains it to me. Because lectures usually have a set structure, I can easily follow along and take notes at my own pace. However, I find that discussions often get off-topic and are hard to follow.

Lily

I prefer classes with a lot of opportunities for discussion. For me, discussions broaden my thinking because I can hear different perspectives from my classmates. Also, I can get feedback by talking with my classmates about a difficult topic. I value this interaction and it helps me to learn things more easily overall.

Cut   Paste   Undo   Redo   Word Count: 0

실전문제 19 – 현대의 건강 vs 과거의 건강

Your professor is teaching a class on sociology. Write a post responding to the professor's question.

In your response, you should do the following.

• Express and support your opinion.
• Make a contribution to the discussion in your own words.

An effective response will contain at least 100 words.

Doctor Foster

People are living longer than ever before. Life expectancy has risen all over the world. However, some people are voicing the opinion that this does not necessarily mean that people are healthier. Before our class next week, I want to know your opinion about this topic. Please write on the discussion board about this question: are people healthier now than they were in the past?

Holly

I think people are much healthier thanks to advancements in medical inventions. Before, people died early because of unexpected illnesses. Now, because of the development of medical equipment such as X-rays and CT scans, doctors are able to diagnose and treat diseases earlier.

Michael

I disagree with Holly. I think that people are more stressed than ever before. The society we live in puts a lot of pressure on people to succeed. More people are stressed from their studies or because of their jobs. These high stress levels can lead people to be more vulnerable to stress-related diseases.

Cut   Paste   Undo   Redo   Word Count: 0

실전문제 20 - 기대 수명 증가

Your professor is teaching a class on social studies. Write a post responding to the professor's question.

In your response, you should do the following.

• Express and support your opinion.
• Make a contribution to the discussion in your own words.

An effective response will contain at least 100 words.

Doctor Adams

Life expectancy has risen globally during the last few centuries. People are now expected to live up to 100 years old, and many older people are crossing this threshold. Before next class, I would like you to respond to the following question on the discussion board: what do you think is the biggest factor in the increase of life expectancy? Why do you think it has this effect?

Jessica

I think improvements in living standards have played a key role in why people are living longer. Before, people threw their waste on the streets, and they caught a lot of sickness from unpurified water. We now live in much more sanitary conditions with a sewer system and easy access to clean water.

Mike

Advancements in medicine are the biggest reason for the increased life expectancy. We are now able to treat illnesses that would have been fatal before. What would have been a pandemic in the past can now be avoided with a simple vaccine. Furthermore, surgeries and other treatments prolong lives, contributing to longer lifespans.

Cut　Paste　Undo　Redo　　　　　　　　　　Word Count: 0

toefl.siwonschool.com

Actual Tests

01 Actual Test 1

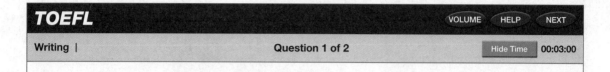

Several years ago, a man went to a sale at a private home in California and bought a box of envelopes filled with photographic negatives (which are images on film or glass that can be used to create photograph prints). The negatives were originally made in the 1920s and depicted some landscapes that are located in the western United States. Although they did not have any names on them, some people claim that the negatives were originally made by one of the greatest American photographers of the 20th century, Ansel Adams. There are several reasons to back up this argument.

Firstly, the landscapes captured in the negatives were the same as some of those that Ansel Adams had photographed. In one of them, a large pine tree leans downward on a cliff. A photograph that was undoubtedly taken by Adams in the 1920s shows a tree with the same unusual characteristics.

Secondly, the negatives had been organized in envelopes that were numbered and labeled by hand. The handwriting on those envelopes is similar to none other than Virginia Adams, who was the wife of Ansel Adams. She was known to help her husband out with his work, so the believers that the negatives were originally taken by Ansel Adams say that Virginia most likely helped Ansel organize the negatives by writing down location names of where they were taken and assigning numbers to them.

Thirdly, quite a few of the negatives showed signs of fire damage, which could have occurred during a studio fire that once destroyed or damaged almost one third of Ansel Adams' negatives. This fire damage is considered another piece of evidence that the negatives purchased at the sale did indeed belong to Ansel Adams.

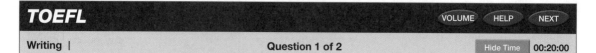
Directions: You have 20 minutes to plan and write your response. Your response will be judged on the basis of the quality of your writing and on how well your response presents the points in the lecture and their relationship to the reading passage. Typically, an effective response will be 150 to 225 words.

Question: Summarize the points made in the lecture, being sure to explain how they cast doubt on specific points made in the reading passage.

Several years ago, a man went to a sale at a private home in California and bought a box of envelopes filled with photographic negatives (which are images on film or glass that can be used to create photograph prints). The negatives were originally made in the 1920s and depicted some landscapes that are located in the western United States. Although they did not have any names on them, some people claim that the negatives were originally made by one of the greatest American photographers of the 20th century, Ansel Adams. There are several reasons to back up this argument.	Cut Paste Undo Redo Word Count: 0

Firstly, the landscapes captured in the negatives were the same as some of those that Ansel Adams had photographed. In one of them, a large pine tree leans downward on a cliff. A photograph that was undoubtedly taken by Adams in the 1920s shows a tree with the same unusual characteristics.

Secondly, the negatives had been organized in envelopes that were numbered and labeled by hand. The handwriting on those envelopes is similar to none other than Virginia Adams, who was the wife of Ansel Adams. She was known to help her husband out with his work, so the believers that the negatives were originally taken by Ansel Adams say that Virginia most likely helped Ansel organize the negatives by writing down location names of where they were taken and assigning numbers to them.

Thirdly, quite a few of the negatives showed signs of fire damage, which could have occurred during a studio fire that once destroyed or damaged almost one third of Ansel Adams' negatives. This fire damage is considered another piece of evidence that the negatives purchased at the sale did indeed belong to Ansel Adams.

Writing for an Academic Discussion

For this task, you will read an online discussion. A professor has posted a question about a topic, and some classmates have responded with their ideas.

Write a response that contributes to the discussion. You will have 10 minutes to write your response. It is important to use your own words in the response. Including memorized reasons or examples will result in a lower score.

Your professor is teaching a class on computer science. Write a post responding to the professor's question.

In your response, you should do the following.

• Express and support your opinion.
• Make a contribution to the discussion in your own words.

An effective response will contain at least 100 words.

Doctor Allen

An increasing number of companies are investing in new AI technologies. These technologies are being applied to more areas in new ways. Over the next few weeks, we will cover these technologies and how they affect society. But first, I would like you to think about this question: is AI dangerous to society, or is it a tool that can improve people's lives?

Jeremy

I think AI is a dangerous technology that will be harmful to society. As new AI technologies are developed, more and more jobs are at the risk of being taken over by AI. This would displace a lot of workers and increase unemployment. We need to be careful that advancements in AI technology do not negatively affect people's livelihoods.

Lisa

AI is an enormously powerful tool that can solve many of the problems we face today. Unlike humans, AI can go through huge amounts of data very quickly and identify underlying patterns. If this technology is applied well, think of the potential solutions it can present for diseases and global warming!

Cut Paste Undo Redo   Word Count: 0

02 Actual Test 2

Milk is commonly consumed in cultures around the world, but is it actually as good as we think it is? Modern science has found several reasons for us to eliminate milk from our diets entirely.

First, according to a study in the British Medical Journal, there seems to be a correlation between drinking milk regularly and suffering bone fractures. The study followed approximately 61,400 women over a period of 20 years. Among those women, those who drank three or more glasses of milk per day were 60% more likely to develop a hip fracture, and 16% overall to fracture any bone in their body.

Second, it is a well-known fact that toxins in a woman's body can be passed on from a mother to a baby through breast milk. The same is true for milk that is obtained from cows. When a cow becomes sick and is given antibiotics by the farmers that care for it, those antibiotics can contaminate the milk from that cow. A healthy human does not need antibiotics, and consuming them causes the body to develop an immunity to them. That means that when a person does become sick, the antibiotics that would normally be used to treat their illness would be less effective, and possibly even useless.

Third, the nutrients found in milk can easily be found in other foods. For example, fish are an excellent source of protein that is low in fat. If you are on a vegan diet, you can obtain protein from beans, nuts, or tofu. To find the B vitamins that your body needs, consume plenty of leafy green vegetables. These options would be preferable over drinking the milk of another mammal, which is not something that normally happens in nature.

Directions: You have 20 minutes to plan and write your response. Your response will be judged on the basis of the quality of your writing and on how well your response presents the points in the lecture and their relationship to the reading passage. Typically, an effective response will be 150 to 225 words.

Question: Summarize the points made in the lecture, being sure to explain how they challenge the specific points made in the reading passage.

Milk is commonly consumed in cultures around the world, but is it actually as good as we think it is? Modern science has found several reasons for us to eliminate milk from our diets entirely.

First, according to a study in the British Medical Journal, there seems to be a correlation between drinking milk regularly and suffering bone fractures. The study followed approximately 61,400 women over a period of 20 years. Among those women, those who drank three or more glasses of milk per day were 60% more likely to develop a hip fracture, and 16% overall to fracture any bone in their body.

Second, it is a well-known fact that toxins in a woman's body can be passed on from a mother to a baby through breast milk. The same is true for milk that is obtained from cows. When a cow becomes sick and is given antibiotics by the farmers that care for it, those antibiotics can contaminate the milk from that cow. A healthy human does not need antibiotics, and consuming them causes the body to develop an immunity to them. That means that when a person does become sick, the antibiotics that would normally be used to treat their illness would be less effective, and possibly even useless.

Third, the nutrients found in milk can easily be found in other foods. For example, fish are an excellent source of protein that is low in fat. If you are on a vegan diet, you can obtain protein from beans, nuts, or tofu. To find the B vitamins that your body needs, consume plenty of leafy green vegetables. These options would be preferable over drinking the milk of another mammal, which is not something that normally happens in nature.

Cut   Paste   Undo   Redo   Word Count: 0

Writing for an Academic Discussion

For this task, you will read an online discussion. A professor has posted a question about a topic, and some classmates have responded with their ideas.

Write a response that contributes to the discussion. You will have 10 minutes to write your response. It is important to use your own words in the response. Including memorized reasons or examples will result in a lower score.

Your professor is teaching a class on political science. Write a post responding to the professor's question.

In your response, you should do the following.

• Express and support your opinion.
• Make a contribution to the discussion in your own words.

An effective response will contain at least 100 words.

Doctor Ward

Over the next few weeks, we will cover urbanization and its effects on city infrastructure. In the next class, we will discuss possible solutions city governments could implement to reduce heavy traffic. But first, I would like you to consider this question: what are some measures city governments could take to reduce traffic?

Cathy

I think the government can encourage more companies to implement remote work policies. When employees commute to work, they either drive or use public transportation, causing more traffic, especially during rush hour. If more employees work from home, the number of people on the roads will decrease.

Patrick

One way would be to tax private car owners. Too many people own cars in the city despite the traffic and limited parking space. A tax on private cars will discourage people from buying or using their cars. Instead, people will walk or take public transportation.

 Cut   Paste   Undo   Redo   Word Count: 0

시원스쿨 토플 전문강사
박주영 선생님

시원스쿨
TOEFL Writing
온라인 강의

빈출 토픽별 학습으로 최신 트렌드 파악
시원스쿨 TOEFL Writing 강의 POINT 3

실제 시험에 적용할 수 있는
주제별 배경지식 및
어휘, 작문 표현 정리

토픽별 문제모음을 통해
배경지식과 관련된
작문 표현 습득

토픽 내 다양한
기출 변형문제를 통해
시험 트렌드 파악 및 작문 연습

시원스쿨LAB(lab.siwonschool.com)에서 유료강의를 수강하실 수 있습니다.

고득점을 위한 토플 라이팅 기본서

SIWONSCHOOL
TOEFL

Writing

정답 및 해설

시원스쿨 LAB

고득점을 위한 **토플** 라이팅 **기본서**

SIWONSCHOOL
TOEFL

Writing

정답 및 해설

시원스쿨 LAB

실전문제 1 – 생물 주제 (1)

Reading Passage	Listening Script
Over the past 150 years, scientists have tracked a steady decline in populations of yellow cedar, a species of tree that is commonly found throughout parts of the northwestern United States and Canada. Numerous hypotheses have been put forward to account for this decline.	The reading passage offers a few explanations regarding the population decline of the yellow cedar, but unfortunately, none of them are truly convincing.
The first hypothesis centers on changes in climate as the main cause of the decline in yellow cedar populations. Seasonal temperatures have been changing in the regions where yellow cedars grow. As a result, the growth of the surface roots of the trees no longer begins in the early spring, but in the late winter. This change has a considerable impact on overall tree health. Because the young roots are sensitive to temperature change, they are prone to freezing during cold winter nights, and such root damage may eventually lead to the death of many trees.	First, there is the hypothesis about roots being damaged by cold temperatures. Well, the passage fails to point out one very important factor. At higher elevations, where the temperature is lower, there are far fewer trees dying than at lower elevations, where it is relatively warm. So, if the decline were due to freezing temperatures, we would see a larger number of trees dying at higher elevations. With that in mind, even if colder temperatures weaken the roots of the trees, it seems unlikely that this is what is killing the trees.
A second hypothesis is that parasites such as the cedar bark beetle are largely responsible for the decline. The larvae of cedar bark beetles are known to eat the wood of the trees, damaging them severely. Several cases have been documented where the beetles attacked yellow cedars so extensively that hundreds of trees died, so these parasites are certainly capable of causing a decrease in tree population.	Second, the problem with the cedar bark beetle hypothesis is that yellow cedars have a higher resistance to insect parasitism than the majority of tree species. To be specific, yellow cedars contain chemicals in their leaves and bark that are toxic to the insects. As such, the chances of healthy yellow cedars dying as a result of insect damage are low. In cases where dead yellow cedars were found to be infested with beetles, it seems more likely that the trees were already diseased or damaged, and close to death, prior to the arrival of the beetles. So, we cannot claim that the beetles are directly responsible for a decline in yellow cedar populations.
A third hypothesis singles out brown bears as the cause of the decline. The bark of the yellow cedar is high in sugar and bears often tear the bark off with their claws to eat it. In fact, the sugar content of the yellow cedar bark is even higher than that of the forest berries that the bears regularly consume. While the stripping of the bark is unlikely to kill the trees outright, the feeding habits of the bears leave the trees in a vulnerable state, indirectly contributing to their decline.	And finally, while it is true that bears damage trees, I doubt they are responsible for the yellow cedar's decline. Yellow cedars have been dying off in large numbers all across the northwest United States, both in mainland coastal regions and also on islands off the coast. The thing is, these islands are not home to any bears, but we still see the same decrease in the number of yellow cedars. This tells us that bears are not responsible for the population decline.

해석

지난 150년 동안에 걸쳐, 과학자들은 미국 북서부 및 캐나다 여러 지역에 걸쳐 흔히 보이는 나무 종의 하나인 미국 편백나무의 지속적인 개체군 감소 과정을 추적해 왔다. 이 감소 문제를 설명하기 위해 다수의 가설이 제시되어 왔다.

첫 번째 가설은 미국 편백나무 개체군의 감소에 대한 주된 원인으로서 기후 변화를 중심으로 한다. 미국 편백나무가 자라는 지역에서 계절적 기온이 변화하고 있다. 그 결과, 이 나무의 지표면 뿌리 성장이 더 이상 이른 봄에 시작되지 않고 늦은 겨울에 시작되고 있다. 이러한 변화는 나무의 전반적인 건강에 상당한 영향을 미치고 있다. 어린 뿌리가 기온 변화에 민감하기 때문에, 추운 겨울 밤에는 얼어붙기 쉬우며, 그러한 뿌리 손상은 결국 많은 나무의 죽음으로 이어질 수 있다.

두 번째 가설은 편백나무좀 같은 기생 생물이 감소 문제의 주된 원인이라는 점이다. 편백나무좀의 유충은 이 나무의 목질부를 먹으면서 심각하게 손상시키는 것으로 알려져 있다. 이 나무좀이 미국 편백나무를 너무 광범위하게 공격한 나머지 수백 그루의 나무가 죽은 것으로 기록된 여러 사례가 있기 때문에, 이 기생 생물은 분명 나무 개체수의 감소를 초래할 수 있다.

세 번째 가설은 감소 문제의 원인으로 불곰을 지목하고 있다. 미국 편백나무의 껍질은 당분이 높기 때문에 곰이 흔히 발톱으로 이 껍질 부분을 떼어내 먹는다. 실제로, 미국 편백나무 껍질의 당분 함량은 곰이 주기적으로 소비하는 숲 속 산딸기류 열매보다 훨씬 더 높다. 껍질을 벗기는 것이 나무를 완전히 죽일 가능성은 없지만, 곰의 먹이 섭취 습성이 이 나무를 취약한 상태로 만들면서, 간접적으로 감소 문제의 원인이 되고 있다.

독해 지문이 미국 편백나무의 개체군 감소와 관련해 몇 가지 설명을 제공하고 있기는 하지만, 유감스럽게도, 그 중 어느 것도 정말로 설득력이 있지는 않습니다.

첫 번째로, 추운 기온으로 인해 손상되는 뿌리에 관한 가설이 있습니다. 음, 독해 지문은 한 가지 아주 중요한 요인을 지적하지 못하고 있습니다. 기온이 더 낮은, 높은 고도에서는, 상대적으로 따뜻한, 더 낮은 고도에 비해 죽는 나무가 훨씬 더 적습니다. 따라서, 감소 문제가 차가운 기온 때문이라면, 고도가 더 높은 곳에서 더 많은 나무가 죽는 것을 보게 될 겁니다. 이를 감안하면, 설사 더 추운 기온이 나무의 뿌리를 약화시킨다 하더라도, 이것이 나무를 죽이고 있을 가능성은 없어 보입니다.

두 번째로, 편백나무좀 가설과 관련된 문제는 미국 편백나무가 대다수의 나무 종보다 해충 기생에 대한 저항력이 더 높다는 점입니다. 구체적으로, 미국 편백나무는 잎과 껍질 속에 해충에 유독한 화학 물질을 포함하고 있습니다. 따라서, 건강한 미국 편백나무가 해충 피해에 따른 결과로 죽을 가능성은 낮습니다. 죽은 미국 편백나무에 나무좀이 들끓고 있었던 것으로 밝혀진 경우에는, 그 나무가 나무좀이 나타나기에 앞서 이미 병이 들었거나 손상되어 죽음에 가까워져 있었을 가능성이 더 컸던 것으로 보입니다. 따라서, 우리는 나무좀이 미국 편백나무 개체군의 감소에 대한 직접적인 원인이라고 주장할 수 없습니다.

그리고 마지막으로, 곰이 나무를 손상시키는 것이 사실이기는 하지만, 저는 미국 편백나무 감소 문제의 원인이라고 보진 않습니다. 미국 편백나무는 미국 북서부 지역 전체에 걸쳐 본토의 해안 지역과 해안에서 떨어져 있는 여러 섬에서도 대규모로 계속 소멸되는 중입니다. 문제는, 이 섬들은 곰이 사는 서식지가 전혀 아니지만, 우리는 여전히 동일하게 미국 편백나무의 숫자 감소를 겪고 있다는 점입니다. 이는 곰이 그 개체수 감소의 원인이 아니라는 사실을 우리에게 말해주는 것입니다.

강의에서 언급된 요점들이 어떻게 독해 지문에 제시된 특정 주장들에 대해 이의를 제기하는지 설명하면서 그 내용을 요약해 보시오.

노트테이킹

↓ YC account for	none convin.
changes climate young roots / prone to freezing → death	fails / factor. ↑ - temp. ↓ fewer trees dying - ↓ / warm. colder weaken unlikely kill
parasites / cedar bark beetle larvae eat the wood	problem ↑ resis. bark leaves toxic damage already disease / damage X / directly respons.
brown bears tear the bark off	true → doubt X all across X home → still X respons.

모범 답안

The reading passage and the lecture both discuss the decline of yellow cedar trees. The writer states that three explanations can account for the reason why the populations of the trees have been steadily reduced. However, the lecturer disagrees with the argument, saying that none of them are convincing.

First of all, the lecturer doubts the writer's point that climate change has caused the yellow cedar populations to decline. He claims that the argument fails to consider one important factor: elevation. Fewer trees at higher elevations with lower temperatures die than at lower elevations with warmer temperatures. Although the writer states that the surface roots of the trees are prone to freezing during the cold winter and eventually lead to their death, the lecturer points out that colder temperatures weaken the roots but do not seem to kill the trees.

Secondly, the lecturer refutes the argument in the reading passage that the cedar bark beetle, a parasite, can be responsible for the decline in the population of yellow cedar. He states that this argument has a problem. Yellow cedars have a resistance to the parasite. While the writer states that the larvae of the beetles severely damage the trees, the lecturer highlights that the chances of insect damage are low. This is because the leaves and bark of yellow cedars have toxic chemicals resistant to the insects. In addition, already damaged or sick trees were found to be infected by the beetles, which means that the parasite is not directly responsible for the decline.

Finally, the lecturer doubts the writer's argument that brown bears can be the indirect cause of the decline. **He contends that** it is partly true, but it is doubtful as well. The decline of yellow cedars has been happening all across the northwest United States. **While the writer and the lecturer both agree that** bears tear the bark off and damage the tree, **in the listening part, the lecturer says** there is a decrease in the population in some places where no bears live. Therefore, it can be concluded that bears are not the cause of the population decline.

(353 words)

독해 지문과 강의는 모두 미국 편백나무의 감소 문제를 이야기한다. 글쓴이는 세 가지 설명이 왜 이 나무의 개체군이 지속적으로 감소되어 왔는지에 대한 이유를 말해줄 수 있다고 언급한다. 하지만, 강의 진행자는 그 중 어느 것도 설득력이 있지 않다고 말하면서 그러한 주장에 동의하지 않는다.

가장 먼저, 강의 진행자는 기후 변화가 미국 편백나무 개체군이 감소하도록 초래했다는 글쓴이의 주장에 의구심을 갖는다. 강의 진행자는 그러한 주장이 한 가지 중요한 요인, 즉 고도를 고려하고 있지 않다고 주장한다. 기온이 더 낮고 더 높은 고도에 위치한 나무가 기온이 더 따뜻한 더 낮은 고도에 있는 나무보다 더 적게 죽는다. 글쓴이는 이 나무의 지표면 뿌리가 추운 겨울 중에 얼어붙는 경향이 있어서 결국 죽음에 이른다고 언급하고 있지만, 강의 진행자는 더 차가운 기온이 뿌리를 약화시키기는 하지만 나무를 죽이는 것으로 보이지는 않는다는 점을 지적하고 있다.

두 번째로, 강의 진행자는 독해 지문에서 기생 생물인 편백나무좀이 미국 편백나무 개체수의 감소에 대한 원인일 수 있다고 제시한 주장에 반박하고 있다. 강의 진행자는 이러한 주장에 문제가 있다고 언급한다. 미국 편백나무는 그 기생 생물에 대한 저항력을 지니고 있다. 글쓴이는 이 나무좀의 유충이 나무를 심각하게 손상시킨다고 언급하는 반면, 강의 진행자는 해충 피해 가능성이 낮다는 점을 강조한다. 이는 미국 편백나무의 잎과 껍질에 해충에 저항하는 독성 화학 물질이 들어 있기 때문이다. 추가로, 이미 손상되거나 병든 나무가 그 나무좀에 감염된 것으로 밝혀졌으며, 이는 그 기생 생물이 개체수 감소 문제에 대한 직접적인 원인이 아니라는 것을 의미한다.

마지막으로, 강의 진행자는 불곰이 감소 문제의 간접적인 원인일 수 있다는 글쓴이의 주장에 의구심을 지니고 있다. 강의 진행자는 일부 맞는 말이기는 하지만, 의심스럽기도 하다고 주장한다. 미국 편백나무의 감소는 미국 북서부 지역 전체에 걸쳐 계속 발생되고 있다. 글쓴이와 강의 진행자 둘 모두 불곰이 해당 나무의 껍질을 떼어낸다는 점에 동의하기는 하지만, 청해 파트에서는, 곰이 전혀 살지 않는 몇몇 장소에도 개체군 감소 문제가 존재한다고 강의 진행자가 말한다. 따라서, 곰이 개체군 감소의 원인은 아닌 것으로 결론 내릴 수 있다.

어휘

decline in ~의 감소 **population** 개체군, 개체수 **species** (동식물의) 종 **hypothesis** 가설(hypotheses는 복수) **put forward** ~을 제시하다, 제안하다 **account for** ~을 설명하다, 해명하다 **have a considerable impact on** ~에 상당한 영향을 미치다 **overall** 전반적인 **parasite** 기생 생물 **be responsible for** ~에 대한 원인이다 **larvae** 유충 **single out** ~을 지목하다 **bark** 나무껍질 **stripping** 벗겨내기 **outright** 완전히 **vulnerable** 취약한 **contribute to** ~의 원인이 되다

convincing 설득력 있는 **fail to do** ~하지 못하다 **point out** ~을 지적하다 **elevation** 고도 **relatively** 상대적으로, 비교적 **resistance** 저항(력) **parasitism** 기생 (상태) **be infested with A** A가 들끓다 **diseased** 병든

be prone to ~하는 경향이 있다, ~하기 쉽다 **be infected by** ~에 감염되다

실전문제 2 – 생물 주제 (2)

Reading Passage	Listening Script
Genetically modified (GM) crops are produced using recombinant DNA technology that allows favorable genes to be transferred from one organism to another. The successful expression of transferred genes may have a variety of advantages in GM crops, such as increased growth rate or an ability to grow in harsh conditions. As such, this technology has several far-reaching benefits on a global scale.	It may be true that there are some benefits of growing genetically modified crops, but it is also important to look at the risks involved. When you look at the GM farming industry in depth, there are some major disadvantages and risks associated with genetically modified crops.
First, GM crops can improve human health as they contain fewer potential allergens and higher levels of essential amino acids, essential fatty acids, vitamins, and minerals. They can also play a potential role in fighting malnutrition in developing countries where poor people rely heavily on single food sources such as rice for their diet. Typically, rice does not contain sufficient quantities of essential nutrients required to prevent malnutrition, but GM rice has a much higher nutritional value, making it more beneficial to human health.	First, while there might be potential for GM crops to improve human health, none of these claims are based on real scientific data. Very few extensive studies have been carried out on the potential human health impacts of GM crop consumption and many of the studies that have been conducted have been met with skepticism and criticism. Moreover, several leading agricultural scientists have expressed concerns about allergenicity. Because genetic modification usually adds or mixes proteins that were not native to the original crop, it carries the massive potential for causing new allergic reactions in the human body.
Moreover, a direct benefit of GM crops is the reduction of pesticide applications. This means that farmers have less exposure to harmful chemicals, and there will be lower amounts of pesticide residues in food and feed crops. For example, insect resistance in GM maize has been achieved by transferring the gene for toxin creation from the bacterium, *Bacillus thuringiensis* (Bt). This toxin is commonly used as an insecticide in agriculture and is considered safe to use on food and feed crops. GM crops that have the ability to produce this toxin themselves require no additional pesticide application.	With regard to the second point, the need for fewer pesticides for GM crops may sound good, but the repeated use of a single pesticide over time increases pesticide resistance in the target species. So, the extensive use of a limited number of pesticides has a high likelihood of speeding up the evolution of resistant pest populations. For instance, in India, farmers have reported that the pink bollworm has become resistant to GM Bt cotton, and similar cases of pest resistance have been reported in Australia and the United States.
Lastly, due to the higher yield and lower production cost of GM crops, farmers who purchase GM seeds will benefit economically and produce more food at affordable prices. With more and more multinational GM seed companies emerging, it is getting easier for farmers in developing nations to purchase GM seeds and enjoy the financial benefits of GM crop cultivation.	Finally, the increased dependence on multinational seed companies can be problematic for many farmers, particularly those in poorer regions. The companies that patent and control GM seeds are known to inflate seed prices, and this is already having a significant effect on the global economy. In the end, global food production will be dominated by a few seed companies, and this will massively increase the dependence of developing countries on industrialized nations.

해석

유전자 변형(GM) 작물은 유리한 유전자를 한 유기체에서 다른 유기체로 이식될 수 있게 해주는 재조합 DNA 기술을 활용해 만들어진다. 이식된 유전자의 성공적인 발현은 성장률 증가 또는 가혹한 환경에서의 성장 능력 같이 GM 작물에 있어 다양한 장점이 될 수 있다. 따라서, 이 기술은 전 세계적인 규모로 여러 가지 지대한 영향을 미치는 이점을 지니고 있다.

우선, GM 작물은 알레르기 유발 항원은 더 적으면서 더 높은 수준의 필수 아미노산과 필수 지방산, 비타민, 그리고 무기질을 포함하고 있기 때문에 인간의 건강을 향상시켜줄 수 있다. 또한 가난한 사람들이 식사로 쌀처럼 단 한 가지의 식량 공급원에 크게 의존하는 개발 도상국 내의 영양 실조 문제와 맞서 싸우는 데 있어 잠재적인 역할을 할 수 있다. 일반적으로, 쌀은 영양 실조를 막는 데 필요한 충분한 양의 필수 영양소를 함유하고 있지는 않지만, GM 쌀은 영양적 가치가 훨씬 더 높으며, 이로 인해 인간의 건강에 더 유익하다.

게다가, GM 작물의 직접적인 혜택은 살충제 사용량의 감소이다. 이는 농부들이 유해 화학 물질에 덜 노출되고, 식품 및 사료용 작물에 더 적은 양의 살충제 잔여물이 존재하게 된다는 것을 의미한다. 예를 들어, GM 옥수수의 내충성은 '바실러스 튜링겐시스(Bt)'라는 박테리아에 들어 있는 독소 생성 유전자를 이식함으로써 이뤄졌다. 이 독소는 농업용 살충제로 흔히 쓰이고 있으며, 식품 및 사료용 작물에 사용하기에 안전한 것으로 여겨지고 있다. 스스로 이 독소를 만들어낼 수 있는 능력이 있는 GM 작물은 별도의 살충제 사용이 필요치 않다.

마지막으로, GM 작물의 더 높은 수확량 및 더 낮은 생산비로 인해, GM 종자를 구입하는 농부들이 경제적으로 혜택도 보고 알맞은 가격에 더 많은 식물도 생산하게 된다. 점점 더 많은 다국적 GM 종자 생산업체들이 나타나면서, 개발 도상국 내의 농부들이 GM 종자를 구입하고 GM 작물 재배에 따른 경제적 이득을 누리는 것이 더 수월해지고 있다.

유전자 변형 작물을 기르는 데 몇 가지 이점이 있다는 것이 사실일 수도 있지만, 관련 위험 요소들을 살펴보는 것 또한 중요합니다. GM 농업을 심층적으로 들여다보면, 유전자 변형 작물과 연관되어 있는 몇몇 중대한 단점과 위험 요소들이 존재합니다.

첫 번째로, GM 작물이 인간의 건강을 향상시켜줄 수 있는 잠재성이 있을 수도 있지만, 이러한 주장들 중 그 어떤 것도 실제 과학적인 자료를 기반으로 하고 있지 않습니다. GM 작물 소비가 인간의 건강에 미치는 잠재적인 영향에 관해 실시된 광범위한 연구가 거의 없으며, 실시된 연구들 중 많은 것이 회의론과 비판론에 부딪혀 왔습니다. 게다가, 여러 선구적인 농업 과학자들은 알레르기 항원성에 대해 우려를 표명해 왔습니다. 유전자 조작이 일반적으로 원래의 작물에 고유하지 않은 단백질을 추가하거나 혼합하기 때문에, 사람의 신체에 새로운 알레르기 반응을 유발할 잠재성을 아주 크게 지니고 있습니다.

두 번째 주장과 관련해서는, GM 작물에 필요한 살충제가 더 적다는 건 좋게 들릴 수도 있지만, 시간을 두고 단 한 가지 살충제만 반복적으로 사용하는 건 목표 생물 종의 살충제 내성을 높이게 됩니다. 따라서, 제한된 숫자의 살충제를 광범위하게 사용하면 해충 개체군의 내성 물질 발전 속도를 빠르게 할 가능성이 높습니다. 예를 들어, 인도에서는, 농부들이 분홍솜벌레가 GM Bt 목화에 내성이 생긴 사실을 알렸으며, 유사한 해충 내성 사례들이 호주와 미국에서도 보고된 바 있습니다.

마지막으로, 다국적 종자 생산 업체들에 대한 의존도 증가가 많은 농부들에게 문제가 될 수 있는데, 특히 더 가난한 지역에 있는 농부들에게 그렇습니다. GM 종자에 대해 특허를 내고 통제하는 회사들은 종자 가격을 부풀리는 것으로 알려져 있으며, 이는 이미 세계 경제에 상당한 영향을 미치고 있습니다. 결국, 전 세계의 식품 생산이 몇몇 종자 생산업체에 의해 좌지우지될 것이며, 이는 개발 도상국의 선진국 의존도를 대단히 크게 높이게 될 것입니다.

강의에서 언급된 요점들이 어떻게 독해 지문에 제시된 특정 주장들에 대해 이의를 제기하는지 설명하면서 그 내용을 요약해 보시오.

노트테이킹

GM bene.	disad. / risks
↑ human health ↓ allergen higher nutritional value	none / real scien. data. very few stud. skep. critic. allergen. X native - origin. → new allergic
↓ pesticide GM maize	↑ resis. evolution → resis. ex) pink bollworm report Aus. U.S
yield / ↓ production cost benefit economically	↑ depen. / multina. seed prob. companies ↑ prices → global eco → depen. ↑ - indust. nation

모범 답안

The reading passage and the lecture both discuss genetically modified crops (GM). The writer states that GM crops globally have some advantages. However, the lecturer disagrees with the argument, saying that they have some disadvantages and risks associated with each benefit in the reading.

First of all, the lecturer doubts the writer's point that GM crops help to improve human health with their higher nutritional value. She argues that this advantage might be true, but this is not based on real scientific data. Very few studies on the impact of GM crops on human health have been conducted and many of the cases faced skepticism and criticism. Although the writer states that GM crops contain fewer potential allergens, the lecturer points out that agricultural scientists are worried about allergic reactions in the human body. This is because added proteins in GM crops are not native to the original ones.

Secondly, the lecturer refutes the argument in the reading passage that pesticide applications can be reduced. She states that using a specific pesticide repeatedly can cause an increase in pesticide resistance to a particular species. This is because there is the possibility of resistant pest populations to evolve. While the writer states that GM maize with the gene for toxin creation does not need additional pesticide, the lecturer highlights that the pink bollworm in India has resistance to GM cotton, and similar cases have been reported in some countries.

Finally, the lecturer doubts the writer's argument that GM seeds with a higher yield and lower production cost will give financial benefits to farmers and produce more at affordable prices. **She contends that** it is problematic that many farmers rely on multinational seed companies. **In the reading passage,** farmers in developing countries can easily purchase GM seeds and achieve some financial benefits from it, **but in the listening part, the lecturer says** this will make the farmers highly dependent on industrialized nations. In fact, the companies have already increased the prices of seeds and negatively affected the global economy.

(337 words)

독해 지문과 강의는 모두 유전자 변형 작물(GM)을 이야기한다. 글쓴이는 GM 작물이 세계적으로 몇몇 장점이 있다는 점을 언급한다. 하지만, 강의 진행자는 독해 지문에 제시된 각 이점과 연관되어 있는 몇몇 단점 및 위험 요소들이 있다고 말하면서 그러한 주장에 동의하지 않는다.

가장 먼저, 강의 진행자는 GM 작물이 더 높은 영양적 가치로 인간의 건강을 향상시키는 데 도움이 된다는 글쓴이의 주장에 의구심을 갖는다. 강의 진행자는 이러한 장점이 사실일 수도 있지만, 실제 과학적인 자료를 기반으로 하지 않는다고 주장한다. GM 작물이 인간의 건강에 미치는 영향과 관련해 실시된 연구가 거의 없으며, 그 사례들의 많은 것이 회의론 및 비판론에 직면했다. 글쓴이가 GM 작물이 잠재적인 알레르기 유발 항원을 더 적게 함유하고 있다고 언급하고 있지만, 강의 진행자는 농업 과학자들이 사람 신체 내의 알레르기 반응에 대해 우려하고 있다는 점을 지적한다. 이는 GM 작물에 추가되는 단백질이 원래의 작물에 고유한 것이 아니기 때문이다.

두 번째로, 강의 진행자는 독해 지문에서 살충제 사용이 줄어들 수 있다고 제시한 주장에 반박하고 있다. 강의 진행자는 반복적으로 특정 살충제를 사용하면 특정 종에 대한 살충제 내성 증가를 유발할 수 있다고 언급한다. 이는 내성을 지닌 해충 개체군으로 발전될 가능성이 있기 때문이다. 글쓴이가 독성 생성 유전자를 지닌 GM 옥수수는 별도의 살충제가 필요치 않다고 언급하고 있지만, 강의 진행자는 인도의 분홍솜벌레가 GM 목화에 내성을 지니고 있고, 유사한 사례들이 몇몇 국가에서 보고된 점을 강조하고 있다.

마지막으로, 강의 진행자는 수확량은 더 높고 생산비는 더 낮은 GM 종자가 농부들에게 재정적 이점을 제공해주면서 알맞은 가격으로 더 많은 양을 생산할 것이라는 글쓴이의 주장에 의구심을 지니고 있다. 강의 진행자는 많은 농부들이 다국적 종자 생산업체에 의존하는 것이 문제가 된다고 주장한다. 독해 지문에는, 개발 도상국 농부들이 쉽게 GM 종자를 구입해 그것으로부터 일부 재정적 이점을 이룰 수 있다고 나타나 있지만, 청해 파트에는, 이러한 점으로 인해 농부들이 선진국에 크게 의존하게 될 것이라고 강의 진행자가 말한다. 실제로, 그 업체들은 이미 종자의 가격을 인상해 세계 경제에 부정적으로 영향을 미쳐 왔다.

어휘

genetically modified crops 유전자 변형 작물 **recombinant** (유전자에 대한) 재조합의 **transfer** ~을 이식하다 **far-reaching** 지대한 영향을 미치는 **allergen** 알레르기 유발 항원 **play a potential role in** ~에 있어 잠재적인 역할을 하다 **malnutrition** 영양 실조 **rely heavily on** ~에 크게 의존하다 **benefit** n. 이점, 혜택 v. 이득을 얻다, 혜택을 보다 **pesticide** 살충제(= insecticide) **application** 사용, 적용 **residue** 잔여물 **resistance** 내성, 저항성 **yield** 수확(량), 산출(량) **emerge** 나타나다, 출현하다

involved 관련된, 수반된 **associated with** ~와 연관된 **carry out** ~을 실시하다(= conduct) **be met with** ~에 부딪히다, ~을 접하다 **skepticism** 회의론 **allergenicity** 알레르기 항원성 **native to** ~에 고유한 **target species** 목표 생물 종 **population** 개체군, 개체수 **dependence on** ~에 대한 의존(도) **inflate** ~을 부풀리다

face ~에 직면하다, ~와 맞닥뜨리다 **affect** ~에 영향을 미치다

실전문제 3 – 생물 주제 (3)

Reading Passage	Listening Script
Paleontologists recently uncovered 66-million-year-old fossilized remains of a Tyrannosaurus rex and were surprised to discover that the specimen still contained some actual living tissues. The find is virtually unprecedented, as fossils typically contain only minerals that have replaced an animal's tissues. The paleontologists made their groundbreaking discovery when they cracked open one of the fossilized bones and found what appeared to be the remains of collagen, red blood cells, and blood vessels inside the exposed cavity.	The idea of detecting the remains of actual T-rex tissue is as exciting to me as it is to anyone, but in reality, many of the claims made in the reading passage should be viewed with skepticism.
First, upon analyzing the inside of the broken bone, the scientists observed numerous hollow grooves that branched off in various directions. They concluded that these were likely the channels where blood vessels were once located in the bone. Closer inspection revealed a soft organic substance within the grooves. This caused much excitement among the scientists, as they believed it could be the remnants of the Tyrannosaurus rex's actual blood vessels.	First, the organic substance found inside the bone grooves could be any number of substances, so we should not jump to the conclusion that it represents the remains of blood vessels. For instance, bacteria often inhabit bone cavities, such as the channels where blood vessels used to be, long after an animal has died. So, it is common to find scraps of organic material when bacteria have lived inside bones. The material identified as blood vessels by the scientists may simply be the remnants of bacteria.
Second, the scientists examined the interior structures of the bone using powerful microscopes, and they detected rounded particles that may once have been red blood cells. Further analysis showed the presence of iron within the spherical particles. Iron is critical to the transportation of oxygen by red blood cells. Furthermore, the center of each particle was dark red in color, and each particle was of comparable size to a red blood cell.	Second, the passage mentions the significance of the dark red rounded particles that could contain iron. Well, the problem with that is that similar particles have been found in other fossils in that region, including fossils of organisms that never had red blood cells. So, thinking logically, these particles are probably the remains of something else - such as a mineral that is red in color - rather than evidence of red blood cells.
Third, another test indicated that collagen - a key component of living bone tissue - was still contained within the bone. This fibrous protein combines with other proteins to form a matrix that basically acts as a strong scaffolding inside living bones. So, its presence supported the notion that actual bone tissue still existed in the bone.	Third, with regard to the supposed presence of collagen, there is a big problem. Collagen has never been detected in animal remains that are older than one hundred thousand years, and collagen is not believed to be able to last any longer than that. So, it is highly improbable that collagen would remain in fossilized remains for 66 million years. A more likely scenario is that the collagen came from a more recent source and was never actual tissue from the Tyrannosaurus rex. It's even possible that it came from the fingertips of the scientists examining the specimen, as human skin contains collagen.

해석

고생물학자들이 최근 6,600백만 년이나 된 티라노사우루스 렉스 화석 유해를 발굴했으며, 그 표본이 여전히 일부 실제 생체 조직을 포함하고 있다는 사실을 발견하고는 놀라워했다. 이 발견물은 거의 전례 없는 일인데, 화석이 일반적으로 동물의 생체 조직을 대체한 무기질만 포함하고 있기 때문이다. 고생물학자들은 화석화된 뼈들 중의 하나를 쪼개서 연 다음, 노출된 구멍 안쪽에 콜라겐과, 적혈구, 그리고 혈관으로 보이는 것을 찾아내면서 획기적인 발견을 이뤘다.

첫 번째로, 깨진 뼈 내부를 분석하면서, 과학자들은 여러 방향으로 가지처럼 뻗어 있는 수많은 가늘고 긴 홈들이 비어 있는 것을 관찰했다. 과학자들은 이것들이 한때 혈관들이 뼈 속에 자리잡고 있던 가는 홈일 가능성이 있는 것으로 결론 내렸다. 더욱 면밀한 조사를 통해 그 가늘고 긴 홈들 내부에 부드러운 유기 물질이 있는 것으로 드러났다. 이는 과학자들 사이에서 대단한 흥분을 일으켰는데, 이들은 그 물질이 티라노사우루스 렉스의 실제 혈관이 남은 부분일 수 있다고 생각했기 때문이다.

두 번째로, 과학자들은 강력한 현미경을 활용해 뼈의 내부 구조를 검사했는데, 한때 적혈구였을 수도 있는 둥근 입자들을 발견했다. 더욱 심층적인 분석을 통해 그 구형 입자들 내에서 철분의 존재가 드러났다. 철분은 적혈구에 의한 산소 운반에 있어 대단히 중요하다. 더욱이, 각 입자의 중심부는 검붉은색이었으며, 각 입자는 적혈구와 비슷한 크기로 되어 있었다.

세 번째로, 또 다른 테스트를 통해 생체 뼈 조직의 핵심 구성 요소인 콜라겐이 여전히 뼈 내부에 남아 있었던 것으로 나타났다. 이 섬유질 단백질은 다른 단백질들과 결합해 기본적으로 생체 뼈 내부에서 튼튼한 골격 역할을 하는 세포간질을 형성한다. 따라서, 그 존재는 실제 뼈 조직이 여전히 뼈 내에 존재하고 있다는 개념을 뒷받침해주었다.

실제 티렉스 생체 조직의 유해를 발견한다는 생각은 누구에게나 그렇듯 저에게도 흥미롭긴 하지만, 현실적으로는, 독해 지문에 제기된 주장들 중 많은 부분은 회의적인 시각으로 바라봐야 합니다.

첫 번째로, 뼈의 가늘고 긴 홈에서 찾은 유기 물질은 얼마든지 많은 물질들일 수 있기 때문에 그것이 혈관 유해를 나타낸다고 단정짓지 말아야 합니다. 예를 들어, 박테리아는 동물이 죽고 오랜 시간이 지난 후에도 전에 혈관이 있던 가는 홈 같은 뼈 속 구멍에 흔히 서식합니다. 따라서, 박테리아가 뼈 내부에 살아 있던 경우에 남은 유기 물질을 흔히 찾을 수 있습니다. 과학자들에 의해 혈관으로 확인된 물질은 단순히 박테리아 잔여물일 수 있습니다.

두 번째로, 독해 지문은 철분을 함유하고 있을 수 있는 검붉은색 둥근 입자의 중요성을 언급합니다. 음, 그에 대한 문제는 유사한 입자들이 그 지역 내 다른 화석들에서도 발견된 바가 있다는 점이며, 여기에는 적혈구를 전혀 갖고 있지 않는 생물체의 화석도 포함됩니다. 따라서, 논리적으로 생각해보면, 이 입자들은 아마 적혈구에 대한 증거가 아니라 붉은색으로 된 무기물 같은 무언가 다른 것의 유해일 수 있습니다.

세 번째로, 이른바 콜라겐의 존재와 관련해서는, 큰 문제가 있습니다. 콜라겐은 10만년보다 오래된 동물 유해에서 한 번도 발견된 적이 없었으며, 콜라겐은 그보다 조금이라도 더 오래 지속될 수 있는 것으로 여겨지지 않습니다. 따라서, 콜라겐이 6,600백만 년 동안이나 화석화된 유해 속에 남아 있을 가능성은 거의 없습니다. 좀 더 가능성 있는 시나리오는 그 콜라겐이 더 최근의 출처에서 나온 것이었고 절대로 실제 티라노사우루스 렉스의 생체 조직이 아니었다는 점입니다. 인간의 피부가 콜라겐을 포함하고 있기 때문에, 심지어 그 표본을 검사하던 과학자들의 손가락 끝부분에서 나온 것일 가능성도 있습니다.

강의에서 언급된 요점들이 어떻게 독해 지문에 제시된 특정 주장들에 대해 대응하는지 설명하면서 그 내용을 요약해 보시오.

노트테이킹

T.rex living tissue blood vessels, red blood cells, collagen	skeptic.
hollow grooves soft organic - remnants	X ex bacteria after ani. died com. orga. mater. bacteria live
rounded particles = red blood cells iron critical - transport. of oxyg.	prob. simil. particles / X red blood cells remains
collagen	big prob. X last longer from fingertips - exam.

모범 답안

The reading passage and the lecture both discuss whether the fossilized remains of a Tyrannosaurus rex contained some actual living tissue. The writer states that the remains of blood vessels, red blood cells and collagen were discovered inside the exposed cavity of the bone. However, the lecturer disagrees with the argument, saying that the evidence suggested by the writer should be viewed with skepticism.

First of all, the lecturer doubts the writer's point that hollow grooves were likely to be where blood vessels were once located based on a remaining organic substance. He argues that it cannot be concluded that the organic substance is the remains of blood vessels. Although the writer states that the soft organic substance within the grooves could be the remnants of the blood vessels by closer inspection, the lecturer points out that it could possibly be the remains of bacteria. In fact, it is common for bacteria to live inside bones after an animal has died.

Secondly, the lecturer refutes the argument of the reading passage that red blood cells were detected in the form of rounded particles. He states that this argument has a problem. While the writer states that the rounded particles have iron critical to the transport of oxygen by red blood cells, the lecturer highlights that other fossils in the same region have similar particles but never had red blood cells. Therefore, these particles could be the remains of something else.

Finally, the lecturer doubts the writer's argument that collagen was detected within the bone. He contends that this evidence has a big problem. In the reading passage, the presence of collagen can support the existence of actual bone tissue, but in the listening part, the lecturer says that collagen cannot last any longer than one hundred thousand years. Rather, collagen could have come from the fingertips of the scientists while examining the Tyrannosaurus rex, not from the specimen.

(317 words)

독해 지문과 강의는 모두 티라노사우루스 렉스 화석 유해가 일부 실제 생체 조직을 포함하고 있었는지 이야기한다. 글쓴이는 혈관과 적혈구, 그리고 콜라겐 유해가 뼈의 노출된 구멍 내부에서 발견되었다고 언급한다. 하지만, 강의 진행자는 글쓴이에 의해 제시된 증거를 회의적인 시각으로 바라봐야 한다고 말하면서 그러한 주장에 동의하지 않는다.

가장 먼저, 강의 진행자는 비어 있는 가늘고 긴 홈들이 남아 있는 유기 물질을 바탕으로 한때 혈관이 자리잡고 있던 곳이었을 가능성이 있다는 글쓴이의 주장에 의구심을 갖는다. 강의 진행자는 그 유기 물질이 혈관 유해인 것으로 결론 내릴 수 없다고 주장한다. 글쓴이는 그 가는 홈 내부의 부드러운 유기 물질이 더욱 면밀한 조사를 통해 혈관 잔여물일 수 있다고 언급하고 있지만, 강의 진행자는 그것이 아마 박테리아 유해일 수 있다고 지적한다. 실제로, 동물이 죽은 후에도 박테리아가 뼈 속에 사는 것이 흔하다.

두 번째로, 강의 진행자는 적혈구가 둥근 입자 형태로 발견되었다고 말하는 독해 지문 내의 주장에 반박하고 있다. 강의 진행자는 이러한 주장에 문제가 있다고 언급한다. 글쓴이가 그 둥근 입자가 적혈구의 산소 운반에 대단히 중요한 철분을 지니고 있다고 언급하는 반면, 강의 진행자는 같은 지역의 다른 화석들이 유사한 입자들을 지니고 있긴 하지만, 적혈구는 전혀 없었다는 점을 강조한다. 따라서, 이 입자들은 뭔가 다른 것의 유해일 수 있다.

마지막으로, 강의 진행자는 콜라겐이 뼈 내부에서 발견되었다는 글쓴이의 주장에 의구심을 갖는다. 강의 진행자는 이 증거에 큰 문제가 있다고 주장한다. 독해 지문에는, 콜라겐의 존재가 실제 뼈 조직의 존재를 뒷받침해줄 수 있다고 나타나 있지만, 청해 파트에는, 콜라겐이 10만년보다 조금이라도 더 오래 지속될 수 없다고 강의 진행자가 말한다. 오히려, 콜라겐이 그 표본이 아니라 티라노사우루스 렉스를 검사하던 중에 그 과학자들의 손가락 끝부분에서 나왔을 수도 있다.

실전문제 4 – 생물 주제 (4)

Reading Passage	Listening Script
Among all of the marine species endangered by the fishing industry, sea turtles face the gravest threat. When turtles get tangled up in nets used by commercial shrimp-fishing boats, they are unable to swim to the surface for air. An invention called a turtle excluder device (TED) has been proposed as a solution to this problem. A TED is incorporated into the nets and functions by letting captured turtles escape through a door in the net. However, many people are opposed to the use of TEDs for a variety of reasons.	We have just read about several criticisms that have been made about TEDs, or turtle excluder devices. However, many leading experts maintain that TEDs are an excellent way to protect endangered turtles, and these are some of their arguments for their use on shrimping vessels.
First, TEDs may not be as effective as other strategies when it comes to limiting the threat to sea turtles. One strategy that has been suggested is enforcing a law that restricts the amount of time that nets can be kept underwater. Before a set time limit, the shrimp boats must raise their nets so that any turtles tangled up in them can have a chance to breathe and subsequently be set free by the shrimp boat crew.	First, a law that imposes a time limit on fishing net use might sound like a good idea, but it would be too difficult to enforce. There are thousands upon thousands of shrimp boats in the seas and oceans, most of which are hundreds of miles from the nearest land. It would be virtually impossible for government officials to monitor all these vessels. In contrast, it would be relatively simple to mandate the use of TEDs by requiring all shrimp boats to have them installed prior to leaving port.
Second, certain species of threatened sea turtles grow to such large sizes that TEDs would be ineffective in saving them. For instance, adult leatherbacks and loggerheads - two of the largest species of sea turtles - would be unable to pass through the relatively narrow escape passages that are installed in TEDs. So, for these species, even nets equipped with TEDs would still pose a threat to adult turtles.	Second, there is some truth to the argument that some turtle species are too large for TEDs, but these turtles are not present in large numbers in many shrimping locations. Moreover, it would not be too hard to modify TEDs in regions where large turtles live, making them large enough to accommodate those species. So, if larger TEDs could be easily implemented, this would overcome the issue of large turtles being unable to pass through the nets.
Third, many shrimp boat captains report that turtles rarely ever get tangled up in nets. Fishing industry data indicate that a shrimp boat may accidentally catch only around ten turtles per year. Moreover, TEDs will reduce the amount of shrimp that the boats can catch, and the profitability of each catch, because a significant number of them will escape through the turtle passage. Shrimpers argue that this is a disproportionately high cost to pay just to save ten turtles per year.	Third, even if a single shrimp boat only accidentally catches around ten turtles per year, that still results in a huge number of dead turtles, considering that there are thousands of shrimp boats in operation. And we are talking about species that are already endangered, so the loss of thousands of turtles each year will bring their populations down to significantly low numbers. The rapid decline of sea turtle populations is a far worse outcome overall than shrimp boats losing some of their catch and profits.

수산업에 의해 멸종 위기에 처한 모든 해양 생물 종 중에서, 바다거북은 가장 심각한 위협에 직면해 있다. 거북이들이 상업용 새우잡이 배에서 사용하는 그물망에 걸려 뒤엉키게 되면, 공기를 얻기 위해 수면을 향해 헤엄칠 수 없다. 거북 탈출 장치(TED)라고 불리는 발명품이 이 문제에 대한 해결책으로 제안되었다. TED는 그물망 내에 포함되어 있는 것으로서 갇힌 거북이 그물망 내의 출구를 통해 빠져나갈 수 있게 해주는 것으로 기능한다. 하지만, 많은 사람들이 다양한 이유로 TED의 사용에 반대한다.

첫 번째로, TED는 바다거북에 대한 위협을 제한하는 일과 관련해서는 다른 전략들만큼 효과적이지 않을 수 있다. 제안된 바 있는 한 가지 전략은 그물망이 바다 속에서 유지될 수 있는 시간 길이를 제한하는 법을 시행하는 것이다. 정해진 제한 시간이 되기 전에, 새우잡이 배가 반드시 그물망을 걷어 올려 그 안에 걸려 엉켜있는 어떤 거북이든 숨도 쉬고 그 뒤로 새우잡이 배의 선원에 의해 풀려날 기회를 얻을 수 있게 해주는 것이다.

두 번째로, 멸종 위기에 처한 특정 바다거북 종은 너무 크게 자라서 TED가 구출하는 데 효과적이지 못할 것이다. 예를 들어, 성체가 된 장수거북과 붉은바다거북은 가장 큰 두 가지 바다거북 종으로서, TED 내에 설치된 상대적으로 좁은 탈출 통로를 통해 빠져나가지 못할 것이다. 따라서, 이러한 종에 대해서는, 심지어 TED가 장착된 그물망이 성체 거북에게 여전히 위협을 가하게 될 것이다.

세 번째로, 많은 새우잡이 배 선장들은 거북이 좀처럼 그물망에 걸려 엉켜 있지 않다고 전한다. 수산업 자료에 따르면 새우잡이 배 한 척이 일 년에 오직 약 10마리의 거북이만 우연히 잡을 수 있는 것으로 나타나 있다. 더욱이, TED는 새우잡이 배가 잡을 수 있는 새우의 양과 각 어획량의 수익성을 떨어뜨리게 되는데, 상당수가 거북 탈출 통로를 통해 빠져나가기 때문이다. 새우잡이 어부들은 이것이 단지 일 년에 10마리의 거북을 살리기 위해 치르는 대가로는 지나치게 값비싼 것이라고 주장한다.

우리는 방금 TED, 즉 거북 탈출 장치와 관련해 제기된 여러 비판과 관련된 내용을 읽어봤습니다. 하지만, 손꼽히는 많은 전문가들은 TED가 멸종 위기에 처한 거북을 보호하는 훌륭한 방법이라고 주장하고 있으며, 이는 그들이 새우잡이 배에서 활용하자고 주장하는 것의 일부입니다.

첫 번째로, 어망에 대해 제한 시간을 부과하는 법은 좋은 아이디어인 것처럼 들릴 지도 모르지만, 시행하기 너무 어려울 것입니다. 바다와 해양에는 수천 수만 척의 새우잡이 배가 있으며, 그 대부분은 가장 가까운 육지에서 수백 마일 떨어져 있습니다. 정부 당국자들이 이 배들을 모두 감시한다는 건 사실상 불가능할 것입니다. 이와 대조적으로, 출항하기에 앞서 모든 새우잡이 배에 설치해 놓도록 요구함으로써 TED 활용을 의무화하는 것은 비교적 간단할 것입니다.

두 번째로, 일부 거북 종이 TED에 비해 너무 크다는 주장은 일부 사실이긴 하지만, 이 거북들은 많은 새우잡이 조업 지역에 대규모로 존재하지 않습니다. 게다가, 대형 거북이 사는 지역에서 TED를 개조해 그러한 종을 수용할 정도로 충분히 크게 만드는 게 아주 어렵진 않을 것입니다. 따라서, 더 큰 TED가 쉽게 시행될 수 있다면, 이것으로 대형 거북이 그물망을 통과해 지나갈 수 없는 문제를 극복하게 될 것입니다.

세 번째로, 설사 단 한 척의 새우잡이 배가 단지 우연히 일 년에 약 10마리의 거북을 잡는다 하더라도, 수천 척의 새우잡이 배가 조업하고 있다는 것을 감안하면, 이로 인해 여전히 엄청난 숫자의 죽은 거북이 생기게 됩니다. 그리고 우리는 이미 멸종 위기에 처한 종에 관해 이야기하고 있기 때문에, 매년 죽음에 이르는 수천 마리의 거북으로 인해 개체수가 상당히 낮은 수치로 떨어질 것입니다. 바다거북 개체수의 빠른 감소는 새우잡이 배들이 어획량과 수익의 일부를 잃는 것보다 전반적으로 훨씬 더 좋지 않은 결과입니다.

강의에서 언급된 요점들이 어떻게 독해 지문에 제시된 특정 주장들에 대해 대응하는지 설명하면서 그 내용을 요약해 보시오.

노트테이킹

sol. oppos.	excel.
time limit	good / diffi. enforce boats ↑ - X monitor simple install before leave
ineff. large pass X	O / rare modi. large enough → overcome
rare	huge number popul ↓ rapid ↓ → worse

모범 답안

The reading and the lecture both discuss whether a turtle excluder device (TED) can be a solution to turtles becoming tangled in nets. The writer states that there are opposing opinions on using TEDs. However, the lecturer disagrees with the argument, saying that TEDs are an excellent method to protect endangered turtles.

First of all, the lecturer doubts the writer's point that a time limit to keep nets underwater would be a good strategy. She argues that the way of limiting time sounds good, but it is difficult to enforce. This is because there are so many boats in the sea that officials could not monitor all of them. The lecturer also argues that using TEDs would be relatively simpler than a time limit method in that boats are required to install TEDs just before leaving a port.

Secondly, the lecturer refutes the argument of the reading passage that the large size of turtles could make TEDs ineffective. She states that this is partially true, but the specific turtle species with a large body is rare in shrimping locations. While the writer states that large turtles could not escape through the turtle passage, the lecturer highlights that TEDs can be made large enough for larger turtles to pass through. Therefore, this problem could be easily overcome.

Finally, the lecturer doubts the writer's argument that catching turtles rarely happens, only about ten turtles per year. She contends that the accidental catching eventually results in a huge number of deaths. Plus, the population of endangered species would go down. In the reading passage, the writer claims that implementing TEDs is a high cost to pay, but in the listening part, the lecturer says that the rapid decrease of the populations is worse than losing some profits.

(294 words)

독해 지문과 강의는 모두 거북 탈출 장치(TED)가 거북이 그물망에 걸려 엉키게 되는 문제에 대한 해결책이 될 수 있는지 이야기한다. 글쓴이는 TED 이용을 반대하는 의견이 있다고 언급한다. 하지만, 강의 진행자는 TED가 멸종 위기에 처한 거북을 보호할 수 있는 훌륭한 방법이라고 말하면서 그러한 주장에 동의하지 않는다.

가장 먼저, 강의 진행자는 그물망을 물속에 넣어두는 시간에 대한 제한이 좋은 전략이 될 것이라는 글쓴이의 주장에 의구심을 갖는다. 강의 진행자는 시간 제한 방법이 좋은 것처럼 들리기는 하지만, 시행하기 어렵다고 주장한다. 이는 바다에 배가 너무 많이 있어서 당국자들이 그것을 모두 감시할 수 없기 때문이다. 강의 진행자는 또한 배가 출항 직전에 TED를 설치해야 한다는 점에서 TED 이용이 시간 제한 방법보다 상대적으로 더 간단할 것이라고 주장한다.

두 번째로, 강의 진행자는 크기가 큰 거북이 TED를 효과적이지 못하게 만들 수 있다고 말하는 독해 지문 내의 주장에 반박하고 있다. 강의 진행자는 이것이 일부 사실이긴 하지만, 몸이 큰 특정 거북 종이 새우잡이 조업 지역에 흔치 않다고 언급한다. 글쓴이는 큰 거북이 거북 탈출 통로를 통해 빠져나갈 수 없을 거라고 언급하고 있지만, 강의 진행자는 TED가 더 큰 거북이 통과해 지나갈 수 있을 정도로 충분히 크게 만들어질 수 있다는 점을 강조한다. 따라서, 이 문제는 쉽게 극복할 수 있을 것이다.

마지막으로, 강의 진행자는 일 년에 불과 약 10마리밖에 되지 않을 정도로 거북을 잡는 일이 좀처럼 발생되지 않는다는 글쓴이의 주장에 의구심을 갖는다. 강의 진행자는 그렇게 우연한 포획이 결국 엄청난 숫자의 죽음을 초래한다고 주장한다. 게다가, 멸종 위기에 처한 종의 개체수가 줄어들게 될 것이다. 독해 지문에서, 글쓴이는 TED 시행이 지불해야 하는 값비싼 대가라고 주장하지만, 청해 파트에서, 강의 진행자는 빠른 개체수 감소가 일부 수익을 잃는 것보다 더 좋지 않다고 말한다.

어휘

species (동식물의) 종 endangered 멸종 위기에 처한 grave 심각한 get tangled up in ~에 걸려 뒤엉키게 되다 incorporate ~을 통합하다, 합치다 be opposed to ~에 반대하다 when it comes to ~와 관련해서는, ~라는 측면에 있어 enforce (법 등) ~을 시행하다, 집행하다 subsequently 그 뒤에, 나중에 equipped with ~가 장착된, ~을 갖춘 pose a threat to ~에 위협을 가하다 profitability 수익성 disproportionately 지나치게, 불균형적으로

impose ~을 부과하다 virtually 사실상, 거의 mandate ~을 의무화하다 modify ~을 개조하다, 변경하다 accommodate ~을 수용하다 implement ~을 시행하다 overcome ~을 극복하다 outcome 결과 overall 전반적으로

population 개체수, 개체군

실전문제 5 - 생물 주제 (5)

Reading Passage	Listening Script
The underwater noises, or songs, produced by whales can be useful for tracking the migration routes of whale populations. Scientists studying whale song recently discovered one unique whale who makes noises like no other whale. To be specific, the song of this whale is unique in that it is sung at 52 hertz, which is an unusually high pitch or frequency. The 52-hertz whale's distinctive ability confused scientists when they first detected the animal, but they have now put forward a few theories to explain the phenomenon.	Scientists have put forward three theories to explain why the 52-hertz whale sings so uniquely, but there are flaws in each one that I'd like to discuss.
The first theory is that the 52-hertz whale may simply be a highly uncommon species of whale - a species that has so few members that scientists have never encountered one before. The species may have been more abundant in the past, but its population may have significantly declined. The 52-hertz whale may even be the only surviving member of the species.	First, it is very improbable that the 52-hertz whale is the last member, or one of the last members, of a rare species. Even if that were the case, the whale obviously had parents, and those whales would also have sung at a pitch of 52 hertz. But, scientists have been using technology to listen to whale song for several decades, and they have never before heard a song like the one produced by the 52-hertz whale. So, there must be another reason for this whale's unique vocalizations.
A second theory is that two different species of whales mated and gave birth to the 52-hertz whale, making it a hybrid. It is known that when different species of whales mate, it is common for the offspring to carry species-specific traits from both parents. The 52-hertz whale may sing in such a distinctive way because its song is a unique combination of its parents' songs, rather than being the same as either parent's song.	Second, there is a very low chance that the 52-hertz whale is the offspring of two different species. We know that its migration pattern is very unique, whereas the migration patterns of genuine hybrid whales typically follow those of non-hybrid whales. So, we would expect the 52-hertz whale to follow the patterns of non-hybrid whales, if it were truly a hybrid. But, in reality, scientists who have tracked the songs of the 52-hertz whale have found that it migrates by itself, following a very unusual route.
A third theory is that the hearing of the 52-hertz whale is impaired in some way. Whales learn to make sounds in the same way that humans do - by mimicking the sounds they hear. When humans are born with hearing deficiencies, their speech develops very differently from that of someone with perfect hearing. So, the 52-hertz whale may sing uniquely because it has been unable to hear the songs produced by other whales.	Third, hearing impairment or deafness does not adequately explain why the frequency or pitch of the 52-hertz whale's song is so high. As is the case with humans, the sounds that whales make originate from the throat, so the song pitch is dependent on the structure of a whale's throat. The 52-hertz whale's throat structure must be very unique for it to produce sounds at such a high pitch, and this has no connection to any kind of hearing deficiency.

해석

고래가 수중에서 만들어내는 소리, 즉 노래는 고래 개체군의 이주 경로를 추적하는 데 유용할 수 있다. 고래의 노래를 연구하는 과학자들이 최근 다른 모든 고래와 완전히 다른 소리를 만들어내는 특별한 고래 하나를 발견했다. 구체적으로, 이 고래의 노래는 52헤르츠에서 불려진다는 점에서 특별한데, 이는 흔치 않게 높은 음조, 즉 높은 주파수에 해당된다. 52헤르츠로 노래하는 고래의 독특한 능력은 이 동물을 처음 발견했을 때 과학자들을 혼란스럽게 했지만, 지금은 이러한 현상을 설명하기 위해 몇 가지 이론까지 제시한 상태이다.

첫 번째 이론은 52헤르츠로 노래하는 고래가 그야말로 대단히 흔치 않은 고래 종, 즉 극소수 구성원만 속해 있어서 과학자들이 전에 한 번도 접해본 적이 없었던 종일 수 있다는 점이다. 이 종은 과거에 더 많았을 수도 있지만, 그 개체수가 상당히 줄어들었을 수 있다. 52헤르츠로 노래하는 고래는 심지어 그 종에서 유일하게 생존해 있는 일원일 수 있다.

두 번째 이론은 두 가지 다른 고래 종이 짝짓기를 해 52헤르츠로 노래하는 고래를 낳으면서, 혼종이 생겨났다는 것이다. 서로 다른 고래 종이 짝짓기할 때, 그 새끼가 부모 둘 모두에게서 물려받은 종 특유의 특성을 지니는 것이 흔한 일로 알려져 있다. 52헤르츠로 노래하는 고래는 그 노래가 부모 중 어느 한쪽의 노래와 같은 것이 아니라 부모의 노래들이 독특하게 조합되어 있어서 그렇게 특색 있는 방식으로 노래할 수 있다.

세 번째 이론은 52헤르츠로 노래하는 고래의 청력에 어떤 면에서 장애가 있다는 점이다. 고래는 사람이 소리를 듣고 모방하는 것과 동일한 방식으로 소리 내는 법을 배운다. 사람이 청각 장애를 갖고 태어나는 경우에, 그 사람의 말하기 능력은 완벽한 청력을 지닌 사람과 매우 다르게 발달된다. 따라서, 52헤르츠로 노래하는 고래는 다른 고래들이 만들어내는 노래들을 들을 수 없었기 때문에 독특하게 노래할 수 있는 것이다.

과학자들이 왜 52헤르츠로 노래하는 고래가 그렇게 독특하게 노래하는지 설명하기 위해 세 가지 이론을 제시했지만, 각 이론에 결점이 있으며 그 얘기를 해보고자 합니다.

첫 번째로, 52헤르츠로 노래하는 고래가 희귀 종의 마지막 일원, 즉 마지막으로 남은 일원들 중 하나라는 점은 거의 불가능한 일입니다. 설사 그것이 가능한 경우라 하더라도, 그 고래에겐 부모가 있었기 때문에, 그 고래들 또한 52헤르츠의 음조로 노래했을 것입니다. 하지만, 과학자들은 수십 년 동안 기계를 활용해 고래의 노래를 계속 들어오고 있으며, 52헤르츠로 노래하는 고래가 만들어내는 것과 같은 노래를 전에 한 번도 들어본 적이 없습니다. 따라서, 이 고래의 독특한 발성에는 틀림없이 다른 이유가 존재합니다.

두 번째로, 52헤르츠로 노래하는 고래가 두 가지 다른 종의 새끼일 가능성은 대단히 낮습니다. 우리는 그 고래의 이주 패턴이 매우 독특한 반면, 진정한 혼종 고래의 이주 패턴이 일반적으로 혼종이 아닌 고래의 패턴을 따른다는 사실을 알고 있습니다. 따라서, 우리는 52헤르츠로 노래하는 고래가 정말 혼종이라면, 혼종이 아닌 고래의 패턴을 따를 것으로 예상할 수 있습니다. 하지만, 실제로는, 52헤르츠로 노래하는 고래의 노래를 추적했던 과학자들은 그 고래가 매우 특이한 경로를 따라 혼자 이주한다는 사실을 알게 되었습니다.

세 번째로, 청각 장애, 즉 난청은 왜 52헤르츠로 노래하는 고래의 주파수 또는 음조가 그렇게 높은지 충분히 설명해주지 못합니다. 인간의 경우와 마찬가지로, 고래가 만들어내는 소리는 목에서 비롯되기 때문에, 노래의 음조는 고래 목의 구조에 의해 좌우됩니다. 52헤르츠로 노래하는 고래의 목 구조는 그렇게 높은 음조로 된 소리를 만들어낼 정도로 대단히 특별한 것이 틀림없으며, 이는 어떤 종류의 청각 장애와도 연관성이 없습니다.

강의에서 언급된 요점들이 어떻게 독해 지문에 제시된 특정 주장들에 대해 이의를 제기하는지 설명하면서 그 내용을 요약해 보시오.

노트테이킹

unique theories	flaws
X common	improb. parents o / X heard another
hybrid – two	low chance mig. pattern – non-hyb. unusual
hearing impairment	X adequ. throat unique X connec.

모범 답안

The reading and the lecture both discuss the uniqueness of the 52-hertz whale. The writer states that there are three theories why the whale sound is unique. However, the lecturer disagrees with the argument, saying that each of the explanations has flaws.

First of all, the lecturer doubts the writer's point that the 52-hertz whale may be an unusual species that is rarely encountered. He argues that this point is improbable. Although the writer states that the significant decline of its population may lead to it being rare, the lecturer points out that there would have been parents that made the 52-hertz sound too, but scientists have never heard a song like this. Therefore, it is possible that there is another reason for the unique sound.

Secondly, the lecturer refutes the argument of the reading passage that the 52-hertz whale could be a hybrid with specific traits from two different types of whales. He states that there is a very low chance for this to be true. This is because the whale shows unique migration patterns distinctive from hybrid whales, which follow the routes of non-hybrid whales. The lecturer also points out that the 52-hertz whale migrates following an unusual route based on tracking its song.

Finally, the lecturer doubts the writer's argument that a hearing impairment could be the reason for the high pitch. He contends that the argument does not adequately explain the high frequency. In the reading passage, the writer claims that whales with hearing deficiencies make high pitch sounds because of the lack of opportunity to learn how to make sounds from others, but in the listening part, the lecturer says there is no connection between the high pitch and hearing deficiencies. This is because the whale sounds originate from the unique structure of its throat, not as a result of hearing impairment.

(307 words)

독해 지문과 강의는 모두 52헤르츠로 노래하는 고래의 독특함을 이야기한다. 글쓴이는 왜 이 고래의 소리가 독특한지에 관한 세 가지 이론이 있다고 언급한다. 하지만, 강의 진행자는 각 설명에 결점이 있다고 말하면서 그러한 주장에 동의하지 않는다.

가장 먼저, 강의 진행자는 52헤르츠로 노래하는 고래가 좀처럼 접할 수 없는 흔치 않은 종일 수 있다는 글쓴이의 주장에 의구심을 갖는다. 강의 진행자는 이러한 주장이 가능성이 없다고 주장한다. 글쓴이는 그 고래 개체수의 상당한 감소가 희귀 상태로 이어질 수 있다고 언급하지만, 강의 진행자는 52헤르츠의 소리를 낸 부모들도 있었겠지만 과학자들은 이러한 노래를 한 번도 들어본 적이 없었다고 지적한다. 따라서, 그 독특한 소리에 대한 다른 이유가 존재할 가능성이 있다.

두 번째로, 강의 진행자는 52헤르츠로 노래하는 고래가 두 가지 다른 종류의 고래에게서 물려 받은 특정한 특징을 지닌 혼종일 수 있다고 말하는 독해 지문의 주장에 반박하고 있다. 강의 진행자는 이것이 사실일 가능성이 매우 낮다고 언급한다. 이는 그 고래가 혼종이 아닌 고래의 경로를 따르는 혼종 고래와 뚜렷이 구별되는 독특한 이주 패턴을 보이기 때문이다. 강의 진행자는 또한 52헤르츠로 노래하는 고래가 자신의 노래에 대한 추적을 바탕으로 흔치 않은 경로를 따라 이주한다는 점을 지적한다.

마지막으로, 강의 진행자는 청각 장애가 높은 음조에 대한 이유일 수 있다는 글쓴이의 주장에 의구심을 갖는다. 강의 진행자는 그 주장이 높은 주파수를 충분히 설명하지 못한다고 주장한다. 독해 지문에서, 글쓴이는 청각 장애를 지닌 고래가 다른 고래들로부터 소리 내는 방법을 배울 기회가 부족하기 때문에 높은 음조의 소리를 낸다고 주장하지만, 청해 파트에서, 강의 진행자는 높은 음조와 청각 장애 사이에 연관성이 존재하지 않는다고 말한다. 이는 그 고래의 소리가 청각 장애에 따른 결과로서가 아니라 특별한 목 구조에서 비롯되기 때문이다.

어휘

migration 이주, 이동 pitch 음조 frequency 주파수 distinctive 독특한, 특색 있는 put forward ~을 제시하다, 제안하다 phenomenon 현상 species (동식물의) 종 encounter ~을 접하다, ~와 맞닥뜨리다 abundant 많은, 풍부한 population 개체수, 개체군 decline v. 줄어들다, 감소하다 n. 감소 mate 짝짓기를 하다 give birth to (새끼) ~을 낳다 offspring 새끼, 자손 species-specific 종 특유의 trait 특성 impaired 장애가 있는, 제 기능을 하지 못하는 mimic ~을 모방하다, 흉내 내다 hearing deficiency 청각 장애(= hearing impairment)

flaw 결점, 결함 decade 10년 vocalization 발성 genuine 진짜의, 진정한 deafness 난청 originate from ~에서 비롯되다 dependent on ~에 좌우되는, 달려 있는, 의존하는

distinctive from ~와 뚜렷이 구별되는 lack 부족, 결핍

실전문제 6 - 과학 주제 (1)

Reading Passage	Listening Script
These days, many people in the United States are pushing the idea that ethanol fuel, which is made from feedstocks such as potatoes and barley, should be used instead of gasoline. However, opponents of the idea say that ethanol is not a suitable alternative to gasoline for the following reasons.	We have just read about a few reasons why people think ethanol fuel is inferior to gasoline, but the arguments made in the text are not very persuasive. Ethanol is a good alternative, and I'll tell you why.
First, when it comes to price, ethanol fuel simply cannot compete with gasoline. You see, to the average consumer, it might appear that the current prices of ethanol and gasoline are almost identical, but you have to take tax subsidies into account. Over the past 25 years, the US government has been helping ethanol producers by providing them with over $10 million in tax subsidies. If this assistance were ever to end, which seems likely, we would see a significant rise in the price of ethanol.	First, the claim that ethanol will be much more expensive than gasoline in the future is flawed. While it's true that government subsidies are currently offsetting the high cost of ethanol, this will not be the case in the future. Once ethanol fuel use significantly increases, it will be natural to see producers begin to lower the price. In other words, the more popular and widespread ethanol fuel becomes, the cheaper it will get. In fact, one study indicates that the cost of ethanol fuel would fall by around 40 percent if production rises by 300 percent.
Second, gasoline-related environmental issues such as global warming will not be solved by an increase in ethanol fuel use. When it is burned as a fuel, ethanol releases carbon dioxide - a greenhouse gas that traps heat in the atmosphere - in the same way that traditional gasoline does. So, in the end, there are no environmental benefits from using ethanol fuel as opposed to gasoline.	Second, the passage is correct in noting that the burning of ethanol results in the harmful emission of carbon dioxide. However, because ethanol is produced from natural feedstocks like potatoes, the production process actually balances out the emission of carbon dioxide. To be specific, all the plants grown for ethanol production absorb carbon dioxide from the atmosphere, and the amount of CO_2 they absorb will be higher than the amount of CO_2 released through ethanol fuel use.
Third, if the production of ethanol fuel were to rise, it would result in a significant decrease in the number of plants available for food. In particular, a large proportion of the feedstocks that farm animals rely on would likely be diverted for use in the ethanol fuel industry. Even if ethanol fuel were to make up just 15 percent of motor fuel in the US, its production could require up to 65 percent of feedstocks such as corn or grain. This would drastically reduce the availability of animal feedstocks, leading to a decline in the agricultural industry.	Third, it is not certain that the number of feedstocks used for animal food will diminish due to ethanol production. Ethanol can be produced from cellulose, which is found in the cell walls of most plants. The interesting thing is that the highest amounts of cellulose are located in plant structures that are not typically consumed by animals. Therefore, the amount of food available for animals will not be affected if we only produce ethanol from those parts that are highest in cellulose.

해석

요즘, 많은 미국인들은 감자와 보리 같은 공급 원료로 만들어지는 에탄올 연료가 휘발유 대신 사용되어야 한다는 아이디어를 밀어붙이고 있다. 하지만, 이 아이디어에 반대하는 사람들은 다음과 같은 이유로 에탄올이 휘발유에 대한 적절한 대안이 아니라고 말한다.

첫 번째로, 가격과 관련해서, 에탄올 연료는 그야말로 휘발유와 경쟁이 되지 않는다. 말하자면, 일반 소비자에게는, 에탄올과 휘발유의 시세가 거의 동일한 것처럼 보일지도 모르지만, 세금 보조금을 감안해야 한다. 지난 25년 동안에 걸쳐, 미국 정부는 에탄올 생산업체에 1천만 달러가 넘는 금액을 세금 보조금으로 제공함으로써 도움을 제공해 오고 있다. 이러한 지원이 언젠가 끝나게 된다면, 우리는 에탄올 가격의 상당한 상승을 겪게 될 것이며, 그럴 가능성도 있어 보인다.

두 번째로, 지구 온난화 같이 휘발유와 관련된 환경 문제들이 에탄올 연료 사용량 증가로 인해 해결되지 않을 것이다. 연료로서 연소되는 경우, 에탄올은 기존의 휘발유와 동일한 방식으로 이산화탄소, 즉 대기 중에 열을 가둬놓는 온실 가스를 방출한다. 따라서, 결국, 휘발유 대신 에탄올 연료를 사용하는 것에 따른 환경적 이득은 존재하지 않게 된다.

세 번째로, 에탄올 연료 생산량이 늘어나게 된다면, 음식으로 이용 가능한 식물 숫자의 상당한 감소를 초래하게 될 것이다. 특히, 가축이 의존하고 있는 많은 부분의 공급 원료가 에탄올 연료 업계에서 이용되도록 전환될 가능성이 있을 것이다. 설사 에탄올 연료가 미국에서 차량 연료의 불과 15퍼센트만 차지하게 된다 하더라도, 그 생산에 옥수수 또는 곡물 같은 공급 원료의 최대 65퍼센트를 필요로 할 수 있다. 이는 동물용 공급 원료의 이용 가능성을 급격히 감소시켜, 농업 분야의 쇠퇴로 이어지게 될 것이다.

우리는 방금 사람들이 에탄올 연료가 휘발유보다 좋지 못하다고 생각하는 몇 가지 이유와 관련된 내용을 읽어봤지만, 이 글에 제시된 주장들은 그렇게 설득력이 있진 않습니다. 에탄올은 좋은 대안이며, 제가 그 이유를 말씀드리겠습니다.

첫째로, 에탄올이 미래에 휘발유보다 훨씬 더 비싸질 것이라는 주장은 결점이 있습니다. 정부 보조금이 현재 비싼 에탄올 비용을 상쇄하고 있다는 점은 사실이지만, 이는 미래에도 해당되는 경우는 아닙니다. 에탄올 연료 사용이 상당히 증가하게 되면, 자연스럽게 그 가격을 낮추기 시작하는 생산업체들을 보게 될 것입니다. 다시 말해서, 에탄올 연료가 더 많은 인기를 얻어 널리 퍼지게 될수록, 더 저렴해질 것입니다. 실제로, 한 연구에 따르면 생산량이 300퍼센트 증가하는 경우에 에탄올 연료 가격은 약 40퍼센트 떨어질 것으로 나타나 있습니다.

두 번째로, 에탄올 연소가 유해 이산화탄소 방출을 초래한다는 점에 주목하는 데 있어 독해 지문의 내용은 옳습니다. 하지만, 에탄올은 감자 같은 천연 공급 원료로 생산되기 때문에, 그 생산 과정은 사실 이산화탄소 방출을 상쇄합니다. 구체적으로, 에탄올 생산을 위해 재배되는 모든 식물이 대기 중의 이산화탄소를 흡수하며, 이 식물이 흡수하는 이산화탄소의 양은 에탄올 연료 사용을 통해 방출되는 이산화탄소의 양보다 더 많을 것입니다.

세 번째로, 동물 먹이로 쓰이는 공급 원료의 숫자가 에탄올 생산으로 인해 줄어들게 된다는 점은 분명하지 않습니다. 에탄올은 대부분의 식물이 지닌 세포벽에서 찾을 수 있는 셀룰로오스로 생산될 수 있습니다. 흥미로운 부분은 가장 많은 양의 셀룰로오스가 일반적으로 동물이 소비하지 않는 식물 구조물에 위치해 있다는 점입니다. 따라서, 우리가 오직 셀룰로오스가 가장 많은 그 부분만으로 에탄올을 생산한다면 동물이 먹을 수 있는 먹이의 양은 영향받지 않게 될 것입니다.

강의에서 언급된 요점들이 어떻게 독해 지문에 제시된 특정 주장들에 대해 의문을 제기하는지 설명하면서 그 내용을 요약해 보시오.

노트테이킹

etho. ↔ gas. X suit	good
X price sup ↑	flawed X future etho. ↑ → ↓ price more → cheaper
X solve envi. issue burn	O / ↓ C.D. balance absorb
↓ food ani.	X certain cell wall cellulose - X ani. X affect.

모범 답안

The reading passage and the lecture both discuss the possibility of ethanol fuel as an alternative to gasoline. The writer states that there are several explanations why this fuel is not a suitable replacement. However, the lecturer disagrees with the argument, saying that the explanations are not persuasive, and, in fact, ethanol can be a good alternative.

First of all, the lecturer doubts the writer's point that ethanol fuel cannot be a competitor with gasoline in price. She argues that this point is flawed. Although the writer states that the current price of ethanol would rise without the financial support of the US government, the lecturer points out that this scenario will not happen in the future. The reason is that the significant increase in ethanol fuel use naturally causes ethanol producers to lower the price. Based on one study, the more ethanol fuel is used, the cheaper it will be.

Secondly, the lecturer refutes the argument in the reading passage that using ethanol fuel will not solve environmental issues such as global warming. She states that it is partially true, but ethanol fuel eventually reduces the level of carbon dioxide in the atmosphere. While the writer and the speaker both agree that carbon dioxide produced by burning ethanol could be harmful to the environment, the lecturer highlights that growing plants for producing ethanol could balance the emission of carbon dioxide. In fact, it is expected that the amount of carbon dioxide that plants absorb would exceed that of the carbon dioxide released.

Finally, the lecturer doubts the writer's argument that the rise of using ethanol fuel would lead to a decrease in food supplies for farm animals. She contends that it is not certain. In the reading passage, the writer claims that the production of ethanol requires about 65 percent of feedstocks, but in the listening part, the lecturer says that this process only needs a part of cell walls, cellulose, that is not eaten by animals. Therefore, this would not affect the food supply for animals.

(338 words)

독해 지문과 강의는 모두 휘발유에 대한 대안으로서 에탄올 연료가 지닌 가능성을 이야기한다. 글쓴이는 왜 이 연료가 적합한 대체재가 아닌지에 대한 여러 가지 설명이 존재한다고 언급한다. 하지만, 강의 진행자는 그 설명들이 설득력이 없는데다, 실제로는, 에탄올이 좋은 대안이 될 수 있다고 말하면서 그러한 주장에 동의하지 않는다.

가장 먼저, 강의 진행자는 에탄올 연료가 가격 면에서 휘발유의 경쟁 상대가 되지 못한다는 글쓴이의 주장에 의구심을 갖는다. 강의 진행자는 이러한 주장에 결점이 있다고 주장한다. 글쓴이는 미국 정부의 재정적인 지원이 없다면 에탄올 시세가 오르게 될 것이라고 언급하지만, 강의 진행자는 이러한 시나리오가 미래에 나타나지 않을 것이라고 지적한다. 그 이유는 에탄올 연료 사용량의 상당한 증가가 자연스럽게 에탄올 생산업체들이 그 가격을 낮추도록 초래한다는 점이다. 한 연구를 바탕으로 볼 때, 에탄올 연료가 더 많이 사용될수록, 더 저렴해질 것이다.

두 번째로, 강의 진행자는 에탄올 연료를 사용하는 것이 지구 온난화 같은 환경 문제를 해결하지 못할 것이라고 말하는 독해 지문 내의 주장에 반박하고 있다. 강의 진행자는 그것이 일부 사실이긴 하지만, 에탄올 연료가 결국 대기 중의 이산화탄소 수준을 낮춘다고 언급한다. 글쓴이와 화자 둘 모두 에탄올 연소에 의해 발생되는 이산화탄소가 환경에 유해할 수 있다는 점에는 동의하고 있지만, 강의 진행자는 에탄올 생산을 위해 식물을 재배하는 것이 이산화탄소 방출을 상쇄할 수 있다고 강조한다. 실제로, 식물이 흡수하는 이산화탄소 양이 방출되는 이산화탄소 양을 초과할 것으로 예상되고 있다.

마지막으로, 강의 진행자는 에탄올 연료 사용량 증가가 가축 먹이 공급량 감소로 이어질 것이라는 글쓴이의 주장에 의구심을 갖는다. 강의 진행자는 그것이 확실치 않다고 주장한다. 독해 지문에서, 글쓴이는 에탄올 생산에 약 65퍼센트의 공급 원료가 필요하다고 주장하지만, 청해 파트에서, 강의 진행자는 이러한 과정에 동물이 먹지 않는 세포벽의 일부, 즉 오직 셀룰로오스만 필요하다고 말한다. 따라서, 이는 동물을 위한 먹이 공급에 영향을 미치지 않을 것이다.

어휘

feedstocks 공급 원료(제조 과정에서 필요로 하는 직접 원료) opponent 반대하는 사람 alternative to ~에 대한 대안 compete with ~와 경쟁하다 identical 동일한 subsidy 보조금 significant 상당한, 많은 benefit from ~로부터 혜택을 보다, 이득을 얻다 as opposed to ~ 대신, ~가 아니라, ~와 대조적으로 a large proportion of 많은 부분의, 대부분의 divert ~을 전환하다 make up ~을 차지하다 up to 최대 ~까지 drastically 급격히

inferior to ~보다 좋지 못한, 열등한 flawed 결점이 있는, 결함이 있는 offset ~을 상쇄하다, 만회하다(= balance out) emission 방출 (물질), 배출(물) absorb ~을 흡수하다 diminish 줄어들다, 감소하다 cellulose 셀룰로오스(고등 식물 .세포막의 주성분) affect ~에 영향을 미치다

replacement 대체(하는 것) competitor 경쟁자 solve ~을 해결하다 exceed ~을 초과하다, 넘어서다

실전문제 7 – 과학 주제 (2)

Reading Passage	Listening Script
Many parts of the Earth underwent a period of extremely low temperature from approximately 1350 to 1900 CE, and this time period is often referred to as the Little Ice Age. During that time, glaciers expanded significantly, and many regions experienced very harsh winter weather. Scientists have debated the possible causes of the Little Ice Age, and several theories have been proposed. First, a disruption of ocean currents may have been responsible for the temperature decrease. Just before the beginning of the Little Ice Age, many of the planet's glaciers melted during a period of uncharacteristically warm weather. This resulted in a large volume of cold fresh water being released into the Gulf Stream, a vast ocean current that directly influences the climate of the Earth. Some scientists think that the Gulf Stream was temporarily disrupted by this rapid influx of fresh water, triggering the Little Ice Age. Second, the cooling of the climate may have indirectly resulted from a decline in human populations. Prior to the Little Ice Age, and in its earliest stage, the human population shrunk due to various factors such as disease and war. Land that was once used for agriculture was abandoned, and new forests began to grow in the fields. These trees removed large amounts of carbon dioxide from the atmosphere, and this had a cooling effect on the Earth. Third, some scientists think that the Little Ice Age may have been caused by the eruption of numerous volcanoes at the beginning of that time period. Volcanic eruptions involve the emission of massive, thick clouds of ash and gas into the atmosphere, and these can form a barrier that sunlight cannot pass through. If sunlight was unable to penetrate the ash cloud and reach the Earth's surface, global temperatures would have gone down.	The reading passage offers a few theories to explain the cause of the Little Ice Age, but they are a little outdated. New scientific studies have provided information that makes it highly unlikely that any of the theories in the text could be true. First, let me talk about the Gulf Stream theory. According to recent research, a disruption of this ocean current would cause a temperature drop, but only in North America and Europe. This is important to note because even countries in the southern hemisphere like New Zealand experienced the effects of the Little Ice Age. So, if a Gulf Stream disruption does not affect southern places, it cannot be considered a viable cause of the Little Ice Age. Second, regarding the idea that new trees growing on unused land cooled the atmosphere by absorbing carbon dioxide, this process would take too much time. It did not take long for the human population to increase back to the level it was at before the period of war and disease. So, in order to feed a growing population, these new trees were cut down quickly so that the land could be used for crop production once again. Therefore, these forests discussed in the passage would not have survived long enough to cause any significant cooling of the atmosphere. Third, it is true that ash clouds from volcanic eruptions can lead to a cooler climate. However, if this had occurred, people would definitely have noticed! A massive amount of dust in the atmosphere would cause various phenomena, like luminous sunsets and brown snow. So, how come there are no records of any such things during the Little Ice Age? The volcanic eruptions at that time were clearly not powerful enough to discharge enough dust to cause global cooling.

해석

지구의 많은 부분이 서기 약 1350년에서 1900년까지 기온이 대단히 낮은 기간을 거쳤는데, 이 시기를 흔히 소빙하기라고 일컫는다. 이 기간에, 빙하가 상당히 확대되었으며, 많은 지역이 매우 혹독한 겨울 날씨를 겪었다. 과학자들이 이 소빙하기의 발생 가능 원인들을 두고 논쟁을 벌여왔으며, 여러 이론이 제시되었다.

첫 번째로, 해류에 대한 방해가 기온 하락의 원인이었을 수 있다. 소빙하기가 시작되기 직전에, 지구 빙하의 많은 부분이 평소답지 않게 따뜻했던 날씨가 지속된 기간 중에 녹아내렸다. 이는 많은 양의 차가운 민물이 지구의 기후에 직접적으로 영향을 미치는 거대 해류인 멕시코 만류로 유입되도록 초래했다. 일부 과학자들은 멕시코 만류가 빠르게 유입된 이 민물에 의해 일시적으로 지장을 받아 소빙하기를 촉발했다고 생각한다.

두 번째로, 기후의 냉각화가 인간 개체군의 감소로 인해 간접적으로 초래되었을 수도 있다. 소빙하기에 앞서, 그리고 그 가장 초기 단계에서, 인간 개체군이 질병과 전쟁 같은 다양한 요인으로 인해 축소되었다. 한때 농업에 이용되었던 땅은 버려졌으며, 새로운 숲이 들판마다 성장하기 시작했다. 이 나무들이 대기에서 많은 양의 이산화탄소를 없앴으며, 이로 인해 지구가 냉각되는 효과가 나타났다.

세 번째로, 일부 과학자들은 소빙하기가 그 시대의 초기에 발생된 수많은 화산 분출에 의해 초래되었을 수도 있다고 생각한다. 화산 분출은 화산재와 가스로 이뤄진 대규모의 짙은 구름이 배출되어 대기로 유입되는 과정을 수반하며, 이 구름은 햇빛이 통과할 수 없는 장애물을 형성할 수 있다. 햇빛이 화산재 구름을 관통해 지표면에 이를 수 없었다면, 지구의 기온은 하락했을 것이다.

독해 지문이 소빙하기의 원인을 설명하는 몇 가지 이론을 제공해주고 있긴 하지만, 이 이론들은 약간 구시대적입니다. 새로운 과학 연구가 지문에 제시된 이론들 중 어떤 것도 사실일 가능성을 대단히 낮게 만드는 정보를 제공한 바 있습니다.

첫 번째로, 멕시코 만류 이론에 관해 이야기해 보겠습니다. 최근의 연구에 따르면, 이 해류에 대한 방해가 기온 하락을 초래했겠지만, 오직 북미와 유럽에만 해당됩니다. 이는 심지어 뉴질랜드처럼 남반구에 위치한 국가들도 소빙하기의 영향을 겪었기 때문에 주목하는 것이 중요합니다. 따라서, 멕시코 만류에 대한 방해가 남쪽 지역들에 영향을 미치지 않는다면, 가능성이 있는 소빙하기 원인으로 볼 수 없습니다.

두 번째로, 이용하지 않았던 땅에서 자란 새 나무들이 이산화탄소를 흡수함으로써 대기를 냉각시켰다는 견해와 관련해서는, 이 과정은 너무 많은 시간이 소요될 것입니다. 인간 개체군이 전쟁 및 질병 발생 기간에 앞서 과거의 수준으로 다시 늘어나기까지는 오랜 시간이 걸리지 않았습니다. 따라서, 늘어나는 개체군에 먹을 것을 제공하기 위해, 그 땅이 다시 한번 작물 생산에 이용될 수 있도록 이 새로운 나무들이 빠르게 잘려 나갔습니다. 그러므로, 독해 지문에서 이야기하는 이 숲들은 어떤 상당한 대기 냉각 상태든 초래할 정도로 충분히 오래 생존하지 못했을 것입니다.

세 번째로, 화산 분출을 통해 나온 화산재 구름이 더 차가운 기후로 이어질 수 있다는 점은 사실입니다. 하지만, 이러한 일이 일어났다면, 사람들이 분명 알아차렸을 것입니다! 대기 중에 나타나는 엄청난 양의 먼지는 빛을 발하는 일몰과 갈색 눈 같은 다양한 현상을 초래했을 것입니다. 따라서, 어째서 소빙하기 중에 나타난 그런 일들에 대한 기록이 존재하지 않는 걸까요? 당시의 화산 분출은 분명 지구 냉각화를 초래할 정도로 충분한 먼지를 방출할 만큼 충분히 강력하진 않았습니다.

강의에서 언급된 요점들이 어떻게 독해 지문에 제시된 특정 주장들에 대해 의문을 제기하는지 설명하면서 그 내용을 요약해 보시오.

노트테이킹

causes L. I. A theories	little outdated
temp. ↓	only NA, Euro. X affect. south
human ↓	too much time popul. ↑ back cut trees, used X survive
volcano	X X record X powerful

모범 답안

The reading passage and the lecture both discuss the causes of the Little Ice Age, a period of extremely low temperatures. The writer states three possible explanations regarding the harsh winter weather. However, the lecturer disagrees with the argument, saying that the theories are a little out of date.

First of all, the lecturer doubts the writer's point that a disruption of a major ocean current, the Gulf Stream, may have decreased the temperature. He argues that this theory is only partially true. Although the writer states that a disruption of the Gulf Stream would cause an unusual drop in temperatures, the lecturer points out that this did not only happen in North America and Europe. In fact, some countries in the southern hemisphere experienced the Little Ice Age as well. If this cooling affected global temperatures, the disruption of ocean currents could not be responsible for the Little Ice Age.

Secondly, the lecturer refutes the argument in the reading passage that the decline of human populations could cool the climate. He states that it would take too much time to bring about the result of the Little Ice Age. In fact, it was easy for the number of people to get back to its previous level. While the writer states that new forests on abandoned land would remove enough carbon dioxide to cool the Earth, the lecturer highlights that people likely cut down the trees and used the land for agriculture once again. Therefore, these forests could not have survived long enough to cause the Little Ice Age.

Finally, the speaker doubts the writer's argument that a volcanic eruption could have caused the Little Ice Age. He contends that this hypothesis is not true. In the reading passage, the writer claims that a massive, thick cloud of ash and gas could block the sunlight and cause a decrease in global temperatures, but in the listening part, the lecturer says that there are no records regarding various phenomena possibly caused by the cloud of ash and gas. It can be assumed that the eruption of a volcano was not powerful enough to cause global cooling.

(355 words)

독해 지문과 강의는 모두 소빙하기, 즉 극도로 기온이 낮았던 시대의 원인을 이야기한다. 글쓴이는 이 가혹한 겨울 날씨와 관련된 세 가지 가능한 설명을 언급한다. 하지만, 강의 진행자는 그 이론들이 약간 시대에 뒤떨어진 것이라고 말하면서 그러한 주장에 동의하지 않는다.

가장 먼저, 강의 진행자는 주요 해류인 멕시코 만류에 대한 방해가 기온을 하락시켰을 수 있다는 글쓴이의 주장에 의구심을 갖는다. 강의 진행자는 이 이론이 오직 일부만 사실이라고 주장한다. 글쓴이는 멕시코 만류에 대한 방해가 흔치 않은 기온 하락을 초래했을 것이라고 언급하지만, 강의 진행자는 이것이 오직 북미와 유럽에서만 발생한 것은 아니라고 지적한다. 실제로, 남반구에 위치한 일부 국가들도 소빙하기를 겪었다. 이러한 냉각 효과가 전 세계 기온에 영향을 미쳤다면, 해류에 대한 방해는 소빙하기의 원인일 수 없을 것이다.

두 번째로, 강의 진행자는 인간 개체군의 감소가 기후를 차갑게 만들었을 수 있다고 말하는 독해 지문 내의 주장에 반박하고 있다. 강의 진행자는 소빙하기라는 결과를 초래하는 데 너무 많은 시간이 소요될 것이라고 언급한다. 실제로, 사람 수가 이전의 수준으로 되돌아가는 것은 쉬운 일이었다. 글쓴이는 버려진 땅에 새로 생긴 숲들이 지구를 냉각시킬 정도로 충분한 이산화탄소를 없앴을 것이라고 언급하고 있지만, 강의 진행자는 아마 사람들이 그 나무들을 잘라내고 농업용으로 그 땅을 다시 이용했을 것이라는 점을 강조한다. 따라서, 이 숲들은 소빙하기를 초래할 정도로 충분히 오래 살아남을 수 없었을 것이다.

마지막으로, 화자는 화산 분출이 소빙하기를 초래했을 것이라고 말하는 글쓴이의 주장에 의구심을 갖는다. 강의 진행자는 이 가설이 사실이 아니라고 주장한다. 독해 지문에는, 글쓴이가 화산재 및 가스로 구성된 거대하고 짙은 구름이 햇빛을 가려 지구의 기온 감소를 초래했을 수 있다고 주장하지만, 청해 파트에는, 강의 진행자가 화산재 및 가스로 구성된 구름에 의해 초래되었을 가능성이 있는 다양한 현상과 관련된 기록이 존재하지 않는다고 말한다. 화산의 분출이 지구 냉각화를 초래할 만큼 충분히 강력하지 않았던 것으로 추정할 수 있다.

어휘

undergo ~을 거치다, 겪다 be referred to as ~라고 일컬어지다 glacier 빙하 disruption 방해, 지장 ocean currents 해류 be responsible for ~에 대한 원인이다 uncharacteristically 평소답지 않게 influx 유입 trigger ~을 촉발하다 population 개체군, 개체수 shrink 축소되다, 줄어들다 abandon ~을 버리다, 포기하다 eruption 분출 emission 배출(물) penetrate ~을 관통하다, 투과하다

outdated 구시대적인, 구식의(= out of date) southern hemisphere 남반구 affect ~에 영향을 미치다 viable (실행) 가능한 absorb ~을 흡수하다 phenomena 현상(phenomenon의 복수형) luminous 빛을 발하는 discharge ~을 방출하다

bring about ~을 초래하다, 유발하다 hypothesis 가설

실전문제 8 - 과학 주제 (3)

Reading Passage	Listening Script
Hail can cause serious damage to fields of crops, and this is becoming an increasing problem for farmers throughout the United States. These small pellets of ice form in clouds instead of rain and snow and can fall from the sky with great force, destroying plants and even buildings. A method called cloud seeding has been developed in an effort to make clouds produce harmless rain or snow instead of hail. To do this, airplanes fly over storm clouds and spray them with silver iodide. Several sources indicate that cloud seeding is an effective way to protect crops from hail.	Despite the evidence discussed in the reading passage, it is not guaranteed that cloud seeding is effective. Indeed, each of the cases in the passage should be questioned for various reasons.
First, several countries in Asia have provided evidence that confirms the effectiveness of cloud seeding. For example, in some large cities, the method has been successfully used to regulate precipitation. The success seen in these urban areas suggests that it would be equally successful when used in the rural United States to protect crops and farming facilities.	First, just because cloud seeding has been successful in Asia, it does not necessarily mean it will work as well in the US. The cases where cloud seeding was used in Asia involved cities, where pollution levels are very high due to factory and vehicle emissions. This high level of pollution makes cloud seeding more likely to succeed because the pollutants interact favorably with clouds and the silver iodide. So, the same results are unlikely to be replicated in an unpolluted area. As such, there is no guarantee that the cloud seeding method would be equally effective in agricultural areas of the United States, where barely any pollution occurs.
Second, some local reports also show that cloud seeding is highly beneficial. An extensive research study was recently carried out in the Midwest of the United States. The researchers kept track of crop damage due to hail in various agricultural regions and compared the differences. They found that there was a significant reduction in hail damage in the areas that use the cloud seeding method compared with those that do not.	Second, the passage mentions a US-based research study, but it fails to include some important information. In that study, hail damage did decrease in the cloud seeding regions, but it also decreased in adjacent areas, in all directions, where no cloud seeding was being carried out. So, it seems obvious that the entire region suffered fewer hailstorms than usual during the study, and cloud seeding made very little difference to the amount of damage caused to crops in the region.
Third, laboratory experiments have also strongly indicated that cloud seeding is effective. Scientists have consistently shown that by adding silver iodide to cold water vapor, they can create light snow rather than hail pellets, which would typically form when water vapor reaches the freezing point.	Third, in a laboratory, it is relatively simple to use silver iodide to form snow rather than hail. But, in an actual real-world setting, silver iodide has a tendency to disrupt the formation of all types of precipitation, even snow and rain, and this can have negative consequences. I mean, if we were to perform cloud seeding in areas, which receive very little rainfall, there is a chance of causing drought and seeing crops die as a result.

해석

우박은 작물 밭에 심각한 손해를 초래할 수 있으며, 이는 미국 전역에 걸쳐 농부들에게 점점 더 큰 문제가 되어가고 있다. 이 작은 얼음 알갱이들은 비나 눈 대신 구름속에서 형성되며, 하늘에서 엄청난 힘을 지니고 떨어지면서, 식물뿐만 아니라 심지어 건물까지 손상시킬 수 있다. 구름씨뿌리기라고 부르는 방법이 구름에게 우박 대신 해롭지 않은 비나 눈을 만들어내도록 하기 위한 노력의 일환으로 개발되었다. 이를 실행하려면, 비행기가 먹구름 위로 날아다니면서 그 구름에 요오드화은을 뿌린다. 여러 출처에 따르면 구름씨뿌리기가 우박으로부터 작물을 보호하는 효과적인 방법인 것으로 나타나 있다.

첫 번째로, 아시아의 여러 국가들이 구름씨뿌리기의 효력을 확인해주는 증거를 제공한 바 있다. 예를 들어, 몇몇 대도시에서는, 이 방법이 강우량을 조절하는 데 성공적으로 이용되어 왔다. 이 도시 지역들에서 나타난 성공 사례는 작물과 농업 시설물을 보호하기 위해 미국 시골 지역에서 활용되어도 똑같이 성공적일 수 있음을 시사한다.

두 번째로, 일부 지역 보도에 따르면 구름씨뿌리기가 대단히 유익한 것으로 나타나기도 한다. 한 광범위한 연구 조사가 최근 미국 중서부 지역에서 실시되었다. 해당 연구가들은 다양한 농업 지역에서 발생된 우박으로 인한 작물 피해를 파악해 그 차이점들을 비교했다. 이들은 구름씨뿌리기 방법을 이용하는 지역들마다 그렇지 않은 지역들에 비해 상당한 우박 피해 감소가 나타났다는 것을 알게 되었다.

세 번째로, 실험실 실험을 통해서도 구름씨뿌리기가 효과적인 것으로 분명하게 나타났다. 과학자들은 차가운 수증기에 요오드화은을 추가함으로써, 우박 알갱이가 아니라 일반적으로 수증기가 빙점에 도달할 때 형성되곤 하는 약한 눈을 만들어낼 수 있다는 것을 지속적으로 보여주었다.

독해 지문에서 논의된 증거에도 불구하고, 구름씨뿌리기가 효과적인지는 보장되어 있지 않습니다. 실제로, 독해 지문에 제시된 각각의 사례들은 여러 이유로 의문을 가져봐야 합니다.

첫 번째로, 단지 구름씨뿌리기가 아시아에서 성공을 거뒀다는 이유만으로, 그것이 반드시 미국에서도 효과가 있을 것임을 의미하지는 않습니다. 구름씨뿌리기가 아시아에서 이용된 사례들은 공장 및 차량 배출물로 인해 오염 수준이 매우 높은 도시들과 관련되어 있었습니다. 이렇게 높은 오염 수준으로 인해 구름씨뿌리기가 성공할 가능성이 더 커지는데, 오염 물질이 구름 및 요오드화은과 서로 잘 반응하기 때문입니다. 따라서, 같은 결과가 오염되지 않은 지역에서 그대로 반복될 가능성은 낮습니다. 그러므로, 구름씨뿌리기 방법이 거의 어떤 오염도 발생되지 않는 미국 농업 지역에서 동일하게 효과적일 것이라는 보장은 없습니다.

두 번째로, 독해 지문이 미국을 기반으로 한 연구 조사를 언급하고 있는데, 일부 중요한 정보를 포함하지 못하고 있습니다. 그 연구에서, 우박 피해가 구름씨뿌리기 실시 지역에서 분명 감소하긴 했지만, 구름씨뿌리기가 실시되고 있지 않던 사방의 모든 인근 지역에서도 감소했습니다. 따라서, 그 지역 전체가 조사 기간 중에 평소보다 더 적게 우박을 동반한 폭풍에 시달렸으며, 구름씨뿌리기가 해당 지역 작물에 초래한 피해 수준에 거의 변화를 가져오지 못했다는 것이 명백해 보입니다.

세 번째로, 실험실에서는, 요오드화은을 이용해 우박이 아닌 눈을 형성시키는 것이 비교적 간단합니다. 하지만, 실제 현실 속 환경에서, 요오드화은은 심지어 눈과 비를 포함해 모든 종류의 강수 형성에 지장을 주는 경향이 있으며, 이는 부정적인 결과를 만들어낼 수 있습니다. 제 말은, 우리가 비가 거의 내리지 않는 지역에서 구름씨뿌리기를 실시하게 된다면, 결과적으로 가뭄을 초래하고 죽어가는 작물을 보게 될 가능성이 있습니다.

강의에서 언급된 요점들이 어떻게 독해 지문에 제시된 특정 주장들에 대해 대응하는지 설명하면서 그 내용을 요약해 보시오.

노트테이킹

CS effec.	question.
asia	X nece. work pollut. interact - silver. X effect.
bene. hail ↓	fail to includ. adj. ↓ - X CS little diff.
lab.	X real set. disrupt. all nega.

모범 답안

The reading passage and the lecture both discuss whether cloud seeding is an effective way to protect crops from hail. The writer states that three pieces of evidence prove the advantages of cloud seeding. However, the lecturer disagrees with the argument, saying that these sources are questionable.

First of all, the lecturer doubts the writer's point that it has been proven that cloud seeding is effective in several Asian countries. She argues that cloud seeding would not necessarily work in the United States. Although the writer states that this method succeeded in regulating precipitation in urban areas of Asian countries, the lecturer points out that it is unlikely to bring about the same result in an unpolluted area in the US. This is because cloud seeding was carried out under particular conditions where pollutants in the air interacted with clouds and the silver iodide. Without pollution, it cannot be guaranteed that cloud seeding would be equally effective in agricultural areas of the US.

Secondly, the lecturer refutes the argument in the reading passage that some research conducted in the United States proves that cloud seeding is effective in reducing hail damage. She states that the research fails to include some important information. This is because it was revealed in the study that adjacent areas without cloud seeding also experienced less hail damage. While the writer states that there were differences in hail damage between the areas using cloud seeding and the areas without cloud seeding, the lecturer highlights that cloud seeding made very little difference in the amount of damage.

Finally, the lecturer doubts the writer's argument that cloud seeding worked in laboratory experiments. She contends that this cannot happen in a real-world setting. In the reading passage, the writer claims that scientists can change hail pellets into light snow by adding silver iodide to cold water vapor, but in the listening part, the lecturer says that silver iodide disrupted all kinds of precipitation. This would result in negative consequences such as a drought or dead crops.

(337 words)

독해 지문과 강의는 모두 구름씨뿌리기가 우박으로부터 작물을 보호하는 효과적인 방법인지 이야기한다. 글쓴이는 세 가지 증거가 구름씨뿌리기의 이점을 증명한다고 언급한다. 하지만, 강의 진행자는 이 자료들이 의심스럽다고 말하면서 그러한 주장에 동의하지 않는다.

가장 먼저, 강의 진행자는 구름씨뿌리기가 여러 아시아 국가에서 효과적이라는 것이 입증되었다는 글쓴이의 주장에 의구심을 갖는다. 강의 진행자는 구름씨뿌리기가 미국에서도 반드시 효과를 내진 못할 것이라고 주장한다. 글쓴이는 이 방법이 아시아 국가의 여러 시골 지역에서 강수량을 조절하는 데 성공을 거뒀다고 언급하지만, 강의 진행자는 미국의 오염되지 않은 지역에서 같은 결과를 초래할 가능성이 낮다고 지적한다. 이는 구름씨뿌리기가 공기 중의 오염 물질이 구름 및 요오드화은과 상호 작용하는 특정 조건 하에서 실시되었기 때문이다. 오염되어 있지 않다면, 구름씨뿌리기가 미국의 농업 지역에서 동일하게 효과적일지 보장할 수 없다.

두 번째로, 강의 진행자는 미국에서 실시된 일부 연구가 구름씨뿌리기가 우박 피해를 줄이는 데 효과적임을 증명한다고 말하는 독해 지문 내의 주장에 반박하고 있다. 강의 진행자는 그 연구가 일부 중요한 정보를 포함하지 못하고 있다고 언급한다. 이는 그 연구에서 구름씨뿌리기를 하지 않은 인근 지역들도 더 적은 우박 피해를 경험한 것으로 드러났기 때문이다. 글쓴이는 구름씨뿌리기를 이용하는 지역과 구름씨뿌리기를 하지 않는 지역 사이에서 우박 피해에 차이가 존재했다고 언급하지만, 강의 진행자는 구름씨뿌리기가 피해 수준에 있어 거의 변화를 가져오지 못했다고 강조한다.

마지막으로, 강의 진행자는 구름씨뿌리기가 실험실 실험에서 효과를 나타냈다는 글쓴이의 주장에 의구심을 갖는다. 강의 진행자는 이것이 실제 환경에서는 발생될 수 없다고 주장한다. 독해 지문에서, 글쓴이는 과학자들이 요오드화은을 차가운 수증기에 추가함으로써 우박 알갱이를 약한 눈으로 바꿀 수 있다고 주장하지만, 청해 파트에서, 강의 진행자는 요오드화은이 모든 종류의 강수에 지장을 초래했다고 말한다. 이는 가뭄 또는 죽은 작물 같은 부정적인 결과를 초래할 것이다.

hail 우박 pellet 알갱이 cloud seeding 구름씨뿌리기(구름에 특정 물질을 뿌려 인공 비를 만드는 방법) silver iodide 요오드화은(아이오딘과 은을 반응시켜 얻는 물질로, 인공 강우나 방부제 등에 사용) regulate ~을 조절하다 precipitation 강수(량) beneficial 유익한, 이로운 carry out ~을 실시하다(= conduct) keep track of ~을 파악하다, 추적하다 water vapor 수증기

guarantee v. ~을 보장하다 n. 보장 pollution 오염 emission 배출(물) pollutant 오염 물질 replicate ~을 그대로 반복하다, 복제하다 fail to do ~하지 못하다 adjacent 인근의 suffer ~에 시달리다, ~을 겪다 have a tendency to do ~하는 경향이 있다 disrupt ~에 지장을 주다, ~을 방해하다 drought 가뭄

bring about ~을 초래하다, 유발하다(= result in)

실전문제 9 - 과학 주제 (4)

Reading Passage	Listening Script
Natural reefs are found throughout the world's oceans, and these sturdy structures serve as perfect habitats for a wide variety of marine organisms. Plants and sponges cling to the rigid reefs, providing shelter and food for countless fish. In order to increase the amount of habitat available to fish, companies involved in the fishing industry are building artificial reefs in coastal waters. Such reefs - built from various metal objects and concrete - offer many advantages. The world is filled with unwanted objects and materials, and artificial reefs are an excellent way to recycle them. Some reefs are constructed from old vehicle tires and appliances which would typically be hard to dispose of safely. The objects are thoroughly cleaned to ensure that they pose no harm to marine life or the environment once they are placed in the ocean. So, artificial reefs help us to reuse old materials in an environmentally friendly and affordable manner. Next, small-scale fishing companies can benefit financially from private artificial reefs. When such companies construct their own artificial reefs in locations that are unknown to larger companies, they improve their economic competitiveness. At the moment, smaller companies struggle to have a presence in fertile fishing grounds that are overrun by the larger companies. By building new fishing areas, smaller firms can improve their catch sizes and help their local communities to prosper. Finally, artificial reefs may help fish populations to grow by offering a safe habitat. Several reports from fishing companies have indicated that fish populations are showing steady growth around artificial reefs, and this benefits not only the ecosystem but also the local economy in places where fishing is prevalent.	The passage talks about several advantages brought about by the construction of artificial reefs. However, a large number of scientists believe that these reefs may cause more harm than good. First, even when harmful substances are removed from artificial reefs, they can still negatively impact the environment. Take the Osborne Reef, for example. This artificial reef was primarily made from used car tires that had been fastened together. But, bad weather caused large parts of the reef to detach and fall to the seafloor with great force, killing countless organisms living there. Second, letting smaller fishing companies build their own private reefs will only end badly. Any vessels operating in the vicinity of the reefs run the risk of colliding with them, or having their fishing nets tangled on them. Because of this unacceptable risk, the only way to allow smaller companies to build their own reefs is if they publicly disclose their locations. And, in that case, they will likely lose any economic advantage they might have gained. Third, even though more fish are apparently being caught around artificial reefs, we cannot assume this means there is a rise in fish populations. Remember that reefs function by attracting fish to them from other regions of the ocean. So, it would make sense that the large numbers of fish seen at artificial reefs used to live somewhere else. Moreover, reefs are more likely to cause a population decrease by grouping fish together, making it easier for fishers to catch them in large numbers.

해석

자연 암초는 전 세계의 바다에서 발견되며, 이 견고한 구조물은 아주 다양한 해양 생물체에게 완벽한 서식지의 역할을 한다. 식물과 해면 동물들이 단단한 암초에 붙어 있으면서, 수없이 많은 물고기들에게 피신처와 먹이를 제공한다. 물고기가 이용 가능한 서식지 규모를 늘리기 위해, 어업 분야와 관련된 업체들이 연안 지역에 인공 암초를 만들고 있다. 다양한 금속 물체와 콘크리트로 만들어지는 이 암초는 많은 이점을 제공한다.

전 세계는 원치 않는 물체와 물품들로 가득하며, 인공 암초는 이를 재활용하는 훌륭한 방법이다. 일부 암초는 일반적으로 안전하게 폐기하기 어려울 수 있는 낡은 차량 타이어 및 기기들로 만들어진다. 이 물체들은 일단 바다 속에 놓이고 나면 해양 생물 또는 환경에 어떠한 해도 가하지 않도록 보장하기 위해 철저히 세척된다. 따라서, 인공 암초는 우리가 환경 친화적이고 가격이 알맞은 방식으로 낡은 물품을 재사용하는 데 도움을 준다.

다음으로, 소규모 수산 업체들이 사설 인공 암초를 통해 재정적으로 혜택을 볼 수 있다. 이러한 업체들이 더 큰 업체에게 알려져 있지 않은 지역에 개별 인공 암초를 짓는 경우, 경제적인 경쟁력을 향상시키게 된다. 현재, 소규모 업체들은 더 큰 업체들이 장악하고 있는 풍부한 어장에 진입하는 것을 힘겨워하고 있다. 새로운 어업 구역을 만듦으로써, 소규모 업체들이 어획량을 개선하고 지역 사회가 번성하도록 도움을 줄 수 있다.

마지막으로, 인공 암초는 안전한 서식지를 제공함으로써 물고기 개체군이 늘어나는 데 도움을 줄 수 있다. 수산 업체들이 전한 여러 보고서에 따르면 물고기 개체군이 인공 암초 주변에서 지속적인 증가를 보이고 있는 것으로 나타났으며, 이는 생태계뿐만 아니라 어업이 일반적인 곳의 지역 경제에도 유익하다.

독해 지문은 인공 암초를 만듦으로써 초래되는 여러 가지 이점에 관해 이야기하고 있습니다. 하지만, 아주 많은 과학자들은 이러한 암초가 득보다 실이 더 많을 수 있다고 생각합니다.

첫 번째로, 심지어 인공 암초에서 유해 물질이 제거되는 경우라 하더라도, 여전히 환경에 부정적으로 영향을 미칠 수 있습니다. 오스본 암초를 예로 들어 보겠습니다. 이 인공 암초는 주로 함께 단단히 고정시킨 중고차 타이어들로 만들어졌습니다. 하지만, 악천후로 인해 이 암초의 많은 부분이 분리되어 엄청난 힘과 함께 해저로 가라앉으면서, 그곳에 살고 있던 수없이 많은 생물체를 죽였습니다.

두 번째로, 소규모 수산 업체들에게 개별 사설 암초를 짓게 하는 것은 오직 부정적인 결과만 초래할 것입니다. 암초 주변에서 운항하는 어떤 선박이든 암초와 충돌하거나 어망이 암초에 걸려 뒤엉키게 되는 위험을 감수하게 됩니다. 받아들이기 힘든 이러한 위험 요소로 인해, 개별 암초를 짓게 할 수 있는 유일한 방법은 소규모 업체들이 위치를 공개적으로 밝히는 경우입니다. 그리고, 그럴 경우에는, 그 업체들이 얻었을 수 있는 어떠한 경제적 이점이든 잃게 될 가능성이 있습니다.

세 번째로, 더 많은 물고기가 분명 인공 암초 주변에서 잡히고 있긴 하지만, 우리는 이것을 물고기 개체군의 증가를 의미하는 것으로 생각할 수는 없습니다. 암초는 바다의 다른 지역으로부터 물고기들을 끌어들임으로써 기능한다는 점을 기억하시기 바랍니다. 따라서, 인공 암초가 있는 곳에서 보이는 아주 많은 물고기는 전에 어딘가 다른 곳에서 살았던 것으로 봐야 앞뒤가 맞을 겁니다. 더욱이, 암초는 물고기들을 한데 모이게 해 어부들이 더 수월하게 대량으로 잡을 수 있도록 만들어, 개체수 감소를 초래할 가능성이 더 큽니다.

강의에서 언급된 요점들이 어떻게 독해 지문에 제시된 특정 주장들에 대해 이의를 제기하는지 설명하면서 그 내용을 요약해 보시오.

노트테이킹

adv.	harm > good
recycle	nega. tire bad → detach / fall kill
bene. finan.	end bad risk colli. public → ↓ eco adv.
safe habitat	X ↑ popul. attract group → easi. catch

모범 답안

The reading passage and the lecture both discuss using artificial reefs as habitats for more fish. The writer states that building artificial reefs in coastal areas offers some benefits. However, the lecturer disagrees with the argument, saying that these structures are expected to cause more harm than good.

First of all, the lecturer doubts the writer's point that unwanted materials can be recycled for artificial reefs. She argues that this recycling can have a negative effect on the environment. Although the writer states that abandoned objects such as old tires are thoroughly cleaned and then used, the lecturer points out that an artificial reef made of tires became detached in bad weather and caused extensive damage. Eventually, unseen ramifications of artificial reefs could kill marine animals.

Secondly, the lecturer refutes the argument of the reading passage that private artificial reefs can provide financial benefits to small fishing businesses. She states that this kind of business will end badly. In response to the mentioned evidence in the reading passage, the lecturer presents contrary evidence that artificial reefs cannot provide economic benefits. This is because there is a risk that operating vessels could collide with the reefs. Plus, to avoid this risk, private reefs should be built publicly, which means they will lose any economic advantage.

Finally, the speaker doubts the writer's argument that artificial reefs could grow fish populations because of the safety they provide. She contends that it cannot be assumed that fish populations will rise. Artificial reefs attract more fish to them from other regions. In the reading passage, the writer claims that more fish populations appear around artificial reefs, but in the listening part, the lecturer says this can cause a population decrease eventually. This is because grouping fish makes it easier for fishers to catch them.

(299 words)

독해 지문과 강의는 모두 더 많은 물고기를 위한 서식지로서 인공 암초를 활용하는 것을 이야기한다. 글쓴이는 연안 지역에 인공 암초를 만들면 몇몇 이점을 제공해준다고 언급한다. 하지만, 강의 진행자는 이 구조물이 득보다 실이 더 많은 것으로 예상된다고 말하면서 그러한 주장에 동의하지 않는다.

가장 먼저, 강의 진행자는 원치 않는 물품이 인공 암초용으로 재활용될 수 있다는 글쓴이의 주장에 의구심을 갖는다. 강의 진행자는 이 재활용이 환경에 부정적인 영향을 미칠 수 있다고 주장한다. 글쓴이는 낡은 타이어 같이 버려진 물체들을 철저히 세척한 다음에 사용한다고 언급하지만, 강의 진행자는 타이어로 만들어진 인공 암초가 악천후에 분리되어 대규모 피해를 초래했다는 점을 지적한다. 결과적으로, 인공 암초의 보이지 않는 영향으로 해양 동물을 죽일 수도 있는 것이다.

두 번째로, 강의 진행자는 사설 인공 암초가 소규모 수산 업체들에게 재정적 혜택을 제공해줄 수 있다고 말하는 독해 지문 내의 주장에 반박하고 있다. 강의 진행자는 이런 종류의 사업이 결과가 좋지 못할 것이라고 언급한다. 독해 지문에 언급된 증거에 대응해, 강의 진행자는 인공 암초가 경제적 혜택을 제공해줄 수 없음을 보여주는 대조적인 증거를 제시한다. 이는 운항하는 선박이 암초와 충돌할 수 있다는 위험 요소가 존재하기 때문이다. 게다가, 이러한 위험 요소를 피하기 위해, 사설 암초는 공개적으로 만들어져야 하는데, 이는 어떠한 경제적 이점이든 잃게 된다는 것을 의미한다.

마지막으로, 화자는 인공 암초가 제공하는 안전성으로 인해 물고기 개체군을 증가시킬 수 있다는 글쓴이의 주장에 의구심을 갖는다. 강의 진행자는 물고기 개체군이 늘어날 것으로 추정할 수 없다고 주장한다. 인공 암초는 다른 지역으로부터 더 많은 물고기를 끌어들인다. 독해 지문에서, 글쓴이는 더 많은 물고기 개체군이 인공 암초 주변에 나타난다고 주장하지만, 청해 파트에서, 강의 진행자는 이것이 결과적으로 개체군 감소를 초래할 수 있다고 말한다. 이는 물고기를 한 데 모이게 하는 것으로 인해 어부들이 더욱 쉽게 잡을 수 있기 때문이다.

어휘

reef 암초 **habitat** 서식지 **organism** 생물체 **sponge** 해면 동물 **cling to** ~에 붙어 있다, 매달려 있다 **appliances** (가전) 기기 **dispose of** ~을 폐기하다, 처리하다 **pose no harm to** ~에 해를 가하지 않다 **affordable** 가격이 알맞은 **benefit from** ~로부터 혜택을 보다, 이득을 얻다 **improve** ~을 향상시키다, 개선하다 **competitiveness** 경쟁력 **struggle to do** ~하는 것을 힘겨워하다 **have a presence in** ~에 진입하다, ~에 영향력을 발휘하다 **fertile** 풍부한, 비옥한, 수확량이 많은 **overrun** ~을 장악하다, ~에 널리 퍼지다 **catch** 어획량 **prosper** 번영하다 **population** 개체군, 개체수 **prevalent** 일반적인, 널리 퍼진

cause more harm than good 득보다 실이 더 많다 **substance** 물질 **impact** ~에 영향을 미치다 **fasten** ~을 단단히 고정하다 **detach** 분리되다 **in the vicinity of** ~의 인근에 **collide with** ~와 충돌하다 **tangle** ~을 엉키게 하다 **disclose** ~을 밝히다, 공개하다 **it makes sense that** ~라는 점이 앞뒤가 맞다, 말이 되다

abandon ~을 버리다, 포기하다 **detach** ~을 분리하다 **ramification** 영향, 결과

실전문제 10 - 과학 주제 (5)

Reading Passage	Listening Script
These days, it is common for people to discuss the possibility of sending humans to colonize Earth's Moon, or even Mars, but there may be a better option. Our solar system is home to hundreds of thousands of massive asteroids, and they may be more suitable targets for human colonization for a variety of reasons.	The reading passage outlines a few reasons why asteroids are better options for colonization than planets or moons, but the reasons given are not wholly convincing.
For a start, asteroids are often abundant sources of rare metals and elements that would fetch a high price back on Earth due to their scarcity here. By colonizing an asteroid, we would gain access to huge deposits of gold and platinum among other materials, and these could be mined and transported back to Earth. The profits gained through asteroid mining could greatly offset the costs of the colonization expedition.	First, while it's true that asteroids often contain valuable metals and minerals, it is not simple to turn these into a profit. The costs involved in mining the materials, not to mention shipping them back to Earth, would be very high, and may not even result in a profit at all. Moreover, market values back on Earth are affected by rarity, so precious materials may diminish in value if large amounts are suddenly being brought to Earth from an asteroid colony, further reducing the profitability potential of asteroid mining.
Another reason that asteroids are prime targets for colonization is that they are relatively close to Earth. Every year, many of them briefly enter Earth's orbit, and some of them even come closer to our planet than the Moon! So, it would be fairly easy and affordable to reach these particular asteroids, especially compared with the dangerous and expensive 4-year round-trip that would be required to take colonists to Mars and back.	Second, yes, some asteroids do come within close proximity to the Earth, but just because they might be easy to reach, it doesn't necessarily mean they will be easy to return from. I mean, the vast majority of asteroids that enter, or come near Earth's orbit are on a track that will take them huge distances from Earth. So, while it may be easy to travel to these asteroids when they are passing by Earth, it may take an extremely long time for colonists to get back to Earth, as their colonized asteroid may end up even further away from Earth than Mars is.
Last, due to their relatively small size compared to moons and planets, asteroids have lower gravity. This makes it a lot easier to land a spacecraft on an asteroid than on the Moon or Mars, where the gravity would strongly pull the spacecraft down toward the surface. The same is true when it comes to leaving the asteroid - lower gravity facilitates take-off. So, a spacecraft visiting and returning from an asteroid would require less fuel, and would be able to carry more equipment for the colonization operation.	Third, the passage discusses the benefits of low gravity, but none of the disadvantages. The low-gravity environment might facilitate landing and launching, but it can have adverse effects on the spacecraft personnel. Prolonged exposure to low-gravity conditions would cause a significant decline in the colonists' muscle mass and bone density, as well as numerous other negative health effects. The potential impact this could have on the colonists is far more important than the ability to carry less fuel and more equipment.

해석

요즘은, 사람들이 지구의 달이나 심지어 화성을 식민지화하기 위해 인간을 보내는 것의 가능성을 흔히 이야기하지만, 더 나은 선택권이 있을 수도 있다. 우리 태양계에는 수 십만 개의 거대 소행성이 존재하고 있기 때문에, 이 소행성들이 다양한 이유로 인간의 식민지화에 더 적합한 대상이 될 수 있다.

우선, 소행성은 흔히 희귀 금속 및 원소가 풍부한 공급원으로서, 지구에서의 희소성으로 인해 이곳에서 비싼 값에 다시 팔리게 될 것이다. 소행성 하나를 식민지화함으로써, 우리는 다른 물질들 중에서도 엄청나게 매장되어 있는 금과 백금을 이용할 수 있게 될 것이며, 이는 채굴해 지구로 다시 옮길 수 있다. 소행성 채굴을 통해 얻는 수익은 식민지화 탐험에 드는 비용을 크게 상쇄할 수 있다.

소행성이 식민지화의 주된 대상인 또 다른 이유는 상대적으로 지구와 가깝다는 점이다. 해마다, 많은 소행성이 잠시 동안 지구의 궤도에 진입하며, 그 중 일부는 심지어 달보다 더 가깝게 우리 지구에 다가온다! 따라서, 이 특정 소행성들에 도달하는 것이 꽤 수월하고 비용도 알맞을 수 있는데, 특히 식민지 개척자들을 화성까지 데려갔다가 돌아오는 데 필요할 수 있는 4년간의 위험하고 많은 비용이 드는 왕복 여정과 비교하면 그러하다.

마지막으로, 위성 및 행성들에 비해 상대적으로 작은 크기로 인해, 소행성은 중력이 더 낮다. 이로 인해 중력이 표면으로 우주선을 강하게 끌어 들이게 될 달 또는 화성보다 소행성에 우주선을 착륙시키는 것이 훨씬 더 쉽다. 소행성에서 떠나는 경우와 관련해서도 마찬가지인데, 더 낮은 중력이 이륙을 용이하게 해주기 때문이다. 따라서, 소행성을 방문했다가 복귀하는 우주선은 연료를 더 적게 필요로 할 것이며, 식민지화 활동에 필요한 장비를 더 많이 옮길 수 있을 것이다.

독해 지문은 왜 소행성이 행성 또는 위성들보다 식민지화에 더 좋은 선택권인지 몇 가지 이유를 간략히 설명하고 있지만, 제시된 이유들이 완전히 설득력이 있진 않습니다.

첫 번째로, 소행성이 흔히 가치 있는 금속과 광물을 지니고 있다는 것이 사실이기는 하지만, 이것들을 수익으로 탈바꿈시키는 건 간단하지 않습니다. 그 물질들을 채굴하는 데 수반되는 비용이, 지구로 다시 싣고 오는 일은 언급할 필요도 없이, 매우 높을 것이며, 심지어 전혀 수익을 초래하지 못할 수도 있습니다. 게다가, 지구로 가져온 뒤의 시장 가치는 희소성에 의해 영향을 받기 때문에, 많은 양이 갑자기 소행성에서 지구로 들어오게 되는 경우에는 귀중한 물질의 가치가 떨어져, 소행성 채굴에 따른 수익 발생 잠재성을 더욱 낮출 수 있습니다.

두 번째로, 네, 일부 소행성이 분명 지구와 근접한 범위 내로 접근하긴 하지만, 단지 도달하기 쉬울 수도 있다는 이유만으로, 반드시 소행성으로부터의 복귀가 쉬울 것임을 의미하진 않습니다. 말하자면, 지구 궤도에 진입하거나 가까이 접근하는 대다수의 소행성은 지구로부터 엄청나게 먼 거리로 보내는 궤적에 놓이게 됩니다. 따라서, 지구를 지나쳐 갈 때 이 소행성들로 이동하는 것이 쉬울 수는 있어도, 식민지 개척자들이 다시 지구로 돌아올 땐 대단히 오랜 시간이 걸릴 수도 있는데, 식민지화된 소행성이 결국에는 지구에서 화성과의 거리보다 훨씬 더 멀리 떨어진 곳에 있을 수 있기 때문입니다.

세 번째로, 독해 지문은 낮은 중력의 이점을 이야기하고 있는데, 단점은 아무것도 언급하고 있지 않습니다. 중력이 낮은 환경이 착륙과 이륙을 용이하게 할지는 모르겠지만, 우주선 탑승 인원에게 부정적인 영향을 미칠 수 있습니다. 중력이 낮은 상태에 대한 장기간의 노출은 식민지 개척자들에게 근육량과 골밀도의 상당한 감소를 비롯해 여러 다른 건강상의 부정적인 영향도 초래할 수 있습니다. 이것이 식민지 개척자들에게 미칠 수 있는 잠재적 영향이 더 적은 연료와 더 많은 장비를 나를 수 있는 가능성보다 훨씬 더 중요합니다.

강의에서 언급된 요점들이 어떻게 독해 지문에 제시된 특정 주장들에 대해 이의를 제기하는지 설명하면서 그 내용을 요약해 보시오.

노트테이킹

sending human? asteroid suitable	X convin.
high price ↓	O / X simple ship. ↑ → X rarity ↓ → brought earth prof. ↓
relatively close	X nece. mean easy long time – get back further away
lower gravity	none. dis. adv. → person. ↓ muscle / bone nega. health impor. > fuel. equip.

모범 답안

The reading passage and the lecture both discuss the possibility of sending humans to another planet. The writer states that there are several reasons for asteroids being suitable options for human colonization. However, the lecturer disagrees with the argument, saying that none of the theories in the reading passage are wholly convincing.

First of all, the lecturer doubts the writer's point that mining rare metals and elements from an asteroid could offset the costs of the colonization expedition. He argues that this argument is only partially true. Although the writer and the lecturer both agree that there are valuable metals and minerals in asteroids, the lecturer points out that it is not simple to turn these into a profit. In fact, the shipping fee is very expensive, and the materials may not even result in profitable products at all. Plus, since the market price depends on rarity, the value of the materials may decrease under the condition that large amounts of them could be brought to Earth. Eventually, the profitability could be reduced.

Secondly, the lecturer refutes the argument in the reading passage that it is easy to reach asteroids because of their proximity to Earth. He states that this is not entirely true. While the writer and the lecturer both state that some asteroids come close enough to the Earth and people might easily reach them, the lecturer highlights that it does not necessarily mean that it will be easy to return. In fact, the majority of asteroids coming near Earth's orbit will be far away from Earth at some point and it may take an extremely long time for people to get back to Earth.

Finally, the lecturer doubts the writer's argument that asteroids have lower gravity, which helps to land a spacecraft easily. He contends that nothing about this is advantageous. In the reading passage, the writer claims that lower gravity facilitates landing and take-off, but in the listening part, the lecturer says it can have adverse effects on people in the spacecraft. In fact, too much exposure to low gravity would decrease muscle mass and bone density, and negatively influence health. These health issues are more important than carrying less fuel and more equipment.

(368 words)

독해 지문과 강의는 모두 다른 행성으로 사람을 보내는 것의 가능성을 이야기한다. 글쓴이는 인간의 식민지화에 있어 소행성이 더 적합한 선택권인 것에 대해 여러 가지 이유가 있다고 언급한다. 하지만, 강의 진행자는 독해 지문에 제시된 이론들 중 어떤 것도 완전히 설득력이 있지는 않다고 말하면서 그러한 주장에 동의하지 않는다.

가장 먼저, 강의 진행자는 소행성에서 희귀 금속 및 원소를 채굴하는 것이 식민지화 탐험에 드는 비용을 상쇄할 수 있을 것이라는 글쓴이의 주장에 의구심을 갖는다. 강의 진행자는 이 주장이 오직 일부만 사실이라고 주장한다. 글쓴이와 강의 진행자 둘 모두 가치 있는 금속과 광물이 소행성에 있다는 점에는 동의하지만, 강의 진행자는 그것들을 수익으로 탈바꿈시키는 일이 간단하지 않다고 지적한다. 실제로, 운송 비용이 매우 많이 드는 데다, 그 물질들이 심지어 전혀 수익성 있는 제품이 되지 못할 수도 있다. 게다가, 시장 가격이 희소성에 달려 있기 때문에, 이 물질들의 가치는 많은 양을 지구로 들여올 수 있다는 전제 하에 하락할 수도 있다. 결국, 수익성이 감소될 수 있을 것이다.

두 번째로, 강의 진행자는 지구와의 근접성으로 인해 소행성에 도달하는 것이 쉽다고 말하는 독해 지문 내의 주장에 반박하고 있다. 강의 진행자는 이것이 전적으로 사실이 아니라고 언급한다. 글쓴이와 강의 진행자는 모두 일부 소행성이 지구와 충분히 가깝게 다가오고 사람들이 쉽게 도달할 수도 있다고 언급하지만, 강의 진행자는 그렇다고 해서 돌아오는 게 쉬울 것임을 반드시 의미하는 건 아니라고 강조한다. 실제로, 지구 궤도에 가까이 다가오는 대부분의 소행성은 어느 시점이 되면 지구에서 멀리 떨어지게 될 것이며, 사람들이 지구로 돌아오는 데 대단히 오랜 시간이 걸릴 수도 있다.

마지막으로, 강의 진행자는 소행성이 더 낮은 중력을 지니고 있어서 우주선을 쉽게 착륙시키는 데 도움이 된다는 글쓴이의 주장에 의구심을 갖는다. 강의 진행자는 이 부분과 관련해 이로운 게 없다고 주장한다. 독해 지문에서, 글쓴이는 더 낮은 중력이 착륙과 이륙을 용이하게 한다고 주장하지만, 청해 파트에서, 강의 진행자는 우주선 내의 사람들에게 부정적인 영향을 미칠 수 있다고 말한다. 실제로, 낮은 중력에 너무 많이 노출되면 근육량과 골밀도를 감소시키고, 건강에 부정적으로 영향을 미치게 될 것이다. 이러한 건강 관련 문제는 더 적은 연료와 더 많은 장비를 나르는 것보다 더 중요하다.

어휘

colonize ~을 식민지화하다, 개척하다 asteroid 소행성 element 원소 fetch a high price 비싼 값에 팔리다 scarcity 희소성(= rarity) deposit 매장(량) mine ~을 채굴하다 offset ~을 상쇄하다 orbit 궤도 gravity 중력 land ~을 착륙시키다 when it comes to ~와 관련해서, ~라는 측면에 있어 facilitate ~을 용이하게 하다

turn A into B A를 B로 탈바꿈시키다, 전환하다 affect ~에 영향을 미치다 diminish 떨어지다, 줄어들다, 약화되다 close proximity to ~와 근접한 거리 trajectory 궤적, 궤도 end up 결국 ~하게 되다 have an effect on ~에 영향을 미치다(= have an impact on) adverse 부정적인, 불리한 decline in ~의 감소, 하락 density 밀도

depend on ~에 달려 있다, ~에 따라 다르다 influence ~에 영향을 미치다

실전문제 11 – 인류 주제 (1)

Reading Passage	Listening Script
In 1936, during the construction of a railway line in Iraq, workers unearthed a set of distinctive clay jars. These artifacts were passed on to an archaeologist, who determined that they were approximately 2,200 years old and proposed that they were used as ancient batteries. Inside each jar was an iron rod surrounded by copper wire. As demonstrated by the archaeologist, when the jars were filled with certain liquids, they produced an electric current. However, it is unlikely that these jars actually functioned as electric batteries when they were created.	The reading passage is keen to point out how these clay jars were most probably not constructed in order to provide electricity, but the arguments used in the text are rather weak. In my opinion, the clay jars could indeed have been used as ancient batteries.
First of all, virtually identical clay jars were also discovered at an archaeological site nearby, where the city of Seleucia once stood. These jars also contained the copper wire, but testing determined that the jars were used for storing religious scrolls, not for any electrical purpose. Since the jars believed to be batteries have the same design as those found at Seleucia, it is likely that they were also used for storing scrolls, which would naturally have degraded and vanished over the past 2,200 years.	First, there are the scrolls found at the ancient site of Seleucia. Even though both sets of jars are very similar, it does not necessarily mean that they were both used for holding scrolls. One possibility is that such vessels were originally designed for one purpose - holding scrolls - but were later found to have an additional function. I mean, perhaps an ancient scholar noticed that the clay jars produced electricity when iron, copper, and fluids were introduced to them, and then the jars took on an unknown secondary function.
Second, if the jars were used to generate electricity, we would expect them to be connected to additional metal wires or some other means of conducting electricity. However, nothing was found in the vicinity of the jars that could be used to transfer an electrical current.	Second, it is odd that no wires or other conducting materials were found near the jars, but it's important to remember who found them. Local villagers and railroad workers made the discovery, and they might have removed some materials from the site where the jars were buried. These people were not trained archaeologists, so they might have mistaken conducting material for useless scrap and simply thrown it away.
Finally, why would people who lived 2,200 years ago require electricity in the first place? They had no objects or machines that were powered by electricity. So, the clay jars that people believe are batteries would have been useless to the ancient people who built them.	Finally, the passage questions why anyone in an ancient civilization would need a battery. Well, it was not necessarily used to power a device. The mild shock it could produce may have been used as a form of therapy to cure medical ailments. It could also have been used as a way of showing some kind of magical powers in order to gain influence over people.

해석

이라크에서 철도가 건설 중이던 1936년에, 작업자들이 일련의 독특한 점토 항아리들을 땅속에서 발굴했다. 이 인공 유물이 한 고고학자에게 전달되었고, 이 학자는 그 유물이 대략 2,200년은 된 것으로 결론 내리면서 고대의 배터리로 사용되었다는 의견을 제시했다. 각 항아리 내부에는 구리선으로 둘러싸인 철 막대가 하나 들어있었다. 이 고고학자가 설명한 바와 같이, 이 항아리들은 특정 액체로 가득 채워지면, 전류를 만들어냈다. 하지만, 이 항아리들이 만들어졌을 때 실제로 전기 배터리로서 기능했을 가능성은 낮다.

가장 먼저, 거의 동일한 점토 항아리들이 근처의 한 유적지에서도 발견되었는데, 그곳은 한때 셀레우키아라는 도시가 세워졌던 곳이다. 이 항아리들도 구리선을 포함하고 있었지만, 실험을 통해 이 항아리들은 전기와 관련된 용도는 전혀 지니고 있지 않았으며, 종교적인 두루마리를 보관하는 데 쓰였던 것으로 밝혀졌다. 배터리로 여겨졌던 항아리들이 셀레우키아에서 발견된 것들과 디자인이 동일했기 때문에, 이 항아리들도 지난 2,200년 동안에 걸쳐 자연적으로 분해되어 사라진 두루마리 보관용으로 쓰였을 가능성이 있다.

두 번째로, 그 항아리들이 전기를 만드는 데 쓰였다면, 우리는 또 다른 금속 선이나 어떤 다른 전기 전도 수단과 연결되는 것으로 예상하게 될 것이다. 하지만, 그 항아리들 근처에서 전류를 이동시키는 데 쓰였을 수 있는 것이 전혀 발견되지 않았다.

마지막으로, 애초에 2,200년 전에 살았던 사람들이 왜 전기가 필요했을 것인가? 그 사람들은 전기로 동력이 제공되는 어떤 물체나 기계도 갖고 있지 않았다. 따라서, 사람들이 배터리라고 생각하는 이 점토 항아리들은 그것들을 만든 고대 사람들에겐 무용지물이었을 것이다.

독해 지문은 어떻게 이 항아리들이 전기를 제공하기 위해 만들어진 것이 아닐 가능성이 가장 큰지를 지적하고 싶어하지만, 지문에 쓰여 있는 주장들은 다소 설득력이 부족합니다. 제 생각엔, 그 점토 항아리들이 실제로 고대의 배터리로 활용되었을 수도 있습니다.

첫 번째로, 고대 유적지 셀레우키아에서 발견된 두루마리들이 있습니다. 두 가지 일련의 항아리들이 매우 유사하기는 하지만, 그렇다고 해서 그 두 곳의 항아리들이 두루마리를 담기 위해 쓰였다는 것을 꼭 의미하지는 않습니다. 한 가지 가능성은 그러한 용기들이 원래 하나의 용도, 즉 두루마리 보관을 위해 고안되기는 했지만, 추가적인 기능이 있었던 것으로 나중에 밝혀졌다는 점입니다. 말하자면, 철, 구리, 그리고 액체가 점토 항아리에 넣어지면 전기를 만들어내어, 그 후에 그 항아리가 알 수 없는 부가적인 기능을 지니게 되었다는 사실을 아마도 고대의 한 학자가 알게 되었을 것입니다.

두 번째로, 그 항아리들 근처에서 어떤 선이나 다른 전도성 물체가 발견되지 않았다는 점이 이상하긴 하지만, 누가 찾았는지를 기억하는 게 중요합니다. 현지 마을 주민들과 철도 작업자들이 발견했으며, 그 사람들이 항아리들이 묻혀 있던 곳에서 어떤 물품들을 치웠을지도 모릅니다. 이 사람들은 숙달된 고고학자가 아니기 때문에, 전도성 물체를 쓸모 없는 폐품으로 오해해 단순히 버렸을지도 모릅니다.

마지막으로, 독해 지문은 누구든 고대 문명 사회에 살았던 사람이 왜 배터리가 필요했을지 의문을 제기합니다. 음, 반드시 기계에 동력을 제공하기 위한 용도로만 쓰인 건 아닙니다. 그 항아리가 만들어낼 수 있는 약한 충격이 의학적 질병을 치료하기 위한 요법의 한 종류로 이용되었을 수 있습니다. 사람들을 대상으로 하는 영향력을 얻기 위해 일종의 주술적 힘을 보여주기 위한 한 가지 수단으로도 이용되었을 수 있습니다.

강의에서 언급된 요점들이 어떻게 독해 지문에 제시된 특정 주장들에 대해 이의를 제기하는지 설명하면서 그 내용을 요약해 보시오.

노트테이킹

clay jar - battery? unlikely	indeed
virtu. iden. store scroll	simil. / X nece. later elec - iron, copper, fluids intro.
metal wire conduc. elec.	who found remove. X train. arch. mistake, throw
X object or machi.	X nece. power cure show magical → influen.

모범 답안

The reading passage and the lecture both discuss whether clay jars unearthed in Iraq were used as ancient batteries. The writer states that these artifacts were not likely to function as electric batteries. However, the lecturer disagrees with the argument, saying that the stated evidence is weak and indeed the clay jars were used as ancient batteries.

First of all, the lecturer doubts the writer's point that clay jars were used for a religious purpose based on the similarity of artifacts found at Seleucia. He argues that it does not necessarily mean that the jars stored religious scrolls. Although the writer and the lecturer both state that the discovered clay jars and the jars holding scrolls seem to be very similar, the lecturer points out that the function of the clay jars may have been changed from holding scrolls to producing electricity. This might have happened because iron, copper, and fluids were introduced to the clay jars.

Secondly, the lecturer refutes the argument in the reading passage that nothing, like an additional metal wire, has been found for transferring an electrical current. He states that it is important who found the clay jars. While the writer and the lecturer both agree that it is odd that additional metal wires for conducting were not found, the lecturer highlights that the people who discovered them might have made mistakes such as throwing away the metal wires. This is because they were not archaeologists, so they might have removed some materials.

Finally, the lecturer doubts the writer's argument that ancient people did not need electricity because there were no machines powered by electricity. He contends that it was not necessarily used to power machines. The lecturer believes the mild electric shock may have been used to cure minor illness or to show magical powers to influence others.

(304 words)

독해 지문과 강의는 모두 이라크에서 발굴된 점토 항아리가 고대의 배터리로 쓰였는지를 이야기한다. 글쓴이는 이 인공 유물이 전기 배터리로서 기능했을 가능성이 없다고 언급한다. 하지만, 강의 진행자는 언급된 증거가 설득력이 부족하고 실제로 그 점토 항아리들이 고대의 배터리로 쓰였다고 말하면서 그러한 주장에 동의하지 않는다.

가장 먼저, 강의 진행자는 셀레우키아에서 발견된 인공 유물과의 유사성을 바탕으로 점토 항아리들이 종교적 용도로 쓰였다는 글쓴이의 주장에 의구심을 갖는다. 강의 진행자는 그것이 반드시 그 항아리들이 종교적 두루마리를 보관했다는 것을 의미하지는 않는다고 주장한다. 글쓴이와 강의 진행자 모두 발견된 항아리들과 두루마리를 담고 있던 항아리들이 매우 유사해 보인다는 점을 언급하고 있지만, 강의 진행자는 점토 항아리의 기능이 두루마리 보관에서 전기 생산으로 바뀌었을 수도 있다는 점을 지적한다. 이는 철, 구리, 액체를 점토 항아리에 넣었기 때문에 일어났을지도 모르는 일이다.

두 번째로, 강의 진행자는 추가적인 금속 선처럼, 전류를 이동시키기 위한 그 어떤 것도 발견되지 않았다고 말하는 독해 지문 내의 주장에 반박하고 있다. 강의 진행자는 누가 그 점토 항아리를 발견했는지가 중요하다고 언급한다. 글쓴이와 강의 진행자 모두 전도용 추가 금속 선이 발견되지 않은 점이 이상하다는 데 동의하지만, 강의 진행자는 그것을 발견한 사람들이 해당 금속 선을 버리는 것 같은 실수를 저질렀을지도 모른다는 점을 강조한다. 이는 그 사람들이 고고학자가 아니라서, 일부 물품을 치워버렸을지도 모르기 때문이다.

마지막으로, 강의 진행자는 전기로 동력을 얻는 기계가 없었기 때문에 고대 사람들이 전기를 필요로 하지 않았다는 글쓴이의 주장에 의구심을 갖는다. 강의 진행자는 그것이 반드시 기계에 동력을 공급하는 데 쓰이지 않았다고 주장한다. 강의 진행자는 약한 전기 충격이 작은 질병을 치료하거나 다른 이들에게 영향을 미치는 주술적 힘을 보여주는 데 쓰였을지도 모른다고 생각한다.

어휘

unearth ~을 발굴하다 **artifact** 인공 유물 **rod** 막대 **archaeologist** 고고학자 **archaeological site** 유적지 **scroll** 두루마리 **degrade** 분해되다 **vanish** 사라지다 **conduct** (전기, 열 등) ~을 전도하다 **electrical current** 전류

be keen to do (간절히) ~하고 싶어하다, ~하는 데 열중하다 **vessel** 용기, 그릇 **introduce** ~을 넣다 **take on** (특정 성질 등) ~을 지니다, 띠다, ~을 맡다 **scrap** 폐품, 쓰레기 **ailment** 병, 질병 **influence** 영향(력)

실전문제 12 - 인류 주제 (2)

Reading Passage	Listening Script
The "Voynich manuscript" is a handwritten book that was acquired by Wilfrid Voynich, a Polish book dealer, in 1912. The book contains text and beautiful drawings that were produced on vellum, a material used for manuscripts before the use of paper became common. It has similarities with manuscripts produced in the 15th and 16th centuries, but it is written in a mysterious text that no one has ever been able to decipher. The true origin of the Voynich manuscript has been the subject of several theories.	The reading passage identifies three individuals who may have been the author of the Voynich manuscript, but it is unlikely that any of them actually wrote the book.

The "Voynich manuscript" is a handwritten book that was acquired by Wilfrid Voynich, a Polish book dealer, in 1912. The book contains text and beautiful drawings that were produced on vellum, a material used for manuscripts before the use of paper became common. It has similarities with manuscripts produced in the 15th and 16th centuries, but it is written in a mysterious text that no one has ever been able to decipher. The true origin of the Voynich manuscript has been the subject of several theories.

One theory is that Voynich himself wrote the manuscript in an effort to create a modern fake of a potentially valuable book. Through his work as an antiquarian and book dealer, Voynich certainly knew how to produce a very convincing centuries-old manuscript. So, many people have theorized that he intended to sell his modern fake to a collector of old manuscripts for a large sum of money.

Another theory is that the strange text in the manuscript has no real meaning and was devised by Edward Kelley in order to trick wealthy book collectors. Kelley was notorious in the sixteenth century for traveling around Europe and conning rich people out of their money, normally by making them believe he possessed magical powers. He may have written the book as part of another scam to take somebody's money. He likely would have convinced that person that the random letters that make up the text were actually the words of a spell or incantation.

Finally, according to some other theories, the manuscript may be a legitimate book that was written in a complex code to keep the true meaning of the text hidden from those who did not have the key to decipher it. Some have speculated that it was written in the 16th century by Anthony Ascham, a botanist and physician, because many of the illustrations contained within it bear similarities with those in one of Ascham's published works, *A Little Herbal*.

The reading passage identifies three individuals who may have been the author of the Voynich manuscript, but it is unlikely that any of them actually wrote the book.

Regarding the first theory, scientists have actually run several tests on the manuscript in order to date the ink and the vellum pages. They determined that both are more than 400 years old, so it is not possible for Voynich to have written the book in the early 1900s. Even if he attempted to make a fake, using 400-year-old vellum pages taken from a genuinely old manuscript, he could not have used 400-year-old ink. So, it seems clear that the manuscript was produced in the 16th century, long before Voynich's time.

Second, the theory that Edward Kelley created the Voynich manuscript in order to trick wealthy people with a magical book is very far-fetched. The thing is, whoever wrote the seemingly coded text in the Voynich manuscript made a lot of effort to create a very complicated script. If Kelley had wanted to fool people in this way, he would have done so by writing something far less complex and detailed. Kelley was known for relatively simple tricks and scams, so it simply does not make sense that he would spend this much time and effort to create an elaborate fake manuscript.

Third, there is the theory that the manuscript is a real book that was written in code to hide important information. The reading passage names Anthony Ascham as a potential author, but it does not seem like his style. Ascham was known simply for writing books about plants, and the content of his books was typically widely known information, not new or original ideas. So, it is very unlikely that a fairly unremarkable botanist like Ascham would ever need to create an intricately coded secret document.

해석

"보이니치 필사본"은 1912년에 폴란드의 한 서적 판매상이었던 윌프리드 보이니치가 손에 넣은 수기 책자이다. 이 책은 종이 사용이 흔해지기 전에 필사본을 만드는 데 이용된 재료인 피지에 쓴 글과 아름다운 그림을 포함하고 있다. 이는 15세기와 16세기에 만들어진 필사본과 유사성을 지니고 있지만, 그 누구도 전혀 해독할 수 없었던 불가사의한 글이 쓰여 있다. 보이니치 필사본의 진정한 유래가 그 동안 여러 이론의 주제였다.

한 가지 이론은 보이니치 자신이 잠재적으로 가치 있는 한 책의 현대적인 모조품을 만들기 위한 노력의 일환으로 이 필사본을 썼다는 것이다. 고서적 전문가이자 서적 판매상으로서 자신의 일을 통해, 보이니치는 수 세기나 된 것으로 납득 가게 하는 필사본을 만들어 내는 방법을 분명히 알고 있었다. 따라서, 많은 사람들은 보이니치가 많은 돈을 벌기 위해 오래된 필사본을 모으는 수집가에게 자신의 현대적인 모조품을 판매할 작정이었다는 이론을 제시했다.

또 다른 이론은 그 필사본 내의 이상한 글이 실제로는 아무런 의미도 없고 부유한 도서 수집가들을 속이기 위해 에드워드 켈리가 고안했다는 것이다. 켈리는 16세기에 유럽 전역을 돌아다니면서, 보통 자신이 주술적인 힘을 보유하고 있다고 믿게 만드는 것으로 사기를 쳐 부유한 사람들에게서 돈을 뜯어냈던 것으로 악명 높았다. 그가 누군가의 돈을 갈취하기 위해 또 다른 사기의 일환으로 이 책을 썼을 수도 있다. 그는 그 글을 구성하는 무작위 글자들이 사실 마법의 주문 또는 주술이라고 그 사람을 납득시켰을 가능성도 있다.

마지막으로, 몇몇 다른 이론에 따르면, 그 필사본은 그 내용을 해독할 열쇠를 지니고 있지 않았던 사람들에게 글의 진정한 의미가 숨겨지도록 유지하기 위해 복잡한 암호로 쓰여진 정당한 책일 수도 있다. 일각에서는 이 책이 식물학자이자 의사였던 앤서니 애스컴이 16세기에 쓴 것으로 추측한 바 있는데, 그 책에 포함된 삽화 중 많은 것들이 애스컴의 출간 작품들 중 하나인 <리틀 허벌>에 담긴 것들과 유사성을 지니고 있기 때문이다.

독해 지문은 보이니치 필사본의 저자였을 수도 있는 세 명의 사람을 확인시켜주고 있지만, 그 중 누구도 실제로 그 책을 썼을 가능성은 낮습니다.

첫 번째 이론과 관련해서는, 과학자들이 사실 잉크 및 피지로 된 페이지들의 연대를 파악하기 위해 그 필사본에 대해 여러 실험을 진행한 바 있습니다. 이 과학자들이 두 가지 모두 400년이 넘은 것으로 밝혀냈기 때문에, 보이니치가 1900년대 초에 그 책을 썼을 가능성은 없습니다. 설사 그가 진정으로 오래된 필사본에서 얻은 400년이나 된 피지로 만든 페이지들을 이용해 모조품을 만들려 했다 하더라도, 400년이나 된 잉크를 사용할 수는 없었을 것입니다. 따라서, 그 필사본이 보이니치가 살았던 시대보다 더 오래 전인 16세기에 만들어진 것이 분명해 보입니다.

두 번째로, 에드워드 켈리가 마법의 책으로 부유한 사람들을 속이기 위해 보이니치 필사본을 만들었다는 이론은 너무 설득력이 없습니다. 문제는, 보이니치 필사본에 담긴 외견상 암호화된 글을 쓴 사람이 누구든 매우 복잡한 원고를 만들기 위해 많은 노력을 기울였다는 점입니다. 켈리가 이런 식으로 사람들을 속이고 싶었다면, 훨씬 덜 복잡하고 자세한 무언가를 써서 그렇게 했을 것입니다. 켈리는 비교적 단순한 속임수와 사기 방법으로 알려진 사람이기 때문에, 정교한 모조 필사본을 만들기 위해 이렇게 많은 시간과 노력을 들였다는 건 그야말로 앞뒤가 맞지 않습니다.

세 번째로, 이 필사본이 중요한 정보를 숨기기 위해 암호로 쓰여진 실제 책이라는 이론이 있습니다. 독해 지문은 앤서니 애스컴을 잠재적 저자로 지목하고 있지만, 그의 문체처럼 보이지 않습니다. 애스컴은 그저 식물에 관한 책을 쓴 것으로 알려져 있었는데, 그가 쓴 책의 내용은 일반적으로 널리 알려져 있는 정보이며, 새롭거나 독창적인 아이디어가 아닙니다. 따라서, 애스컴 같이 꽤 평범한 식물학자가 한번이라도 난해하게 암호화된 비밀 문서를 만들었을 가능성은 매우 낮습니다.

강의에서 언급된 요점들이 어떻게 독해 지문에 제시된 특정 주장들에 대해 대응하는지 설명하면서 그 내용을 요약해 보시오.

노트테이킹

V. manu? origin	unlike. any
V. Produ.	X test - date - ink / vell. O 400 y X possi. produ. 16c before
E K trick	far-fetch compl. - fool ↓ compl. detail. known - simple X time - effort.
A A hidden	X seem style plant / typical & X new, origin. X intric.

모범 답안

The reading passage and the lecture both discuss who the author of the Voynich manuscript is. The writer states that some theories explain the origin of the Voynich manuscript. However, the lecturer disagrees with the argument, saying that none of the writers mentioned in the reading passage wrote the book.

First of all, the lecturer doubts the writer's point that Voynich created a modern fake for money. She argues that this argument is not true. Experts ran some tests to verify the date of the materials used in the manuscript. Although the writer states that Voynich knew how to produce an old fake manuscript, the lecturer points out that it was a genuine old manuscript made in the 16th century. According to tests, the ink and vellum pages were more than 400 years old, and he could not possibly have used those old materials in his time.

Secondly, the lecturer refutes the argument in the reading passage that Edward Kelley devised the manuscript to fool wealthy book collectors. She states that this theory is far-fetched. While the writer states that Edward made rich people believe that the book contains magical powers with some spells he made up, the lecturer highlights that he was unlikely to make such an effort to create the complex and detailed writing just to fool people. In addition, Kelley was well-known for using simple tricks, unlike the manuscript.

Finally, the lecturer doubts the writer's argument that Anthony Ascham wrote the manuscript to keep the true meaning of words hidden. She contends that it does not seem like his style. In the reading passage, the writer claims that the numerous illustrations of the manuscript are similar to those in another book, *A Little Herbal*, written by Ascham, but in the listening part, the lecturer says that the contents are common information about plants, not new or original ideas. This leads to the conclusion that Ascham would not need to create a secret document with intricate codes.

(329 words)

독해 지문과 강의는 모두 누가 보이니치 필사본의 저자인지 이야기한다. 글쓴이는 몇몇 이론들이 보이니치 필사본의 유래를 설명해준다고 언급한다. 하지만, 강의 진행자는 독해 지문에 언급된 저자들 중 그 누구도 그 책을 쓰지 않았다고 말하면서 그러한 주장에 동의하지 않는다.

가장 먼저, 강의 진행자는 보이니치가 돈을 위해 현대적인 모조품을 만들었다는 글쓴이의 주장에 의구심을 갖는다. 강의 진행자는 이러한 주장이 사실이 아니라고 주장한다. 전문가들이 이 필사본에 이용된 재료의 연대를 입증하기 위해 몇몇 실험을 진행했다. 글쓴이는 보이니치가 오래된 모조 필사본을 만드는 방법을 알고 있었다고 언급하지만, 강의 진행자는 이 책이 16세기에 만들어진 진짜 오래된 필사본이었다고 지적한다. 이 실험에 따르면, 잉크와 피지 페이지들이 400년도 넘은 것이며, 보이니치가 당시에 그렇게 오래된 재료를 이용할 수는 없었을 것이다.

두 번째로, 강의 진행자는 에드워드 켈리가 부유한 도서 수집가들을 속이기 위해 이 필사본을 고안했다고 말하는 독해 지문 내의 주장에 반박한다. 강의 진행자는 이 이론이 설득력이 없다고 언급한다. 글쓴이는 에드워드가 이 책에 자신이 만들어낸 몇몇 주문과 함께 주술적 힘이 담겨 있는 것으로 부유한 사람들을 믿게 만들었다고 언급하지만, 강의 진행자는 단지 사람들을 속이기 위해 복잡하고 자세한 글을 만들어낼 정도로 많은 노력을 기울였을 가능성이 없다는 점을 강조한다. 게다가, 켈리는 이 필사본과 달리, 단순한 속임수를 이용하는 것으로 잘 알려져 있었다.

마지막으로, 강의 진행자는 앤서니 애스컴이 말의 진정한 의미를 숨기기 위해 이 필사본을 썼다는 글쓴이의 주장에 의구심을 갖는다. 강의 진행자는 이 책이 그의 문체인 것 같지 않다고 주장한다. 독해 지문에서, 글쓴이는 그 필사본에 들어 있는 다수의 삽화가 애스컴이 쓴 또 다른 책 <리틀 허벌>에 담겨 있는 것들과 유사하다고 주장하지만, 청해 파트에서, 강의 진행자는 그 내용이 새롭거나 독창적인 아이디어가 아니라 식물과 관련된 흔한 정보라고 말한다. 이를 통해 애스컴이 난해한 암호를 담은 비밀 문서를 만들 필요가 없었을 것이라는 결론에 이르게 된다.

어휘

vellum (염소나 송아지 가죽으로 만든) 피지 decipher ~을 해독하다, 판독하다 antiquarian 고서적 전문가 theorize that ~라는 이론을 제시하다 devise ~을 고안하다 notorious 악명 높은 con ~에게 사기를 치다 scam 사기 make up ~을 구성하다, ~을 만들어내다 spell (마법의) 주문 incantation 주술 legitimate 정당한, 합법적인 bear similarities with ~와 유사성을 지니고 있다

date v. ~의 연대를 파악하다, 측정하다 genuinely 진정으로, 진짜로 far-fetched 설득력이 없는 detailed 자세한 make sense that ~라는 것이 앞뒤가 맞다, 말이 되다 elaborate 정교한 unremarkable 평범한, 특별하지 않은 intricately 난해하게, 복잡하게

verify ~을 입증하다, 증명하다

실전문제 13 – 인류 주제 (3)

Reading Passage	Listening Script
In 1909, an experienced explorer named Robert E. Peary embarked on an expedition in an attempt to be the first person to visit the North Pole. Upon his return, Peary claimed that he did in fact reach the North Pole on April 7th, and his apparent success brought him international fame. While the truth of his claim has been disputed by many historians over the years, there are three arguments that support Peary's assertion that he successfully made it to the North Pole.	When considering Robert Peary's claim that he reached the North Pole, the three pieces of supporting evidence presented in the reading passage are not very persuasive.
First, according to Peary, he and his party set off from Ellesmere Island and arrived at the North Pole in just 37 days. Many people have disputed this claim, noting that even expedition teams using modern technology take longer than that to traverse the same route. In 2005, however, a British explorer named Tom Avery traveled from Ellesmere Island to the North Pole in four hours less than Peary. Moreover, Avery made sure to replicate the conditions of Peary's journey, using the same number of dogs and the same type of dogsled, so his success indicates that Peary's claim may well have been truthful.	First, the comparison between Peary's and Avery's expeditions proves nothing, as there were several differences not mentioned in the passage. For a start, Avery had food dropped off by airplane, rather than transporting it on his sled, which meant that his sled carried considerably less weight than Peary's did. The different weather conditions also would have made a huge difference. While Peary's group had to endure consistently harsh weather, Avery enjoyed favorable weather for most of his journey. So, it cannot be concluded that Avery's successful trip provides any support for Peary's claim.
Second, Peary took several photographs during his expedition, and some of these pictures help to support his claim. Scientists analyzed Peary's photos and determined the Sun's position in each photo based on the length of shadows. By cross-referencing the positional data with historical charts of the Sun's position, they determined that the photos were very likely taken at the North Pole on April 7th.	Second, the analysis of the photographs would not have provided accurate data, so they do not prove anything. In order to establish the Sun's position in a photograph precisely, scientists must be able to clearly view all the shadows. But, the problem is that Peary's photographs were taken with a very poor-quality camera, so they are barely in focus, and the shadows are hard to identify. Furthermore, the photos are more than a century old, so the images were badly faded when scientists analyzed them. All things considered, it is impossible to truly determine whether the pictures were taken at the North Pole.
Third, a committee was assembled by the National Geographic Society to investigate all of Peary's expedition documentation and equipment. The committee members concluded that Peary's field notes and equipment usage seemed legitimate and that he had indeed been successful in his efforts to reach the North Pole.	Third, although the National Geographic Society Committee did indeed release a statement that Peary had reached the North Pole, many of the committee members were close friends of Peary. Moreover, many of them had even helped to finance Peary's expedition. The committee only took two days to investigate the validity of Peary's claim, and they did not conduct any comprehensive investigation into his equipment or records. So, it seems that the committee's decision was not impartial or objective, as the members had motives to be favorable towards Peary.

해석

1909년에, 로버트 E. 피어리라는 이름의 경험 많은 탐험가가 북극을 방문하는 첫 번째 사람이 되기 위한 시도로 탐험에 나섰다. 복귀하자마자, 피어리는 자신이 실제로 4월 7일에 북극에 도달했다고 주장했으며, 성공한 것으로 보이는 그의 탐험으로 인해 세계적인 명성을 얻게 되었다. 그의 주장에 대한 진실성이 수년 동안에 걸쳐 많은 역사학자들의 반박에 부딪혔지만, 성공적으로 북극에 도달했다는 피어리의 주장을 뒷받침하는 세 가지 논거가 있다.

우선, 피어리의 말에 따르면, 그는 일행과 함께 엘즈미어 섬에서 출발해 불과 37일만에 북극에 도착했다. 많은 사람들이 심지어 현대적인 기술을 이용하는 탐험 팀들조차 동일한 경로를 횡단하는 데 그보다 더 오랜 시간이 걸린다는 점에 주목하면서, 이 주장에 반박했다. 하지만, 2005년에, 톰 에이버리라는 이름의 영국인 탐험가가 피어리보다 네 시간 더 빨리 엘즈미어 섬에서 북극까지 이동했다. 더욱이, 에이버리는 동일한 숫자의 개와 같은 유형의 개 썰매를 이용해 피어리의 여행 조건을 확실히 그대로 반복했기 때문에, 그의 성공은 피어리의 주장이 충분히 진실이었을 수 있음을 나타낸다.

두 번째로, 피어리는 탐험 중에 여러 사진을 촬영했으며, 이 사진들 중 일부가 그의 주장을 뒷받침하는 데 도움이 된다. 과학자들이 피어리의 사진을 분석해 그림자의 길이를 바탕으로 각 사진에 나타난 태양의 위치를 밝혀냈다. 이 위치 자료를 태양의 위치에 대한 경과도표와 교차 참조하는 방법으로, 이 과학자들은 그 사진들이 4월 7일에 북극에서 촬영되었을 가능성이 매우 크다는 것을 밝혀냈다.

세 번째로, 피어리의 탐험 관련 문서 및 장비를 모두 조사하기 위해 내셔널 지오그래픽 협회에서 위원회를 소집했다. 이 위원회 구성원들은 피어리의 현장 기록과 장비 사용이 정당해 보였고 북극에 도달하기 위해 기울인 노력이 실제로 성공적이었다는 결론을 내렸다.

북극에 도달했다는 로버트 피어리의 주장을 고려할 때, 독해 지문에서 뒷받침하기 위해 제시한 세 가지 증거는 그렇게 설득력이 있지 않습니다.

첫 번째로, 피어리의 탐험과 에이버리의 탐험에 대한 비교는 아무것도 증명하지 못하고 있는데, 독해 지문에 언급되어 있지 않은 여러 차이점이 있었기 때문입니다. 우선, 에이버리는 식량을 썰매로 수송하는 대신 비행기로 옮겨 놓았는데, 이는 그의 썰매가 피어리의 썰매보다 상당히 더 가벼운 무게를 실어 날랐다는 것을 의미했습니다. 다른 날씨 조건 또한 큰 차이를 만들어냈을 것입니다. 피어리의 그룹이 지속적으로 혹독한 날씨를 견뎌야 했던 반면에, 에이버리는 여행 기간의 대부분에 순조로운 날씨를 즐겼습니다. 따라서, 에이버리의 성공적인 여행이 피어리의 주장에 대해 어떤 증거도 제공해준다고 결론 내릴 수 없습니다.

두 번째로, 사진 분석이 정확한 데이터를 제공하지 못했을 것이므로, 어떤 것도 입증하지 못합니다. 사진 속에 나타난 태양의 위치를 정확히 규명하려면, 과학자들이 반드시 모든 그림자를 선명하게 볼 수 있어야 합니다. 하지만, 문제는 피어리의 사진들이 품질이 아주 좋지 못한 카메라로 촬영되었기 때문에, 초점이 거의 맞지 않고, 그림자들을 식별하기 어렵습니다. 게다가, 이 사진들은 한 세기도 더 된 것이어서, 과학자들이 분석했을 때 이미지들이 심하게 바랜 상태였습니다. 이 모든 점들을 고려하면, 그 사진들이 북극에서 촬영되었는지 진정으로 밝혀내는 것은 불가능합니다.

세 번째로, 내셔널 지오그래픽 협회의 위원회가 실제로 피어리가 북극에 도달했다는 성명을 분명 발표하긴 했지만, 그 위원회의 많은 구성원들이 피어리와 가까운 친구 사이였습니다. 더욱이, 그들 중 많은 이들이 심지어 피어리의 탐험에 자금을 제공하는 데 도움을 주기도 했습니다. 이 위원회는 피어리의 주장이 지닌 타당성을 조사하는 불과 이틀밖에 시간이 걸리지 않았고, 그의 장비 또는 기록에 대해 어떠한 종합적인 조사도 실시하지 않았습니다. 따라서, 이 위원회의 결정은 공정하거나 객관적이지 않았던 것으로 보이는데, 그 구성원들이 피어리에게 호의적이었던 이유가 있었기 때문입니다.

강의에서 언급된 요점들이 어떻게 독해 지문에 제시된 특정 주장들에 대해 의문을 제기하는지 설명하면서 그 내용을 요약해 보시오.

노트테이킹

Peary – N. P? arguments	X persu.
T A traveled faster	prov. nth. diff. less weight favor. weather X support
photo.	X prov. any shadow – poor cam. barely focus. old, faded – impo. NP?
NGS legit.	X close fr. X compre. X impar. object.

모범 답안

The reading passage and the lecture both discuss whether Robert E. Peary was the first person to reach the North Pole. The writer states that several pieces of evidence support his argument. However, the lecturer disagrees with the argument, saying that the evidence is not persuasive enough to support that Peary was the first arrival at the North Pole.

First of all, the lecturer doubts the writer's point that the journey made by Tom Avery proved that Peary's expedition could be possible. He argues that Avery's expedition proves nothing because there are some different conditions between the two journeys. Although the writer states that Avery replicated the conditions of Peary's journey, such as the same number of dogs and the same type of dogsled, the lecturer points out that he carried less weight in his sled and experienced favorable weather for most of his journey. Considering these differences, Avery's success cannot support Peary's claim.

Secondly, the lecturer refutes the argument of the reading that the analysis of some photographs taken during Peary's journey could support his claim. He states that the analysis proves nothing. While the writer states that the position of the Sun and the length of shadows explained that the photos were taken at the North Pole, the lecturer highlights that the shadows are hard to identify because of the poor condition of the camera and the fact that it was out of focus. Moreover, the photos are so old and faded that it is impossible to tell whether they were taken at the North Pole.

Finally, the lecturer doubts the writer's argument that a committee put together by the National Geographic Society concluded that Peary's argument seemed legitimate based on his notes and equipment usage. **He contends that** this evidence is not legitimate because the members of the committee were close friends of Peary. **In the reading passage, the writer claims that** the members investigated Peary's journey to the North Pole and concluded it was authentic, **but in the listening part, the lecturer says that** the investigation took only two days and the committee did not investigate his equipment and records in a comprehensive way. Plus, given the fact that they sponsored Peary's expedition, the committee's decision is not objective.

(373 words)

독해 지문과 강의는 모두 로버트 E. 피어리가 북극에 도달한 첫 번째 사람이었는지 이야기한다. 글쓴이는 여러 가지 증거가 그의 주장을 뒷받침한다고 언급한다. 하지만, 강의 진행자는 그 증거가 피어리가 북극에 도착한 첫 번째 사람이라는 것을 뒷받침할 정도로 충분히 설득력이 있지 않다고 말하면서 그러한 주장에 동의하지 않는다.

가장 먼저, 강의 진행자는 톰 에이버리가 했던 여행이 피어리의 탐험이 가능했을 것임을 증명했다는 글쓴이의 주장에 의구심을 갖는다. 강의 진행자는 두 여행 사이에 일부 다른 조건들이 존재하기 때문에 에이버리의 탐험이 아무것도 증명하지 못한다고 주장한다. 글쓴이는 에이버리가 동일한 숫자의 개와 같은 종류의 개 썰매 같은 피어리의 여행 조건을 그대로 반복했다고 언급하지만, 강의 진행자는 에이버리가 썰매로 더 적은 무게를 실어 날랐고 여행 기간의 대부분에 순조로운 날씨를 경험했다는 점을 지적한다. 이러한 차이점들을 고려하면, 에이버리의 성공은 피어리의 주장을 뒷받침하지 못한다.

두 번째로, 강의 진행자는 피어리의 여행 중에 촬영된 몇몇 사진들에 대한 분석이 그의 주장을 뒷받침할 수 있다고 말하는 독해 지문의 주장에 반박한다. 강의 진행자는 이 분석이 아무것도 증명하지 못한다고 언급한다. 글쓴이는 태양의 위치 및 그림자의 길이가 그 사진들이 북극에서 촬영되었다는 것을 설명했다고 언급하지만, 강의 진행자는 카메라의 좋지 못한 상태로 인해 그 그림자들이 식별하기 어렵다는 점과 카메라의 초점이 맞지 않았다는 사실을 강조한다. 더욱이, 사진들이 너무 오래되고 바래서 이 사진들이 북극에서 촬영되었는지 알기란 불가능하다.

마지막으로, 강의 진행자는 내셔널 지오그래픽 협회에 의해 구성된 위원회가 피어리의 기록 및 장비 사용을 바탕으로 그의 주장이 정당해 보인다는 결론을 내렸다는 글쓴이의 주장에 의구심을 갖는다. 강의 진행자는 해당 위원회의 구성원들이 피어리의 가까운 친구였기 때문에 이 증거가 정당하지 않다고 주장한다. 독해 지문에서, 글쓴이는 해당 구성원들이 피어리의 북극 여행을 조사해 그것이 진짜인 것으로 결론 내렸다고 주장하지만, 청해 파트에서, 강의 진행자는 그 조사가 불과 이틀 밖에 걸리지 않은데다 해당 위원회가 피어리의 장비 및 기록을 종합적인 방식으로 조사하지 않았다고 말한다. 게다가, 그들이 피어리의 탐험을 후원했다는 사실로 볼 때, 해당 위원회의 결정은 객관적이지 않다.

어휘

embark on ~에 착수하다 **dispute** ~에 반박하다 **assertion** 주장 **set off** 출발하다 **traverse** ~을 가로지르다, 횡단하다 **replicate** ~을 그대로 반복하다 **cross-reference** ~을 교차 참조하다 **historical chart** 경과 도표 **assemble** ~을 소집하다 **investigate** ~을 조사하다 **legitimate** 정당한

endure ~을 견디다 **consistently** 지속적으로 **establish** ~을 규명하다 **fade** 바래다, 희미해지다 **validity** 타당성, 유효함 **comprehensive** 종합적인, 포괄적인 **impartial** 공정한 **authentic** 진짜인, 정통의

실전문제 14 - 인류 주제 (4)

Reading Passage	Listening Script
Before Giacomo Casanova died in 1798, he wrote an extensive memoir that included many amazing tales from his life. Casanova was known for socializing with a wide range of high-profile people during the 18th century, so his memoir has become an important document that gives an insight into European society at the time. However, many critics have argued that the events, adventures, and relationships described in the memoir were fabricated by Casanova in an effort to make his life seem more interesting than it actually was.	Admittedly, Casanova's memoir contains some exaggeration and errors, but overall, it is largely truthful, and it does offer an accurate and descriptive portrayal of his life. The reading passage details three potential discrepancies in the memoir, but they can all be easily explained.
One aspect of the memoir that has been highly doubted by critics is Casanova's account of his escape from prison in Venice, Italy. According to Casanova, he managed to break through the ceiling of his cell and climb onto the roof, before fleeing into the night. While it is an entertaining anecdote, critics believe that it is very far-fetched. They point out that Casanova was friends with very powerful people in Venice, including politicians, so it is more likely that he had someone offer a bribe to the prison warden to secure his freedom.	First, critics have argued that Casanova lied about his prison escape and was probably released due to a bribe. This seems unlikely, as other inmates in the same prison had even more influential friends than Casanova, yet they were unable to get out through bribery. Furthermore, old prison documents indicate that the ceiling of Casanova's cell had to be repaired shortly after he was free. This strongly backs up his claim that he broke through the ceiling in order to escape.
Another part of Casanova's memoir that has been disputed is the way he describes his lifestyle while living in Switzerland. According to Casanova, he was extraordinarily wealthy at that time, throwing lavish parties and betting huge sums of money while gambling. But, recent evidence has emerged that indicates he had to take out numerous loans from a local moneylender. So, critics argue that Casanova would never have needed to borrow money if he had been as rich as he claimed to be in his memoir.	Second, just because Casanova borrowed from a moneylender, it doesn't necessarily mean that he was poor. There is ample evidence that Casanova did spend large amounts of money on gambling and hosting parties. But much of his wealth came from property and possessions that had to be converted into cash. This could take several days, so while Casanova was waiting to receive his money, he may have taken out a loan so that he could maintain his lavish lifestyle.
Finally, there is a lot of skepticism regarding the conversations with the famous writer Voltaire that Casanova describes in his memoir. There is evidence that Voltaire and Casanova were indeed acquaintances, but critics doubt that Casanova could have remembered their conversations in such vivid detail and written about them decades after they occurred. They suspect that Casanova greatly embellished his simple conversations with	Third, regarding Casanova's conversations with Voltaire, he noted in his memoir that he would normally write down these conversations every evening after he bade farewell to Voltaire. Apparently, Casanova stored these notes away for several years and looked at them again when he began working on his memoir. In fact, many people who knew Casanova at that point in his life remarked that he referred to countless notes and diaries while writing his memoir.

Voltaire in his memoir, because the level of detail seems highly suspicious.	

해석

자코모 카사노바는 1798년에 사망하기에 앞서, 자신의 삶에서 많은 놀라운 이야기들을 포함한 아주 긴 회고록을 썼다. 카사노바는 18세기에 세간의 이목을 끄는 아주 다양한 사람들과 어울렸던 것으로 알려졌기 때문에, 그의 회고록은 당시 유럽 사회에 대한 이해를 제공해주는 중요한 문서가 되었다. 하지만, 많은 평론가들은 이 회고록에 묘사된 사건과 모험, 그리고 관계들이 자신의 삶이 실제보다 더 흥미롭게 보이도록 만들기 위한 노력의 하나로 카사노바에 의해 날조되었다고 주장해 왔다.

이 회고록에서 평론가들이 크게 의구심을 가져왔던 한 가지 측면은 카사노바의 이탈리아 베니스 감옥 탈출 이야기이다. 카사노바의 이야기에 따르면, 자신이 있던 감방 천장을 뚫고 천장으로 기어올라간 후에 야간의 어둠 속으로 달아날 수 있었던 것으로 나온다. 재미를 주는 일화이긴 하지만, 평론가들은 이 이야기가 매우 설득력이 떨어진다고 생각한다. 이들은 카사노바가 정치인들을 포함해 베니스에서 매우 영향력이 큰 사람들과 친분이 있었기 때문에, 누군가에게 부탁해 자신의 자유를 보장하도록 교도소장에게 뇌물을 제공했을 가능성이 더 크다는 점을 지적한다.

카사노바의 회고록에서 반박에 부딪힌 또 다른 부분은 스위스에서 살았을 당시의 생활 방식을 설명하는 방법이다. 카사노바의 이야기에 따르면, 당시에 엄청날 정도로 부유했기 때문에, 호화로운 파티를 열고 도박을 하면서 거액의 돈을 걸었던 것으로 나온다. 하지만, 지역의 한 대금업자에게서 많은 사채를 끌어다 써야 했던 사실을 나타내는 증거가 최근 드러났다. 따라서, 평론가들은 카사노바가 회고록에서 주장한 바와 같이 부자였다면 돈을 빌릴 필요가 없었을 것이라고 주장한다.

마지막으로, 카사노바가 회고록에서 묘사한 유명 작가 볼테르와의 대화와 관련해서도 회의적인 시각이 많다. 볼테르와 카사노바가 실제로 지인 관계였음을 보여주는 증거가 있긴 하지만, 평론가들은 카사노바가 서로간의 대화를 그렇게 생생할 정도로 자세히 기억했다가 그 후로 몇 십 년이나 지나서 그 대화와 관련해 쓸 수 있었는지에 대해 의구심을 갖는다. 평론가들은 그 상세함의 정도가 대단히 의심스럽기 때문에 카사노바가 볼테르와 나눈 단순한 대화를 회고록에서 크게 미화시킨 것으로 의심하고 있다.

인정하건대, 카사노바의 회고록이 일부 과장과 오류를 포함하고 있긴 하지만, 전반적으로는, 대부분 진실성이 있으며, 그의 삶에 대해 정확하면서 서술적인 묘사를 분명히 제공합니다. 독해 지문은 이 회고록에 담긴 세 가지 잠재적인 모순을 자세히 이야기하지만, 모두 쉽게 설명될 수 있습니다.

첫 번째로, 평론가들은 카사노바가 탈옥과 관련해 거짓을 말하고 아마 뇌물로 인해 풀려났을 거라고 주장했습니다. 이는 가능성이 낮아 보이는데, 같은 감옥에 있던 다른 수감자들이 카사노바보다 훨씬 더 영향력 있는 사람들과 친분 관계가 있었음에도 불구하고, 뇌물을 통해 나올 수 없었기 때문입니다. 게다가, 오래된 감옥 기록에 따르면 카사노바가 있던 감방의 천장은 그가 풀려난 직후에 수리되어야 했던 것으로 나타납니다. 이는 탈출하기 위해 천장을 뚫고 나갔다는 그의 주장을 크게 뒷받침해주는 부분입니다.

두 번째로, 단지 카사노바가 대금업자에게서 돈을 빌렸다는 이유만으로, 그것이 반드시 그가 빈곤했음을 의미하진 않습니다. 카사노바가 분명 도박과 파티 주최에 거액의 돈을 썼다는 것을 보여주는 충분한 증거가 있습니다. 하지만 그가 소유했던 부의 대부분은 현금화해야 했던 부동산 및 소유물에서 비롯되었습니다. 이는 며칠이 걸릴 수도 있으므로 카사노바가 돈을 받기 위해 기다리는 동안, 호화로운 생활 방식을 유지할 수 있도록 사채를 받아썼을 수도 있습니다.

세 번째로, 카사노바와 볼테르의 대화와 관련해서, 카사노바는 보통 볼테르에게 작별 인사를 하고 나서 매일 저녁에 이 대화 내용을 적어두곤 했던 것으로 회고록에 언급했습니다. 분명, 카사노바는 수년 동안 이 메모들을 따로 보관했다가 회고록 작업을 시작했을 때 다시 살펴봤을 것입니다. 실제로, 당시 그의 삶에서 카사노바를 알았던 많은 사람들이 그가 회고록을 쓰는 동안 수없이 많은 메모와 일기를 참고했다고 언급했습니다.

강의에서 언급된 요점들이 어떻게 독해 지문에 제시된 특정 주장들에 대해 대응하는지 설명하면서 그 내용을 요약해 보시오.

노트테이킹

accu. memo? fabricated.	accu. explained
doubt - escape prison far-fetched	unlikely more influ. X get out repaired short after
loans	X nece. convert. - cash sev. days wait / lavish
skept. conv. w. V	every evening store - work on ppl remark notes diary

모범 답안

The reading passage and the lecture both discuss the accuracy of a memoir written by Giacomo Casanova. The writer states that three adventurous episodes and events in the memoir were made up to seem more interesting. However, the lecturer disagrees with the argument, saying that the memoir is accurate and all three episodes can be explained.

First of all, the lecturer doubts the writer's point that Casanova's escape from prison in Venice was far-fetched. He claims that this argument is unlikely. Although the writer states that it is more likely that he gave a bribe for his escape rather than freeing himself by breaking through the ceiling, the speaker points out that more powerful people, even more powerful than Casanova, in the same prison were not able to get out through bribery. Furthermore, there are old prison records that the ceiling needed to be repaired right after he got out of the prison.

Secondly, the lecturer refutes the argument in the reading passage that Casanova was not wealthy, as described in the memoir, because he took out numerous loans. He states that borrowing money does not necessarily mean that he was poor. In response to the evidence presented in the reading passage, the lecturer highlights that Casanova borrowed some money because it took several days for his property to be converted into cash. Meanwhile, he used loans to maintain his lavish lifestyle.

Finally, the lecturer doubts the writer's argument that conversations with the famous writer Voltaire could not have occurred because it is skeptical that Casanova remembered all the details. In the reading passage, the writer claims that Casanova wrote about the details of conversations decades after he and Voltaire had them, but in the listening part, the lecturer says that Casanova wrote them down every evening after their conversations. In fact, many people around him stated that he used numerous notes and diaries he had written while working on his memoir.

(322 words)

독해 지문과 강의는 모두 자코모 카사노바가 쓴 회고록의 정확성을 이야기한다. 글쓴이는 회고록에 담긴 세 가지 모험적인 일화 및 사건들이 더 흥미로워 보이도록 하기 위해 꾸며냈다고 언급한다. 하지만, 강의 진행자는 그 회고록이 정확하며 세 가지 일화 모두 설명할 수 있다고 말하면서 그러한 주장에 동의하지 않는다.

가장 먼저, 강의 진행자는 베니스에서 있었던 카사노바의 탈옥이 믿기지 않는다는 글쓴이의 주장에 의구심을 갖는다. 강의 진행자는 이러한 주장이 가능성이 낮다고 주장한다. 글쓴이는 천장을 뚫고 나가 직접 자유의 몸이 된 것이 아니라 탈출을 위해 뇌물을 제공했을 가능성이 더 크다고 언급하지만, 강의 진행자는 같은 감옥에서 카사노바보다 훨씬 더 영향력 있고 더 힘 있는 사람들도 뇌물을 통해 나올 수 없었다고 지적한다. 더욱이, 그가 감옥에서 나온 직후에 그 천장이 수리되어야 했다는 것을 보여주는 오래된 교도소 기록이 존재한다.

두 번째로, 강의 진행자는 카사노바가 많은 사채를 받아썼기 때문에 회고록에 묘사된 것처럼 부유하진 않았다고 말하는 독해 지문의 주장에 반박한다. 강의 진행자는 돈을 빌렸다고 해서 반드시 그가 빈곤했음을 의미하진 않는다고 언급한다. 독해 지문에 제시된 증거에 대응해, 강의 진행자는 카사노바가 부동산을 현금화하는 데 며칠은 걸렸기 때문에 돈을 조금 빌렸다는 점을 강조한다. 그 동안에, 그는 사채를 이용해 호화로운 생활 방식을 유지한 것이었다.

마지막으로, 강의 진행자는 카사노바가 모든 세부 사항을 기억했다는 것이 의심스러운 부분이기 때문에 유명 작가 볼테르와의 대화가 있을 수 없었던 일이라는 글쓴이의 주장에 의구심을 갖는다. 독해 지문에, 글쓴이는 카사노바가 볼테르와 대화를 나누고 몇 십 년이 지나 그 상세 내용에 관해 썼다고 주장하지만, 청해 파트에서, 강의 진행자는 카사노바가 대화를 나누고 매일 저녁에 그것을 써놓았다고 말한다. 실제로, 카사노바가 회고록을 작업하는 동안 이미 써놓았던 많은 메모와 일기를 활용했다고 많은 주변인들이 밝혔다.

어휘

memoir 회고록 tale 이야기 high-profile 세간의 이목을 끄는 insight 이해, 통찰력 fabricate ~을 날조하다, 꾸며내다(= make up)
account 이야기 flee 도망 치다, 달아나다 anecdote 일화 far-fetched 믿기지 않는 warden 교도소장 dispute ~에 반박하다 lavish
호화로운 take out (서비스 등) ~을 받다 skepticism 회의론 vivid 생생한 embellish ~을 미화하다, 꾸미다

exaggeration 과장 discrepancy 모순, 불일치 inmate 수감자 bid farewell to ~에게 작별 인사를 하다(bade는 과거형) refer to ~을
참고하다

property 부동산, 건물

실전문제 15 – 인류 주제 (5)

Reading Passage	Listening Script
Sometime during the 12th century, massive stone buildings were constructed in the settlements of Chaco Canyon in the US state of New Mexico. These "great houses," as they have become known, stand up to four stories tall and include hundreds of rooms. Although there is still no consensus on the purpose of such buildings, three main theories have been put forward.	The reading passage puts forward three theories regarding the purpose of the "great houses" in the Chaco Canyon, but none of them are very persuasive.
The first theory is that the buildings were used as venues for special ceremonies. Archaeologists unearthed a large number of fractured pots that had been buried near one of the buildings, known as Pueblo Alto. They concluded that the pots were evidence that Pueblo Alto served as an important site for ceremonial gatherings. It is known that Native American cultures did engage in such ceremonies, so it is assumed that the Chaco people ate meals together at these events and then discarded the empty food pots afterwards.	First, the theory that the buildings were used to host large ceremonies is not very well supported. When archaeologists dug up the broken pots near Pueblo Alto, they also uncovered a wide range of other items that have no connection to ceremonial events. For instance, they found several broken construction tools, as well as materials used for building. This implies that the items were nothing more than trash discarded by the builders after finishing the construction of the great house. The pots may have been used just to store food for the workers. So, the archaeological findings offer no proof that the building was used to host ceremonial gatherings.
Another theory contends that the buildings were simply housing for hundreds of the Chaco people. Proponents of this theory argue that architecture in the Southwest regions of the US has obviously evolved directly from the great houses of the Chaco. For instance, people have been living in large "apartment-style" buildings in Taos, New Mexico for centuries, and these bear an uncanny resemblance to the large structures in Chaco Canyon.	Second, it is true that the great houses look somewhat similar to later Native American apartment buildings on the outside, but their interiors are nothing alike. In fact, there's nothing inside the great houses that would imply they were used as residences. Let's say that hundreds of Chaco people did live in them. Then, there would need to be numerous fireplaces where people could cook their meals every day. But, there are barely any fireplaces in the buildings. One of the largest buildings could easily accommodate four or five hundred people, yet has fewer than ten fireplaces. So, it doesn't seem likely that the houses were built in order to provide accommodation.
A third theory argues that the Chaco "great houses" were used to store important crops such as maize. Maize was a staple food for the Chaco people, who would store the grain for several months and use it to prepare a wide variety of foods. All of this grain needed to be stored somewhere suitable to ensure that it didn't spoil, and the great houses would have been ideal storage buildings for that purpose.	Third, there is little evidence to support the idea that the large buildings were used to store maize grain. During numerous excavations to uncover the great houses, there was no sign of any maize, or containers that might have been suitable for maize storage. It stands to reason that, if these huge rooms were truly used for the storage of maize, archaeologists would have detected at least a little spilled maize on the floor, but they didn't find any at all.

해석

12세기 중에, 미국 뉴 멕시코 주에 위치한 차코 캐니언의 정착지에 거대 석조 건물이 세워졌다. 이 건물들은 "위대한 집"이라고 알려진 바와 같이, 최대 4층 높이로 서 있으며, 수백 개의 방을 포함하고 있다. 이 건물들의 목적에 대해 여전히 의견 일치가 이뤄져 있지는 않지만, 세 가지 주요 이론이 제시된 바 있다.

첫 번째 이론은 이 건물들이 특별한 의식을 위한 장소로 이용되었다는 것이다. 고고학자들이 푸에블로 알토라고 알려진 건물들 중의 한 곳 근처에 묻혀 있던 아주 많은 조각 난 단지들을 발굴했다. 이들은 그 단지들이 푸에블로 알토가 의식 모임을 위한 중요한 장소의 역할을 했음을 보여주는 증거라는 결론을 내렸다. 미국 원주민 문화가 분명 그러한 의식을 행했던 것으로 알려져 있기 때문에, 차코 사람들이 이러한 행사에서 함께 식사한 후에 빈 음식 단지들을 버린 것으로 추정된다.

또 다른 이론은 그 건물들이 단순히 수백 명의 차코 사람들을 위한 거주지였다고 주장한다. 이 이론을 지지하는 사람들은 미국 남서부 지역의 건축술이 분명 차코의 위대한 집으로부터 직접적으로 발전해왔다고 주장한다. 예를 들어, 사람들이 수 세기 동안 뉴 멕시코의 타오스에 위치한 큰 "아파트형" 건물에서 계속 살아오고 있으며, 이 건물들은 차코 캐니언의 대형 구조물들과 묘할 정도로 닮아 있다.

세 번째 이론은 차코의 "위대한 집"이 옥수수 같은 중요 작물을 보관하는 데 쓰였다고 주장한다. 옥수수는 차코 사람들의 주식이었는데, 이들은 이 곡물을 수 개월 동안 보관하면서 아주 다양한 음식을 조리하는 데 이용하곤 했다. 이 곡물이 모두 반드시 상하지 않도록 하기 위해 어딘가 적절한 곳에 보관되어야 했으며, 이 위대한 집이 그러한 용도로 이상적인 보관용 건물이었을 것이다.

독해 지문은 차코 캐니언에 위치한 "위대한 집"의 용도와 관련해 세 가지 이론을 제시하고 있지만, 그 중 어느 것도 아주 설득력이 있진 않습니다.

첫 번째로, 그 건물들이 대규모 의식을 거행하는 데 이용되었다고 말하는 이론은 그렇게 잘 입증되고 있지 않습니다. 고고학자들이 푸에블로 알토 근처에서 깨진 단지들을 파냈을 때, 의식 행사와 아무런 연관성도 없는 다른 물품들도 아주 다양하게 발견했습니다. 예를 들어, 건축용으로 쓰인 물품들뿐만 아니라 여러 가지 깨진 건축용 도구들도 찾아냈습니다. 이는 그 물건들이 위대한 집 건축을 끝마치고 나서 건축 작업자들이 버린 쓰레기에 지나지 않는다는 것을 암시합니다. 그 단지들은 그저 그 작업자들의 식량을 보관하는 데에만 이용되었을 수도 있습니다. 따라서, 이 고고학적 발견물들은 그 건물이 의식을 위한 모임을 여는 데 이용되었다는 것을 전혀 입증하지 못합니다.

두 번째로, 위대한 집이 겉으로는 후기 미국 원주민 아파트 건물과 다소 유사해 보인다는 점이 사실이긴 하지만, 내부는 전혀 닮아 있지 않습니다. 실제로, 위대한 집 내부에는 거주지로 이용되었음을 나타낼 만한 것이 전혀 없습니다. 그곳에 수백 명의 차코 사람들이 실제로 살았다고 가정해 보겠습니다. 그렇다면, 사람들이 매일 식사를 요리할 수 있는 다수의 화로가 있어야 했을 것입니다. 하지만, 그 건물 안에는 화로가 거의 없습니다. 가장 큰 건물들 중의 하나가 400~500명의 사람들을 어렵지 않게 수용할 수 있었지만, 화로는 10개도 되지 않습니다. 따라서, 그 집들이 숙소를 제공하기 위해 지어졌을 가능성은 없어 보입니다.

세 번째로, 그 큰 건물들이 옥수수 곡물을 보관하는 데 이용되었다는 아이디어를 뒷받침하는 증거가 거의 없습니다. 위대한 집을 발견하기 위한 다수의 발굴 작업 중에, 옥수수 또는 옥수수 보관용으로 적합했을지도 모르는 용기에 대한 흔적조차 전혀 없었습니다. 분명한 점은, 이 거대한 방들이 정말 옥수수 보관용으로 이용되었다면, 고고학자들이 적어도 바닥에 흘려져 있는 옥수수를 조금이라도 발견했겠지만, 전혀 아무것도 찾지 못했다는 사실입니다.

강의에서 언급된 요점들이 어떻게 독해 지문에 제시된 특정 주장들에 대해 의문을 제기하는지 설명하면서 그 내용을 요약해 보시오.

노트테이킹

CC purpose theories	none persu.
ceremony	X sup. X connec. mat. building discard store food X prov.
housing	O → X alike fireplace ↑ – cook barely X seem likely
store crop	little evi. X maize / contain. spilled? → X

모범 답안

The reading passage and the lecture both discuss the purpose of great houses, massive stone buildings in Chaco Canyon in the US state of New Mexico. The writer states that there are several possible theories. However, the lecturer disagrees with the argument, saying that none of the theories in the reading are persuasive.

First of all, the lecturer doubts the writer's point that great houses could be used for ceremonies. She argues that this theory is not well supported. Although the writer states that the discovery of fractured pots was evidence, the lecturer points out that many other items discovered are not connected to ceremonial events. For example, broken construction tools were found, as well as other materials discarded by the builders after building the great house. Moreover, it is assumed that the pots were used for storing some food for workers. Therefore, the findings near Pueblo Alto could not prove anything about ceremonial gatherings.

Secondly, the lecturer refutes the argument in the reading passage that the buildings were made for housing for hundreds of the Chaco people. She states that this is not true. While the writer and the lecturer both agree on the resemblance between the great houses and apartment-style buildings in Taos, the lecturer highlights that the interiors of the buildings are nothing alike. In fact, if hundreds of Chaco people had lived in the buildings, there would have been numerous fireplaces for cooking their meals. However, there are barely any fireplaces. Considering this, it does not seem likely that the houses were for accommodation.

Finally, the lecturer doubts the writer's argument that storing crops could be the purpose of the buildings. She contends that there is little evidence. In the reading passage, the writer claims that maize was a staple crop for Chaco people and had to be stored somewhere, but in the listening part, the lecturer says that there was not any maize or containers for it. If the writer's idea were true, archaeologists would have found at least a little spilled maize on the floor. Therefore, it could be concluded that the buildings were not built for storing food.

(355 words)

독해 지문과 강의는 모두 위대한 집, 즉 미국 뉴 멕시코 주에 위치한 차코 캐니언의 거대 석조 건물이 지닌 목적을 이야기한다. 글쓴이는 가능성 있는 이론이 여러 가지 있다고 언급한다. 하지만, 강의 진행자는 독해 지문에 제시된 이론들 중 어느 것도 설득력이 있지 않다고 말하면서 그러한 주장에 동의하지 않는다.

가장 먼저, 강의 진행자는 위대한 집이 의식용으로 이용되었을 수 있다는 글쓴이의 주장에 의구심을 갖는다. 강의 진행자는 이 이론이 잘 입증되고 있지 않다고 주장한다. 글쓴이는 깨진 단지의 발견이 증거였다고 언급하지만, 강의 진행자는 발견된 여러 다른 물품들이 의식 행사와 연관되어 있지 않다고 지적한다. 예를 들어, 깨진 건축용 도구들을 비롯해, 위대한 집을 지은 후 건축 작업자들이 버린 다른 물품들도 발견되었다. 더욱이, 그 단지들은 작업자들의 일부 식량을 보관하는 데 이용되었던 것으로 추정된다. 따라서, 푸에블로 알토 근처에서 찾은 발견물은 의식을 위한 모임과 관련해 어떤 것도 입증할 수 없었다.

두 번째로, 강의 진행자는 그 건물들이 수백 명의 차코 사람들을 위한 주거용으로 지어졌다는 독해 지문의 주장에 반박한다. 강의 진행자는 이것이 사실이 아니라고 언급한다. 글쓴이와 강의 진행자 모두 위대한 집과 타오스에 위치한 아파트형 건물 사이의 유사성에 대해서는 동의하고 있지만, 강의 진행자는 그 건물들 내부가 전혀 닮지 않았다고 강조한다. 실제로, 수백 명의 차코 사람들이 그 건물에 살았다면, 식사 요리용 화로가 다수 있었을 것이다. 하지만, 화로가 거의 남아 있지 않다. 이를 고려하면, 그 집들이 숙소용이었을 가능성은 없어 보인다.

마지막으로, 강의 진행자는 작물 보관이 그 건물의 용도였을 수 있다는 글쓴이의 주장에 의구심을 갖는다. 강의 진행자는 증거가 거의 없다고 주장한다. 독해 지문에서, 글쓴이는 옥수수가 차코 사람들의 주식이어서 어딘가에 보관되어야 했다고 주장하지만, 청해 파트에서, 강의 진행자는 그것을 입증할 옥수수 또는 옥수수를 담을 용기가 전혀 없었다고 말한다. 글쓴이의 생각이 사실이라면, 고고학자들이 적어도 바닥에 흘려져 있는 옥수수를 조금이라도 발견했을 것이다. 따라서, 그 건물이 식량 보관용으로 지어지지 않았다는 결론을 내릴 수 있을 것이다.

어휘

settlement 정착지 consensus 의견 일치 unearth ~을 발굴하다(= uncover) engage in ~에 관여하다 discard ~을 버리다 proponent 지지하는 사람 evolve 발전하다, 진화하다 uncanny 묘한, 이상한 resemblance 닮음, 유사함 staple food 주식 spoil 상하다

nothing more than ~에 지나지 않는 findings 발견물 residence 주거지 accommodate ~을 수용하다 accommodation 숙소 excavation 발굴 It stands to reason that ~이 분명하다, ~은 당연한 이치이다 detect ~을 발견하다

실전문제 16 - 사회 주제 (1)

Reading Passage	Listening Script
These days, there is a push to make forestry practices more ecologically sustainable. In an effort to encourage wood companies to recycle materials and use fewer resources, a committee has been set up to issue certification to companies that meet specific ecological standards. By receiving this certification, companies can label their products as "eco-certified," which can give them an edge over their uncertified competitors. Although many companies around the world have improved their practices in order to receive the certification, American companies are reluctant to do the same, for several reasons.	Well, the reading passage outlines some reasons why it would not be in the best interests of most American wood companies to seek eco-certification, but the reasons provided are rather shortsighted.
First off, if a company wishes to receive certification, it must pay to have the certification committee investigate its business practices. As a result, it will probably need to raise the prices of its wood products to offset this expense. This puts the company at a disadvantage, because consumers in the United States are highly influenced by price and are unlikely to pay more for certified wood products instead of cheaper uncertified options. Therefore, maintaining low prices is more important to American wood companies than receiving eco-certification.	First of all, yes, price is a high priority for most American consumers. But, according to studies on the decision-making process of consumers, price is only a determining factor when there is a significantly large difference in price between two competing products. In cases where there is a relatively small price difference between two products, like in the case of certified wood, Americans tend to base their buying decision on various other factors. And, among those factors, eco-friendliness is becoming increasingly important to a large proportion of American consumers.
Second, some people argue that, in order to remain competitive, American wood companies must keep up with foreign wood companies by adopting the same new ecological practices, but this claim is inaccurate. American wood companies market and sell the vast majority of their products in the domestic market, so pursuing certification in order to compete with foreign companies makes little sense. Moreover, the huge American consumer base is more interested in the quality of the products rather than how they were made.	Second, even though U.S. wood companies largely sell their products in the domestic market, they should still keep a close eye on developments in the international wood market. While foreign companies might not be direct competitors now, they might be in the future. As I mentioned, American consumers are starting to show more interest in eco-friendly products. So, if foreign companies enter the American market and begin selling eco-certified wood, American consumers might flock towards them and turn their backs on the uncertified American companies.
Third, in America, consumers are constantly inundated with advertising and industry buzzwords, so there is a high chance that they will not be impressed by the "eco-certified" label. Almost all products are labeled as being "eco-friendly" or "new and improved" in some	And third, it is not really true that American consumers disregard all positive marketing gimmicks. Perhaps they are wary of companies exaggerating the value of their own products, but they tend to have more faith in the certification issued by independent agencies. With this in mind, Americans are likely to be strongly attracted to wood products that have been eco-certified by an international committee that has no bias toward any particular company.

way - even low-quality products - so American consumers have lost trust in this type of marketing claim. As a result, they are increasingly wary of purchasing products that bear such labels.

해석

요즘, 삼림 관리 관행을 환경 친화적으로 더욱 지속 가능하게 하려는 적극성이 존재한다. 목재 회사들에게 자재들을 재활용하고 자원을 덜 이용하도록 장려하기 위한 노력의 일환으로, 특정 환경 친화적 기준을 충족하는 회사들에게 인증서를 발급해주기 위해 위원회가 발족되었다. 이 인증서를 받음으로써, 회사들은 자사의 제품들을 "친환경 인증 완료"라고 표기할 수 있으며, 이로 인해 인증받지 못한 경쟁자들보다 우위를 점할 수 있다. 전 세계의 많은 회사들이 이 인증서를 받기 위해 자사의 관행을 개선해오고 있긴 하지만, 미국의 회사들은 여러 가지 이유로 똑같이 하기를 주저하고 있다.

우선, 한 회사가 인증서를 받고자 하는 경우, 인증서 발급 위원회가 회사 내의 사업 관행을 조사하는 데 필요한 비용을 반드시 지불해야 한다. 결과적으로, 이 지출 비용을 상쇄하기 위해 아마 자사의 목재 제품 가격을 인상해야 할 것이다. 이는 그 회사를 불리한 입장에 처하게 만드는데, 미국 내의 소비자들은 가격에 크게 영향을 받는데다 더 저렴하면서 인증받지 못한 선택권 대신 인증받은 목재 제품에 대해 더 많은 돈을 지불할 가능성이 낮기 때문이다. 따라서, 낮은 가격을 유지하는 것이 친환경 인증을 받는 것보다 미국의 목재 회사들에게 더 중요한 부분이다.

두 번째로, 일각에서는 경쟁력을 유지하려면, 미국의 목재 회사들이 동일한 새로운 친환경 관행을 채택함으로써 반드시 외국의 목재 회사들에게 뒤처지지 말아야 한다고 주장하지만, 이러한 주장은 부정확하다. 미국의 목재 회사들은 국내 시장에서 자사의 제품 대부분을 마케팅하고 판매하기 때문에, 외국 회사들과 경쟁하기 위해 인증서를 얻으려 애쓰는 것은 거의 앞뒤가 맞지 않는 얘기이다. 게다가, 미국의 거대한 소비자 층은 어떻게 만들어졌는가 하는 것보다 제품의 품질에 관심이 더 많다.

세 번째로, 미국에서는, 소비자들이 지속적으로 넘쳐나는 광고와 업계 전문 용어를 접하고 있기 때문에, "친환경 인증 완료" 라벨에 깊은 인상을 받지 못할 가능성이 높다. 거의 모든 제품이 어떤 식으로든 "친환경" 또는 "새롭고 개선된" 제품으로 라벨 표기되고 있으며, 심지어 품질이 낮은 제품들조차 그렇기 때문에, 미국의 소비자들은 이런 종류의 마케팅 선전 문구에 대해 신뢰를 상실했다. 그 결과, 그런 라벨을 지니고 있는 제품을 구입하는 것에 대해 점점 더 주의를 기울이고 있다.

음, 독해 지문에서 왜 친환경 인증을 받으려 하는 것이 대부분의 미국 목재 회사들에게 가장 큰 이득이 되지 못할 수도 있는가에 대한 몇 가지 이유를 개괄적으로 설명하고 있지만, 제시된 이유들이 다소 근시안적입니다.

가장 먼저, 네, 가격이 대부분의 미국인 소비자들에게 최우선 사항입니다. 하지만, 소비자들의 의사 결정 과정에 관한 연구에 따르면, 가격은 오직 두 가지 경쟁 제품 사이에서 가격 면에 있어 상당히 큰 차이가 존재할 때만 결정적인 요인이 됩니다. 인증된 목재의 경우에서처럼, 두 제품 사이에 비교적 작은 가격 차이가 존재하는 경우에, 미국인들은 다양한 다른 요인을 구매 결정의 근거로 삼는 경향이 있습니다. 그리고, 그 요인들 사이에서, 친환경성이 대부분의 미국인 소비자들에게 점점 더 중요한 부분이 되어가고 있습니다.

두 번째로, 미국 목재 회사들이 주로 국내 시장에서 자사의 제품을 판매하기는 하지만, 여전히 해외 목재 시장의 추이도 크게 눈 여겨 봐야 합니다. 외국 회사들이 지금은 직접적인 경쟁자가 아닐지도 모르지만, 미래에는 그렇게 될 수도 있습니다. 제가 언급했다시피, 미국의 소비자들은 친환경 제품에 더 많은 관심을 보이기 시작하고 있습니다. 따라서, 외국 회사들이 미국 시장에 진입해 친환경 인증을 받은 목재를 판매하기 시작한다면, 미국의 소비자들은 그쪽으로 몰려들어 인증받지 못한 미국 회사들에게 등을 돌릴지도 모릅니다.

그리고 세 번째로, 미국의 소비자들이 모든 긍정적인 마케팅 전략을 무시한다는 말은 정말로 사실이 아닙니다. 아마 자사의 제품이 지닌 가치를 과대 포장하는 회사들에 대해 주의를 기울이긴 하겠지만, 독립적인 기관에서 발급하는 인증서에 대해서는 더 많은 믿음을 갖는 경향이 있습니다. 이를 감안할 때, 미국인들은 어떤 특정 회사에 대해서도 편견을 지니고 있지 않은 국제적인 위원회에 의해 친환경으로 인증된 목재 제품에 크게 이끌릴 가능성이 있습니다.

강의에서 언급된 요점들이 어떻게 독해 지문에 제시된 특정 주장들에 대해 의문을 제기하는지 설명하면서 그 내용을 요약해 보시오.

wood com. eco. certi? reluct.	shortsight.
pay	O / large diff. small – other eco fri. – impor.
X accu. – keep up with foreign	X direct – future interest – eco enter – turn back
X impressed	X wary ↑ faith attract. ↑

The reading passage and the lecture both discuss whether American wood companies are willing to receive eco-certification. The writer states that there are several reasons for their reluctance to achieve eco-certification. However, the lecturer disagrees with the argument, saying that the theories in the reading are shortsighted.

First of all, the lecturer doubts the writer's point that wood companies should pay extra money to receive the certification. He argues that this argument is only partially true. Although the writer and the speaker both agree that price is an important factor and a priority in buying a product, the lecturer points out that this is only when the difference in price between the two products is large. Likewise, in the case of certification, Americans consider various other factors in a relatively small gap of price, and one of those factors, eco-friendliness, is increasingly important.

Secondly, the lecturer refutes the argument in the reading passage that adopting the same new ecological practices, like foreign wood companies do, is not an accurate reason for American wood companies to receive the certification. He states that the argument is not true. While the writer states that American wood companies have a huge domestic market and it does not make sense to pursue the certification to compete with foreign companies, the lecturer highlights that they should consider international markets. This is because foreign companies might be direct competitors in the future. If

American consumers have interests in eco-friendly products and foreign companies enter the American market, they might turn their backs on the uncertified American products.

Finally, the speaker doubts the writer's argument that advertising with the eco-certified label would not impress American consumers. He contends that it is not true. In the reading passage, the writer claims that American consumers do not trust this marketing approach of using eco-friendly labels, but in the listening part, the lecturer says that the American consumers are not wary of all marketing gimmicks. In fact, they are wary of exaggerated claims in advertisements by companies but have trust in certifications issued by independent agencies.

(345 words)

독해 지문과 강의는 모두 미국 목재 회사들이 친환경 인증서를 받을 의향이 있는지에 대해 이야기한다. 글쓴이는 그 회사들이 친환경 인증 달성을 주저하는 것에 대해 여러 가지 이유가 있다고 언급한다. 하지만, 강의 진행자는 독해 지문 내의 이론들이 근시안적이라고 말하면서 그러한 주장에 동의하지 않는다.

가장 먼저, 강의 진행자는 목재 회사들이 인증서를 받기 위해 추가 비용을 지불해야 한다는 글쓴이의 주장에 의구심을 갖는다. 강의 진행자는 이러한 주장이 오직 일부만 사실이라고 주장한다. 글쓴이와 화자 모두 제품을 구매할 때 가격이 중요한 요인이자 우선 사항이라는 점에 동의하고 있지만, 강의 진행자는 이것이 오직 두 제품 사이에서 가격 차이가 큰 경우에만 해당된다고 지적한다. 마찬가지로, 제품 인증의 경우에, 미국인들은 상대적으로 작은 가격 차이에서는 다양한 다른 요인을 고려하며, 그 요인들 중 하나인 친환경성이 점점 더 중요해지고 있다.

두 번째로, 강의 진행자는 외국 회사들과 마찬가지로 동일한 새 친환경 관행을 채택하는 것이 미국 목재 회사들이 인증서를 받는 정확한 이유는 아니라고 말하는 독해 지문 내의 주장에 반박한다. 강의 진행자는 그 주장이 사실이 아니라고 언급한다. 글쓴이는 미국 목재 회사들에게 아주 큰 국내 시장이 있어서 외국 회사들과 경쟁하기 위해 인증서를 받으려 하는 것이 앞뒤가 맞지 않는다고 언급하지만, 강의 진행자는 해외 시장을 고려해야 한다고 강조한다. 이는 외국 회사들이 나중에 직접적인 경쟁자가 될지도 모르기 때문이다. 미국의 소비자들이 친환경 제품에 관심이 있고 외국 회사들이 미국 시장에 진입한다면, 미국의 소비자들이 인증받지 못한 미국 제품에 대해 등을 돌릴지도 모른다.

마지막으로, 화자는 친환경 인증 완료 라벨을 통한 광고가 미국의 소비자들에게 깊은 인상을 남기지 못할 것이라는 글쓴이의 주장에 의구심을 갖는다. 강의 진행자는 그것이 사실이 아니라고 주장한다. 독해 지문에서, 글쓴이는 미국의 소비자들이 친환경 라벨을 이용하는 이러한 마케팅 접근 방식을 신뢰하지 않는다고 주장하지만, 청해 파트에서, 강의 진행자는 미국의 소비자들이 모든 마케팅 전략에 주의를 기울이지는 않는다고 말한다. 실제로, 그들이 회사의 광고에 담긴 과장된 선전 문구에 주의를 기울이기는 하지만 독립적인 기관에서 발급하는 인증서는 신뢰한다.

어휘

push 적극성, 분발, 노력 practice 관행, 관례 ecologically sustainable 환경 친화석으로 지속 가능한 eco-certified 신환경 인증을 받은 give A an edge over B A가 B보다 우위를 점하게 되다 reluctant to do ~하기를 주저하는, 꺼리는 investigate ~을 조사하다 offset ~을 상쇄하다 put A at a disadvantage A를 불리한 입장에 처하게 하다 keep up with ~에 뒤처지지 않다, ~와 발맞춰 가다 compete with ~와 경쟁하다 make sense 앞뒤가 맞다, 말이 되다 be inundated with A A로 넘쳐나다, A가 쇄도하다 buzzword 전문 용어, 유행어 be wary of ~에 주의를 기울이다, ~을 조심하다 claim 선전 문구 bear ~을 지니고 있다

outline ~을 개괄적으로 설명하다 be in the best interests of ~에게 가장 큰 이득이 되다, ~에게 가장 유리하다 shortsighted 근시안적인 priority 우선 순위 determining 결정적인 base A on B B를 A의 근거로 삼다 flock 몰려들다 turn one's back on ~에 대해 등을 돌리다 disregard ~을 무시하다 gimmick 전략, 수법 exaggerate ~을 과대 포장하다, 과장하다 bias 편견

실전문제 17 - 사회 주제 (2)

Reading Passage	Listening Script
In the United States, particularly in the northwestern region, forests suffer tremendous damage each year due to storms and forest fires. Salvage logging is a practice that is used to deal with the destruction left behind by these natural disasters. The dead trees are removed from the destroyed areas and used for lumber and various wood products. The practice of salvage logging is beneficial both environmentally and economically for several reasons.	While it may seem like salvage logging is a beneficial practice for rejuvenating forested areas that have been damaged by fires or storms, it also has several downsides. In fact, it may even do more harm than good to the environment, and the economic advantages mentioned in the reading passage are also highly debatable.
First, if dead trees are left alone after a natural disaster, they can have a negative impact on the environment. The decaying wood serves as an ideal habitat for insects like the spruce bark beetle. If populations of such insects are allowed to thrive, they will eventually infest nearby healthy trees, causing further damage to forests. Salvage logging ensures that this rotten wood is cleared, preventing unchecked insect infestation and maintaining the health of the undamaged trees in the forest.	First, it is known that decaying wood attracts insects, but is that always a bad thing? Spruce bark beetles, for instance, have not caused any significant damage to forests in Alaska, and they have lived there in abundance for centuries. And, aside from these allegedly harmful insects, old rotten trees also serve as habitats for species that actually help improve the overall health of the ecosystem. So, overall, salvage logging might harm forest health more than insects like the spruce bark beetle do.
Second, the local economy can be boosted by salvage logging. Forests are vital to a wide range of industries, so forest fires and severe storms can cause major economic problems for a large number of businesses. In some cases, however, even trees that have been damaged by natural disasters can still provide enough wood to meet the production needs of many companies. Moreover, more workers are required for salvage logging than for standard logging practices, so it has the added advantage of creating more employment opportunities for local workers.	Second, the reading passage greatly overestimates the economic benefits of salvage logging. When forests are destroyed by natural disasters, helicopters and trucks are required in order to remove any remaining usable lumber. And, it actually costs a lot to use and maintain these vehicles. Moreover, while salvage logging may create jobs for local workers, the positions are only temporary, and they are normally offered to experienced, out-of-state workers rather than inexperienced local residents.
Third, there is the issue of wasted space. When a natural disaster decimates a forest, the area is left littered with dead trees. These trees, if they are left alone, take several years to decompose, and this severely limits the space available for new trees. By removing the dead trees through salvage logging, space immediately becomes available for new vegetation, and this allows the affected area to regrow and recover from the disaster at a much quicker rate.	And third, even if dead trees are removed after a natural disaster, it doesn't necessarily guarantee accelerated regrowth in the area. In fact, if the trees were allowed to decompose naturally, they would enrich the soil with vital nutrients, making it more fertile for future tree growth. By removing the decaying trees immediately, we would deprive the area of much-needed nutrients.

해석

미국에서, 특히 북서부 지역에서는, 삼림이 폭풍과 산불로 인해 매년 엄청난 피해에 시달리고 있다. 구조 벌목은 이러한 자연 재해로 인해 남겨진 파괴에 대처하는 데 활용되는 관행이다. 죽은 나무들은 파괴된 지역에서 제거되고 목재 및 다양한 목조 제품에 사용된다. 이 구조 벌목 관행은 여러 가지 이유로 환경적으로, 그리고 경제적으로 모두 유익하다.

첫 번째로, 죽은 나무가 자연 재해 발생 후에 방치되어 있는 경우, 환경에 부정적인 영향을 미칠 수 있다. 썩어가는 나무는 가문비나무좀 같은 벌레에게 이상적인 서식지의 역할을 한다. 이런 곤충의 개체군이 번성할 수 있게 되면, 결국에는 근처의 건강한 나무에도 들끓게 되어, 삼림에 추가적인 피해를 초래한다. 구조 벌목은 이렇게 썩은 나무가 반드시 제거되도록 함으로써, 삼림 내에서 억제되지 않고 벌레가 들끓는 것을 방지하고 피해를 입지 않은 나무의 건강을 유지할 수 있게 된다.

두 번째로, 지역 경제가 구조 벌목으로 인해 촉진될 수 있다. 삼림은 아주 다양한 산업에 필수적이기 때문에, 산불과 극심한 폭풍은 아주 많은 기업들에게 있어 심각한 경제 문제를 초래할 수 있다. 하지만, 일부 경우에, 심지어 자연 재해로 인해 피해를 입은 나무들도 여전히 많은 회사들의 제품 필요성을 충족할 정도로 충분한 나무를 제공할 수 있다. 게다가, 일반적인 벌목 관행보다 구조 벌목에 더 많은 작업자들이 필요하기 때문에, 지역 근로자들을 대상으로 더 많은 고용 기회를 창출하는 추가 이점을 지니고 있다.

세 번째로, 공간 낭비 문제가 있다. 자연 재해가 삼림을 심각하게 훼손할 때, 그 지역은 죽은 나무가 널려 있는 상태가 된다. 이 나무들은 방치해 놓을 경우, 분해되는 데 수년의 시간이 소요되며, 이는 새로운 나무가 자랄 수 있는 공간을 극심하게 제한한다. 구조 벌목을 통해 죽은 나무를 없앰으로써, 새로운 초목에게 필요한 공간이 즉시 이용 가능하게 되며, 이는 영향을 받은 지역이 훨씬 더 빠른 속도로 재성장하고 재해에서 회복할 수 있게 해준다.

구조 벌목이 화재 또는 폭풍으로 인해 피해를 입은 삼림 지역을 되살리는 데 유익한 행위인 것처럼 보일 수 있지만, 여러 가지 부정적인 측면도 있습니다. 사실, 심지어 환경에 대해 득보다 실이 더 많을 수도 있으며, 독해 지문에 언급된 경제적 이점들 또한 대단히 논란의 여지가 많습니다.

첫 번째로, 썩어가는 나무가 벌레를 끌어들이는 것으로 알려져 있지만, 그게 항상 나쁜 것일까요? 예를 들어, 가문비나무좀은 알래스카의 삼림에 어떤 상당한 피해도 초래한 적이 없으며, 그곳에서 수 세기 동안 대규모로 살아오고 있습니다. 그리고, 이른바 유해한 이 벌레뿐만 아니라, 오래된 썩은 나무들은 실제로 생태계의 전반적인 건강을 향상시키는 데 도움을 주는 종의 서식지 역할도 하고 있습니다. 따라서, 전체적으로, 구조 벌목은 가문비나무좀 같은 벌레보다 삼림 건강에 더 많이 해를 끼칠 수도 있습니다.

두 번째로, 독해 지문은 구조 벌목의 경제적 이점을 크게 과대평가하고 있습니다. 삼림이 자연 재해에 의해 파괴되는 경우, 남아 있는 모든 활용 가능한 목재를 치우려면 헬리콥터와 트럭이 필요합니다. 그리고, 사실 이 운송 수단들을 이용하고 유지 관리하는 데 많은 비용이 듭니다. 더욱이, 구조 벌목이 지역 근로자들을 위해 일자리를 창출할 수 있기는 하지만, 그 자리들은 그저 임시직일 뿐이며, 일반적으로 경험이 부족한 지역 주민들이 아닌 다른 주에서 오는 숙련된 근로자들에게 제공됩니다.

그리고 세 번째로, 설사 죽은 나무가 자연 재해 발생 후에 치워진다 하더라도, 반드시 그 지역 내에서 재성장 가속화를 보장하는 것은 아닙니다. 사실, 그 나무들이 자연적으로 분해되도록 놔두게 되면, 필수 영양분으로 토양을 풍요롭게 해 나중의 나무 성장을 위해 비옥한 상태로 만들어 줄 것입니다. 썩어가는 나무를 즉시 제거함으로써, 그 지역에서 크게 필요로 하는 영양분을 빼앗아가게 될 것입니다.

강의에서 언급된 요점들이 어떻게 독해 지문에 제시된 특정 주장들에 대해 의문을 제기하는지 설명하면서 그 내용을 요약해 보시오.

노트테이킹

bene. envi. eco.	debatable
insect	X always X sign. ↑ health harmful > insects
boost eco.	overestimate heli. truck - remove → cost ↑ only tempo. experi. X local
space	X nece. - regrow enrich - vital nut. - fertile → future grow. deprive needed nut.

모범 답안

The reading passage and the lecture both discuss salvage logging, a practice to deal with forest destruction after natural disasters. The writer states that this method is beneficial to the environment and the economy for several reasons. However, the lecturer disagrees with the argument, saying that all of the theories in the reading are debatable.

First of all, the lecturer doubts the writer's point that salvage logging prevents insect infestations by clearing rotten wood suitable for insect habitats. She argues that it is not always bad to have decaying wood. Although the writer states that thriving populations of spruce bark beetle would infest healthy trees and eventually cause damage to forests, the lecturer points out that the insects have not caused significant damage to forests in Alaska for centuries. In fact, old rotten trees provide habitats for species that help improve the overall health of the ecosystem. Therefore, salvage logging might be more harmful than insects are.

Secondly, the lecturer refutes the argument in the reading passage that salvage logging can boost the local economy. She states that this argument overestimates the economic benefits. While the writer states that more workers are required for salvage logging and it creates more employment for local workers, the lecturer highlights that these positions are only temporary. This is because experienced workers are required, not inexperienced local workers. Plus, after natural disasters, special vehicles are required to remove usable trees, which costs a lot.

Finally, the lecturer doubts the writer's argument that salvage logging can provide some space for new vegetation. She contends that it does not necessarily guarantee the rapid regrowth of trees. In the reading passage, the writer claims that natural decomposition takes several years and new trees cannot grow in affected areas, but in the listening part, the lecturer says that this natural process can enrich the soil with vital nutrients, which helps for future tree growth. This is because natural decomposition can make the soil fertile. Unfortunately, salvage logging could deprive the area of needed nutrients.

(336 words)

독해 지문과 강의는 모두 구조 벌목, 즉 자연 재해 발생 후의 삼림 파괴에 대처하는 관행을 이야기한다. 글쓴이는 이 방법이 여러 가지 이유로 환경과 경제에 이롭다고 언급한다. 하지만, 강의 진행자는 독해 지문에 제시된 이론이 모두 논란의 여지가 있다고 말하면서 그러한 주장에 동의하지 않는다.

가장 먼저, 강의 진행자는 구조 벌목이 벌레의 서식지에 적합한 썩은 나무를 제거함으로써 벌레가 들끓는 것을 방지해준다고 말하는 글쓴이의 주장에 의구심을 갖는다. 강의 진행자는 썩어가는 나무가 있다고 해서 항상 나쁜 것만은 아니라고 주장한다. 글쓴이는 번성하는 가문비나무좀 개체군이 건강한 나무에 들끓어 결국 삼림에 피해를 초래하게 될 것이라고 언급하지만, 강의 진행자는 그 벌레가 수 세기 동안 알래스카의 삼림에 상당한 피해를 초래한 적이 없다고 지적한다. 실제로, 오래된 썩은 나무는 생태계의 전반적인 건강을 개선하는 데 도움을 주는 종에게 필요한 서식지를 제공해준다. 따라서, 구조 벌목이 벌레들보다 더 해로울 수도 있다.

두 번째로, 강의 진행자는 구조 벌목이 지역 경제를 촉진할 수 있다는 독해 지문 내의 주장에 반박한다. 강의 진행자는 이러한 주장이 그 경제적 이점을 과대평가하는 것이라고 언급한다. 글쓴이는 구조 벌목에 더 많은 작업자들이 필요하고 그것은 지역 근로자들을 위해 더 많은 일자리를 창출한다고 언급하지만, 강의 진행자는 이 일자리들이 단지 일시적이라는 점을 강조한다. 이는 경험이 부족한 지역 근로자가 아니라 숙련된 근로자들이 필요하기 때문이다. 게다가, 자연 재해 발생 후에, 특수 운송 수단이 이용 가능한 나무를 치우는 데 필요하지만, 이는 많은 비용이 든다.

마지막으로, 강의 진행자는 구조 벌목이 새로운 초목에 필요한 일부 공간을 제공해줄 수 있다는 글쓴이의 주장에 의구심을 갖는다. 강의 진행자는 그것이 반드시 나무의 빠른 재성장을 보장하는 것은 아니라고 주장한다. 독해 지문에서, 글쓴이는 자연적 분해에 수년의 시간이 소요되며 새로운 나무들이 영향받은 지역에서 자랄 수 없다고 주장하지만, 청해 파트에서, 강의 진행자는 이 자연적 과정이 토양을 필수 영양분으로 풍요롭게 해 미래의 나무 성장에 도움이 될 수 있다고 말한다. 이는 자연적 분해가 토양을 비옥하게 만들어줄 수 있기 때문이다. 유감스럽게도, 구조 벌목은 그 지역에서 필요한 영양분을 빼앗아갈 수도 있다.

어휘

suffer (피해, 고통 등) ~에 시달리다, ~을 겪다 tremendous 엄청난 salvage logging 구조 벌목 practice 관행, 관례 have a negative impact on ~에 부정적인 영향을 미치다 decaying 썩어가는, 부패하는 habitat 서식지 population 개체군, 개체수 infest 들끓다, 우글거리다 decimate ~을 심각하게 훼손하다 be left littered with ~가 널려 있다, ~로 어지럽혀지다 decompose 분해되다, 부패되다 recover from ~에서 회복하다

rejuvenate ~을 되살리다, ~에 다시 활력을 불어넣다 do more harm than good 득보다 실이 더 많다 debatable 논란의 여지가 있는 allegedly 이른바 species (동식물의) 종 overestimate ~을 과대평가하다 temporary 임시의, 일시적인 out-of-state 다른 주에서 오는 guarantee ~을 보장하다 accelerated 가속화된 enrich ~을 풍요롭게 하다 nutrient 영양분 fertile 비옥한 deprive A of B A에게서 B를 빼앗다, 박탈하다

실전문제 18 - 사회 주제 (3)

Reading Passage	Listening Script
Great Britain has been intermittently occupied by settlers for hundreds of thousands of years. Countless ruins and ancient artifacts, ranging from tools to decorative art, have been unearthed and dated back to the Stone Age, the Bronze Age, the Iron Age, and later time periods. However, throughout the 20th century, archaeology was a science that failed to reach its true potential in Great Britain, because it faced many obstacles.	The field of archaeology was significantly altered in Great Britain when new rules and guidelines were implemented in 1990. These changes helped to improve conditions for archaeologists and rectify all of the problems mentioned in the reading passage.
First, pursuing a career in archaeology was an incredibly difficult thing to do. Employment opportunities for budding archaeologists were occasionally offered through universities and the government, but these were in short supply. As a result, many people who had hoped to make a living as archaeologists were forced to branch off onto different career paths, while some worked as part-time amateurs on archaeological projects for little or no pay.	First, thanks to the new guidelines, archaeologists now have many more employment opportunities. Experienced archaeologists are offered a more diverse range of work assignments, such as preliminary site investigations, supervision of dig sites, scientific background research and data analysis, and creation and publication of reports and articles. This demand for archaeologists has led to a surge in archaeology interest in Britain, with more people entering the field than ever before.
Second, the large number of construction projects that took place in the 20th century resulted in the loss of many historical artifacts. Starting in the 1950s, Britain experienced a population boom, so many of its cities and towns underwent rapid development and expansion. Construction workers often accidentally uncovered archaeologically significant ruins and artifacts. Unfortunately, in most cases, these were either discarded or destroyed in order to proceed with construction as quickly as possible.	Second, according to the new guidelines, archaeologists must be brought in to examine construction sites before any work gets underway. If an archaeologist determines that a site is of archaeological value, a meeting will take place between the construction company, local government representatives, and archaeology experts. Together they will establish a plan to ensure the preservation, removal, and documentation of archaeological artifacts that might be uncovered during the construction process.
Third, there was not enough funding available for archaeological expeditions. During the twentieth century, archaeology was financially supported primarily through grants issued by government agencies. These grants only allowed archaeologists to investigate a few key sites of interest, while thousands of other potentially significant archaeological projects were left unfunded. Moreover, as government priorities shifted, funding for archaeologists decreased even further.	Last, one of the new rules adopted states that the construction company - not the government - must pay for any archaeological work carried out at construction sites. This even applies to preliminary investigations of the site and the work involved in planning how to preserve any ruins or artifacts on the site. This provides much-needed additional funding to the field of archaeology. With increased financial support, archaeologists now have the resources to investigate a far greater number of sites than they previously could.

영국은 수십만 년 동안 정착민들이 간헐적으로 차지해왔던 곳이다. 수없이 많은 유적, 그리고 도구에서부터 장식 예술에까지 이르는 고대 인공 유물이 발굴되어 왔으며, 그 시기는 석기 시대와 청동기 시대, 철기 시대, 그리고 그 이후의 여러 시대로까지 거슬러 올라간다. 하지만, 20세기 내내, 고고학은 많은 장애물에 직면했기 때문에, 영국에서 진정한 잠재력에 도달하지 못했던 학문이었다.

첫 번째로, 고고학 분야에서 경력을 추구하는 것은 믿을 수 없을 정도로 하기 어려운 일이다. 신진 고고학자들을 위한 고용 기회가 대학과 정부를 통해 이따금씩 제공되었지만, 그 기회는 턱없이 부족했다. 결과적으로, 고고학자로서 살아가기를 바랐던 많은 사람들은 어쩔 수 없이 다른 진로로 들어서야 했고, 일부는 급여도 거의 또는 전혀 받지 못하고 시간제 아마추어로 고고학 프로젝트에 참여했다.

두 번째로, 20세기에 있었던 아주 많은 건축 프로젝트들로 인해 많은 역사적 인공 유물이 소실되는 결과를 초래했다. 1950년대부터, 영국은 인구 호황을 겪었기 때문에, 많은 도시와 마을이 빠른 발전 및 팽창 과정을 거치게 되었다. 공사 작업자들은 흔히 우연하게 고고학적으로 중요한 유적과 인공 유물을 발견했다. 유감스럽게도, 대부분의 경우, 가능한 한 빨리 건축 공사를 진행하기 위해 버려지거나 파괴되었다.

세 번째로, 고고학적 탐사에 이용 가능한 자금이 충분하지 않았다. 20세기에, 고고학은 주로 정부 기관들이 지급하는 보조금을 통해 재정적으로 지원을 받았다. 이 보조금으로 고고학자들은 그저 관심을 끄는 주요 부지 몇 곳만 조사할 수 있었던 반면, 잠재적으로 중요한 수천 가지 다른 고고학 프로젝트는 자금도 제공받지 못한 상태였다. 더욱이, 정부의 우선 순위가 바뀌면서, 고고학자들을 대상으로 하는 자금은 훨씬 더 감소했다.

영국의 고고학계는 1990년에 새로운 규정과 가이드라인이 시행되면서 상당히 변화되었습니다. 이러한 변화는 고고학자들에 대한 대우를 개선하고 독해 지문에 언급된 모든 문제를 바로잡는 데 도움이 되었습니다.

첫 번째로, 새로운 가이드라인으로 인해, 고고학자들은 현재 더 많은 고용 기회를 얻고 있습니다. 경험 많은 고고학자들은 예비 현장 조사, 발굴 장소 감독, 과학적 배경 연구 및 자료 분석, 그리고 보고서 및 기사의 작성과 출간 같은 더욱 다양한 할당 업무를 제공받고 있습니다. 고고학자에 대한 이러한 수요가 영국에서 고고학에 대한 관심 급증으로 이어지면서, 과거 그 어느 때보다 더 많은 사람들이 이 분야에 발을 들이고 있습니다.

두 번째로, 새로운 가이드라인에 따르면, 어떤 작업이든 진행되기 전에 반드시 고고학자를 참여시켜 공사 현장을 조사해야 합니다. 고고학자가 어떤 장소를 고고학적 가치가 있는 것으로 결정하면, 해당 건설회사와 지역 정부 대표자들, 그리고 고고학 전문가들 사이에서 회의가 열립니다. 이 사람들이 함께 공사 과정 중에 발굴될지도 모르는 고고학적 인공 유물의 보존과 수거, 그리고 문서화 작업을 보장하는 계획을 세웁니다.

마지막으로, 채택된 새로운 규정들 중의 한 가지는 정부가 아닌 건설회사가 반드시 공사 현장에서 실시되는 어떤 고고학적 작업에 대한 비용이든 지불해야 한다고 명시하고 있습니다. 이는 심지어 현장 예비 조사와 현장에서 어떤 유적 또는 인공 유물이든 보존하는 방법을 계획하는 과정과 관련된 작업에도 적용됩니다. 이는 고고학계에 크게 필요한 추가 자금을 제공해줍니다. 재정 지원의 증가로 인해, 현재 고고학자들은 이전에 할 수 있었던 것보다 훨씬 더 많은 현장을 조사하는 데 필요한 재원을 확보하고 있습니다.

강의에서 언급된 새로운 가이드라인이 어떻게 독해 지문에 논의된 특정 문제들을 해결하는 데 도움이 되었는지 설명하면서 그 내용을 요약해 보시오.

노트테이킹

arch GB obstacles	help
diffi. pursue career	↑ empl. ↑ divers. assign. → ↑ interest ↑ enter
construct. historical artifact X	must examine before cons. gov. expert – plan document. uncovered
X enough fund.	const. X gov pay → pre. inve. – work addit. – ↑ resour. > pre.

모범 답안

The reading passage and the lecture both discuss archaeology in Great Britain throughout the 20th century. The writer states that there were several obstacles. However, the lecturer describes how new guidelines adopted by the government in 1990 helped to overcome each of the issues described in the reading.

First of all, the lecturer deals with the writer's point that it was difficult to pursue a career in archaeology. She argues that thanks to the new guidelines, archaeologists can now find more job opportunities. Although the writer states that many people were forced to start on different career paths, or worked as part-time amateurs, the lecturer points out that they are now offered more diverse work assignments. Plus, this demand for archaeologists has led to more interest in archaeology, so more people are entering this field than ever before.

Secondly, the lecturer addresses the argument in the reading passage that many historical artifacts have been lost due to construction projects in the 20th century. She states that archaeologists must examine construction sites before starting any work. While the writer states that archaeologically significant ruins and artifacts were discarded or destroyed by construction workers, the lecturer highlights that now the construction company, government officials, and archaeologists have to meet to make a plan for preservation. Also, they document archaeological artifacts uncovered during the construction project.

Finally, the lecturer considers the writer's argument that there was not enough financial support for archaeology. She contends that the construction company should pay for archaeological work at construction sites, not the government. In the reading passage, the writer claims that only a few archaeological projects could be funded, and others were left unfunded, but in the listening part, the lecturer says that even preliminary investigations and relevant work can be financially supported now. Therefore, this requires much additional funding, so archaeologists have more resources to investigate more sites than before.

(314 words)

독해 지문과 강의는 모두 20세기 전체에 걸친 영국의 고고학을 이야기한다. 글쓴이는 여러 장애물이 있었다고 언급한다. 하지만, 강의 진행자는 1990년에 정부가 채택한 새로운 가이드라인이 독해 지문에서 설명하는 각각의 문제를 극복하는 데 어떻게 도움이 되었는지 설명한다.

가장 먼저, 강의 진행자는 고고학 분야에서 경력을 쌓기 어려웠다고 말하는 글쓴이의 주장을 다룬다. 강의 진행자는 새로운 가이드라인으로 인해, 고고학자들이 현재 더 많은 고용 기회를 찾을 수 있다고 주장한다. 글쓴이는 많은 사람들이 어쩔 수 없이 다른 진로를 찾아 일을 시작하거나 시간제 아마추어로 일해야 했다고 언급하지만, 강의 진행자는 그 사람들이 지금은 더 다양한 할당 업무를 제공받는다고 지적한다. 더욱이, 고고학자에 대한 이러한 수요가 고고학에 대한 더 큰 관심으로 이어졌기 때문에, 과거 그 어느 때보다 더 많은 사람들이 이 분야에 뛰어들고 있다.

두 번째로, 강의 진행자는 20세기에 있었던 공사 프로젝트들로 인해 많은 역사적 인공 유물이 소실되었다고 말하는 독해 지문 내의 주장을 다룬다. 강의 진행자는 어떤 작업이든 시작하기 전에 반드시 고고학자들이 공사 현장을 조사해야 한다고 언급한다. 글쓴이는 고고학적으로 중요한 유적과 인공 유물이 공사 작업자들에 의해 버려지거나 파괴되었다고 언급하지만, 강의 진행자는 이제 건설회사와 정부 당국자들, 그리고 고고학자들이 만나 보존 계획을 세워야 한다는 점을 강조한다. 또한, 이들은 공사 프로젝트 중에 발굴되는 고고학적 인공 유물에 대해 문서화 작업도 한다.

마지막으로, 강의 진행자는 고고학에 필요한 재정적 지원이 충분하지 않았다는 글쓴이의 주장을 살피고 있다. 강의 진행자는 정부가 아닌 건설회사가 공사 현장에서 진행되는 고고학 작업에 대한 비용을 지불해야 한다고 주장한다. 독해 지문에서, 글쓴이는 오직 몇 가지 고고학적 프로젝트만 자금을 제공받을 수 있었고 다른 것들은 자금이 제공되지 않은 상태로 있었다고 주장하지만, 청해 파트에서, 강의 진행자는 이제 심지어 예비 조사 및 관련 작업까지 재정적으로 지원될 수 있다고 말한다. 따라서, 이것이 많은 추가 자금을 필요로 하기 때문에, 고고학자들이 과거보다 더 많은 현장을 조사할 수 있는 재원을 더 많이 확보하고 있다.

어휘

intermittently 간헐적으로 ruins 유적, 폐허 artifact 인공 유물 unearth ~을 발굴하다(= uncover) date back to (유래 등이) ~로 거슬러 올라가다 fail to do ~하지 못하다 be forced to do 어쩔 수 없이 ~하다 branch off onto ~로 들어서다, 접어들다 take place (일, 행사 등이) 일어나다, 발생되다 undergo ~을 서시다, 겪다 discard ~을 비리디, 폐기 처분하다 proceed with ~을 진행하다 grant 보조금 investigate ~을 조사하다 priority 우선 순위 shift 바뀌다

alter ~을 바꾸다, 변경하다 implement ~을 시행하다 rectify ~을 바로잡다 preliminary 예비의 supervision 감독, 관리 surge in ~의 급등, 급증 underway 진행 중인 representative 대표자 adopt ~을 채택하다 carry out ~을 실시하다, 수행하다

overcome ~을 극복하다 official 당국자, 관계자

Reading Passage	Listening Script
It is a sad fact that rhinoceroses are still being hunted illegally for their horns, even though the sale of rhinoceros horns is illegal all over the world. Rhino horns remain extremely valuable on the black market, often being sold for tens of thousands of dollars per kilogram, and rising demand for them has already led to one species of rhino becoming extinct due to poaching. If nothing is done to protect rhinos, many more species will eventually go extinct. People have suggested several ways to address this issue.	Without a doubt, action must be taken to prevent the extinction of more rhinoceros species. However, the solutions described in the reading passage are inadequate for several reasons.
The first way is to make government sales of rhinoceros horns legal. In some countries, governments arrest hundreds of poachers and confiscate the horns they took from rhinos. If governments were allowed to legally sell the huge number of horns they accumulate, they would do so at reasonable prices. This would drive down the market price of rhino horns and make poaching less profitable. This in turn would result in a decline in poaching, giving endangered rhino populations a chance to recover.	First, it is difficult to predict the effects of governments legally selling rhino horns. There might be more consumer interest in rhino horn than we think, but most people do not currently buy it because it's illegal. So, the legal sale of rhino horns might result in an unprecedented surge in demand, which would, in turn, lead to higher rises. This would cause an increase in poaching, which would be more profitable than ever, and a further decline in rhino populations.
The second way is for rhinos to be "dehorned" by trained professionals. By removing the horns of rhinos living in the wild, we could greatly reduce the chance of them being targeted by poachers. Assuming that proper medical equipment and drugs are used, the dehorning procedure can be carried out quickly and painlessly. This approach was attempted on a limited basis in the early 1990s, and none of the rhinos who had their horns removed were hunted by poachers.	Second, the dehorning approach is very impractical. Finding rhinos in the wild and preparing them for the procedure actually requires a lot of time and money. Moreover, the removal of horns may even decrease the chance of survival for rhinos. Rhinos rely on their horns for various purposes, such as digging for water and food, guiding their offspring, and defending themselves from predators. So, while dehorned rhinos may face less threat from poachers, they will struggle to survive in the wild.
The third way is to educate the public. Rhino horn is very commonly used as a medicinal ingredient, as many consumers believe it to have various health benefits. However, there is no scientific evidence that this is true. In fact, rhino horns are primarily composed of keratin, the same material that is found in human fingernails and hair. If we could educate consumers so that they understand keratin has no medicinal value and offers no health benefits, the demand for rhino horn products would drastically decrease.	Third, educating the public is easier said than done. The majority of consumers who purchase rhino horn medicines have strong cultural beliefs about their healing properties, and they are highly unlikely to change their minds. Consumer education rarely works in cases where consumers have strong beliefs about ancient cultural practices, and scientific evidence is typically largely ignored.

해석

코뿔소 뿔의 매매가 전 세계에서 불법임에도 불구하고, 코뿔소가 뿔 때문에 여전히 불법적으로 사냥되고 있다는 건 안타까운 사실이다. 코뿔소 뿔은 암시장에서 여전히 매우 가치 있는 상태이기 때문에, 흔히 킬로그램당 수만 달러에 매매되고 있으며, 그에 대한 수요 증가는 밀렵으로 인해 이미 한 가지 코뿔소 종이 멸종되는 사태에 이르렀다. 코뿔소를 보호하기 위한 조치가 취해지지 않는다면, 더 많은 종이 결국 멸종될 것이다. 사람들이 이 문제를 해결하기 위해 여러 가지 방법을 제안한 바 있다.

첫 번째 방법은 정부 차원에서 코뿔소 뿔 매매를 합법화하는 것이다. 일부 국가에서는, 정부가 수백 명의 밀렵꾼들을 체포해 그들이 코뿔소에게서 떼어 낸 뿔을 몰수하고 있다. 각국 정부가 모으고 있는 엄청난 수의 뿔을 직접 합법적으로 판매할 수 있게 된다면, 그들은 합리적인 가격에 그렇게 할 것이다. 이는 코뿔소 뿔의 시세를 끌어내리고 밀렵의 수익성을 낮출 것이다. 이는 결과적으로 밀렵의 감소를 초래해, 멸종 위기에 처한 코뿔소 개체수가 회복될 가능성이 생길 것이다.

두 번째 방법은 숙련된 전문가들이 코뿔소의 "뿔을 잘라내는" 것이다. 야생에 살고 있는 코뿔소의 뿔을 제거함으로써, 우리는 코뿔소가 밀렵꾼들의 대상이 되는 가능성을 크게 줄일 수 있다. 적절한 의료 장비와 약품을 이용한다면, 뿔 제거 절차는 빠르고 고통 없이 진행될 수 있다. 이러한 접근 방식이 1990년대 초에 제한적으로 시도되었으며, 뿔이 제거된 그 어떤 코뿔소도 밀렵꾼에 의해 사냥되지 않았다.

세 번째 방법은 일반인들을 교육하는 것이다. 코뿔소 뿔은 약재료로 아주 흔히 이용되고 있는데, 많은 소비자들이 건강상의 다양한 이점이 있다고 생각하기 때문이다. 하지만, 이것이 사실임을 보여주는 과학적 증거가 존재하지 않는다. 실제로, 코뿔소 뿔은 주로 케라틴으로 구성되어 있는데, 사람의 손톱과 머리카락에서 발견되는 것과 동일한 물질이다. 케라틴이 어떠한 의학적 가치도 있지 않고 건강상의 이점도 제공하지 않는다는 점을 이해하도록 소비자를 교육할 수 있다면, 코뿔소 뿔 제품에 대한 수요가 급격히 감소할 것이다.

의심의 여지없이, 더 많은 코뿔소 종의 멸종을 막기 위한 조치가 반드시 취해져야 합니다. 하지만, 독해 지문에 설명된 해결책은 여러 가지 이유로 부적절합니다.

첫 번째로, 정부가 합법적으로 코뿔소 뿔을 판매하는 것에 따른 효과를 예측하기 어렵습니다. 우리가 생각하는 것보다 코뿔소 뿔에 대한 소비자의 관심이 더 클지도 모르지만, 대부분의 사람들은 불법이라는 이유로 현재 구입하고 있지 않습니다. 따라서, 합법적인 코뿔소 뿔 판매는 전례 없는 수요 급증을 초래할 수도 있으며, 결국 더 높은 증가로 이어질 것입니다. 이는 그 어느 때보다 더 수익성이 커질 것이기 때문에 밀렵의 증가와 코뿔소 개체수의 추가적인 감소를 초래하게 될 것입니다.

두 번째로, 뿔 제거 접근 방식은 매우 비현실적입니다. 야생에서 코뿔소를 찾아 그런 절차를 위해 준비시키는 일이 실제로는 많은 시간과 비용을 필요로 합니다. 게다가, 뿔 제거는 심지어 코뿔소의 생존 가능성을 떨어뜨릴 수 있습니다. 코뿔소는 물과 먹이를 얻기 위해 땅을 파거나, 새끼를 인도하는 일, 그리고 포식자로부터 자신을 방어하는 일 등, 다양한 목적으로 그 뿔에 의존합니다. 따라서, 뿔이 잘려나간 코뿔소는 밀렵꾼의 위협에 덜 직면할 수는 있지만, 야생에서 힘겹게 생존하게 될 것입니다.

세 번째로, 일반인들을 교육하는 것이 말은 쉽지만 실제로 하긴 어렵습니다. 코뿔소 뿔 약품을 구입하는 대부분의 소비자들은 그 치유 특성에 대한 강한 문화적 믿음을 지니고 있으며, 그러한 생각을 바꿀 가능성은 매우 낮습니다. 소비자 교육은 소비자들이 아주 오래된 문화적 관행에 대한 강한 믿음을 지니고 있는 경우에 좀처럼 효과가 없으며, 과학적 증거는 일반적으로 대부분 무시됩니다.

강의에서 언급된 요점들이 어떻게 독해 지문에 제시된 특정 주장들에 대해 이의를 제기하는지 설명하면서 그 내용을 요약해 보시오.

노트테이킹

rhino. extinct address	inade.
gov → legal	diffi. - predict ↑ demand ↑ poaching → ↓ popul.
dehorn	imprac. ↑ time money ↓ survive. - dig, guide, defend struggle wild
educate	X easy strong bel. - heal X change rarey work sci. ignore.

모범 답안

The reading passage and the lecture both discuss the eventual extinction of the rhinoceros because of illegal hunting for their horns. The writer states that there are several ways to address this problem. However, the lecturer disagrees with the argument, saying that all of the approaches in the reading are inadequate.

First of all, the lecturer doubts the writer's point that one way is to make the sale of rhinoceros horns legal at the state level. He argues that it is difficult to predict the result after legalizing the selling of rhino horns. Although the writer states that confiscating rhino horns from poachers and decreasing their price can make poaching less profitable, the lecturer points out that it might cause an increase in poaching based on a surge in demand. In fact, there might be more consumers interested in rhino horns. This would cause a further decline in rhino populations.

Secondly, the lecturer refutes the argument in the reading passage that the dehorning approach is another effective way. He states that it is very impractical. The lecturer argues that this dehorning procedure requires a lot of time and money. Moreover, this may decrease the possibility of survival for rhinos. In fact, horns are used for various purposes related to the survival of rhinos, such as digging for food, guiding their offspring, and defending themselves. Therefore, although they might face less threat from poachers, they will struggle to survive in the wild.

Finally, the lecturer doubts the writer's argument that education can be a good solution. He contends that educating the public is not easy. In the reading passage, the writer claims that letting people know that there is no scientific evidence about the health benefits of rhino horns would greatly decrease the demand for rhino horn products, but in the listening part, the lecturer says that the majority of consumers have strong cultural beliefs that will make it unlikely for them to change their minds. In fact, education rarely works in such cases where people have strong beliefs related to ancient cultural practices. Usually, scientific evidence is easily ignored.

(349 words)

독해 지문과 강의는 모두 뿔을 얻으려는 불법 사냥으로 인한 궁극적인 코뿔소의 멸종을 이야기한다. 글쓴이는 이 문제를 해결할 수 있는 여러 가지 방법이 있다고 언급한다. 하지만, 강의 진행자는 독해 지문에 제시된 접근 방식이 모두 부적절하다고 말하면서 그러한 주장에 동의하지 않는다.

가장 먼저, 강의 진행자는 한 가지 방법이 국가적인 차원에서 코뿔소 뿔의 판매를 합법적으로 만드는 것이라는 글쓴이의 주장에 의구심을 갖는다. 강의 진행자는 코뿔소 뿔 판매를 합법화한 후에 나타나는 결과를 예측하기 어렵다고 주장한다. 글쓴이는 밀렵꾼들에게서 코뿔소 뿔을 몰수하고 그 가격을 내리는 것이 밀렵의 수익성을 떨어뜨릴 수 있다고 언급하지만, 강의 진행자는 그것이 수요의 급증을 바탕으로 밀렵의 증가를 초래할 수도 있다고 지적한다. 실제로, 코뿔소 뿔에 관심이 있는 소비자들이 더 많을 수도 있다. 이는 코뿔소 개체수의 추가적인 감소를 초래할 것이다.

두 번째로, 강의 진행자는 뿔 제거 접근 방식이 또 다른 효과적인 방법이라고 말하는 독해 지문 내의 주장에 반박한다. 강의 진행자는 그것이 매우 비현실적이라고 언급한다. 강의 진행자는 이 뿔 제거 접근 방식이 많은 시간과 비용을 필요로 한다고 주장한다. 더욱이, 이 방식은 코뿔소의 생존 가능성을 떨어뜨릴 수 있다. 실제로, 뿔은 먹이를 얻기 위해 땅을 파거나 새끼를 인도하는 일, 그리고 자신을 방어하는 일 같이 코뿔소의 생존과 관련된 다양한 목적을 위해 이용된다. 따라서, 밀렵꾼의 위협에 덜 직면할 수는 있지만, 야생에서 생존하기 힘겨울 것이다.

마지막으로, 강의 진행자는 교육이 좋은 해결책이 될 수 있다는 글쓴이의 주장에 의구심을 갖는다. 강의 진행자는 일반인들을 교육하는 것이 쉽지 않다고 주장한다. 독해 지문에서, 글쓴이는 사람들에게 코뿔소 뿔이 지닌 건강상의 이점과 관련된 과학적 증거가 존재하지 않는다고 알리는 것이 코뿔소 뿔 제품에 대한 수요를 크게 감소시킬 것이라고 주장하지만, 청해 파트에서, 강의 진행자는 대부분의 소비자들이 강한 문화적 믿음을 지니고 있어서 그것으로 인해 생각을 바꿀 가능성이 낮아질 것이라고 말한다. 실제로, 교육은 사람들이 아주 오래된 문화적 관행과 관련된 강한 믿음을 지니고 있는 경우에 좀처럼 효과가 없다. 일반적으로, 과학적 증거는 쉽게 무시된다.

어휘

species (동식물의) 종 extinct 멸종된 poaching 밀렵 address v. (문제 등) ~을 해결하다, 처리하다 arrest ~을 체포하다 confiscate ~을 몰수하다 accumulate ~을 모으다, 축적하다 drive down (물가 등) ~을 끌어내리다 profitable 수익성이 좋은 in turn 결과적으로, 그 결과 endangered 멸종 위기에 처한 population 개체수, 개체군 recover 회복되다 dehorn ~의 뿔을 잘라내다 carry out ~을 실시하다, 수행하다 on a limited basis 제한적으로 ingredient (식품 등의) 재료, 성분 be composed of ~로 구성되다 drastically 급격히

take action 조치를 취하다 inadequate 부적절한, 불충분한 unprecedented 전례 없는 surge in ~의 급증, 급등 impractical 비현실적인 rely on ~에 의존하다 predator 포식자 face v. ~에 직면하다, ~을 접하다 struggle to do 힘겹게 ~하다, ~하는 것을 버거워하다 property 특성 ancient 아주 오래된 practice 관행, 관계

extinction 멸종 legalize ~을 합법화하다 procedure 절차 related to ~와 관련된

실전문제 20 – 사회 주제 (5)

Reading Passage	Listening Script
In Canada, most workers normally spend 8 hours a day for 5 days a week at their jobs. However, many of them are pushing for a 4-day week and are even willing to get paid less in order to do so. A national policy requiring companies to give their employees the option of working a 4-day workweek for 4/5 (80%) of their normal salary would be beneficial to the economy overall as well as the individual companies and the employees who choose to take advantage of that option.	Giving employees the option of a 4-day workweek would not have the positive effects on company profits, the overall economy, or the lives of employees in the ways that the reading claims it would.
A shortened workweek would increase profits for companies because workers would be more rested and focused, and as a result, they would be less likely to make errors while they work. Recruiting more staff to ensure that the same amount of work gets done would not lead to additional payroll costs because the 4-day staff would only be paid at 4/5 of the normal rate. In the end, companies would have less staff who are overworked and prone to making errors, for the same total sum of money, which would increase company profits.	First, providing the option of a 4-day workweek would likely require companies to spend more, maybe even a lot more. Recruiting more staff means spending more on training and medical benefits. Don't forget that the costs of things like health benefits can be the same regardless of whether someone works 4 or 5 days a week. And employing more staff members also means that more space and computers are needed. Those extra costs would put a dent in company profits.
For the country in general, one of the primary benefits of this option being made available would be reduced unemployment rates. If large numbers of full-time employees reduced their working hours, the remainder of their workload would have to be covered by others. Therefore, for every 4 employees who choose the 80% week, a new employee could be hired at the same reduced 4/5 rate.	Second, in regards to overall employment, it doesn't necessarily follow that many more jobs will open up once some people decide to work 4 days a week. As I mentioned a moment ago, hiring new workers is expensive. And there are other things companies might do. They could just have their employees work overtime to make up the difference. Even worse, they could raise their expectations of their staff. They might say that the 4-day staff members should complete the same amount of work as they used to do in 5 days. If they do that, then new job openings would not be created and current working conditions for staff would just get worse.
Finally, having the option of a 4-day workweek would be more beneficial for individual employees. Those who could afford to accept the lower salary in exchange for more personal time throughout the week could improve their quality of life by spending more time with family and friends, pursuing private interests, or just simply enjoying hobbies.	Finally, even though a 4-day workweek gives workers more free time in their personal lives, it also presents some risks that might have a negative impact on their overall quality of life. By working a shorter week, a worker's job stability and chances for advancing their career could be reduced. 4-day workers would probably be the first ones to be let go during an economic downturn. They might also be overlooked for promotions because a company would prefer to have a 5-day employee in a management position to ensure reliable coverage and consistent supervision throughout the whole workweek.

해석

캐나다에서, 대부분의 근로자들은 일반적으로 직장에서 일주일에 5일 동안 하루에 8시간을 보낸다. 하지만, 그들 중 많은 사람들은 주 4일제를 요구하고 있고 심지어 그렇게 하기 위해 돈을 더 적게 받을 의향이 있다. 회사들이 직원들에게 정상 급여의 4/5(80%)로 주 4일 근무제를 선택할 수 있도록 하는 국가 정책은 그 선택 사항을 활용하려는 개별 회사들과 직원뿐만 아니라 경제 전반에 도움이 될 것이다.

단축된 근무 시간은 회사들의 이익을 증가시킬 것인데, 그 이유는 근로자들이 더 많이 쉬고 집중하게 되어, 결과적으로 근로자들이 일하는 동안 실수를 할 가능성이 줄어들 것이기 때문이다. 주 4일 근무 직원은 정상 임금의 5분의 4만 지급될 것이기 때문에, 동일한 양의 업무를 수행하기 위해 더 많은 직원을 고용하는 것은 추가 급여 비용으로 이어지지 않을 것이다. 결국, 회사는 같은 금액으로 과로하고 실수를 저지르기 쉬운 직원을 더 적게 보유하게 될 것이고, 이는 회사의 이익을 증가시킬 것이다.

국가 전반적으로, 이 선택 사항이 가능해지는 것에 따른 주요 이점 중 하나는 실업률 감소일 것이다. 많은 수의 정규직 직원들이 근무 시간을 줄인다면, 나머지 업무량은 다른 직원들이 대신해야 할 것이다. 따라서, 주 80%를 선택한 직원 4명당 한 명의 신규 직원을 동일하게 감소한 4/5 임금 비율로 채용할 수 있다.

마지막으로, 주 4일 근무제의 선택 사항을 갖는 것이 개별 직원들에게 더 유익할 것이다. 한 주 동안 더 많은 개인적인 시간을 대가로 더 낮은 급여를 받아들일 여유가 있는 사람들은 가족 및 친구들과 더 많은 시간을 보내거나, 개인적인 관심사를 추구하거나, 단순히 취미 생활을 즐기면서 삶의 질을 향상시킬 수 있다.

직원들에게 주 4일 근무제 선택권을 제공하는 것은 독해 지문이 주장하는 방식으로 회사 수익, 전반적인 경제 또는 직원들의 삶에 긍정적인 영향을 미치지 않을 것입니다.

첫째, 주 4일 근무제 선택권을 제공하면 회사들은 더 많은, 어쩌면 훨씬 더 많은 돈을 써야 할 것입니다. 직원을 더 채용한다는 것은 업무 교육과 의료 보험에 더 많은 돈을 쓴다는 것을 의미하죠. 건강 보험과 같은 것들의 비용은 누군가가 일주일에 4일이나 5일을 일하든 상관없이 같을 수 있다는 것을 잊지 마세요. 그리고 더 많은 직원을 고용하는 것은 더 많은 공간과 컴퓨터가 필요하다는 것을 의미합니다. 그 추가 비용은 회사 수익에 타격을 줄 것입니다.

둘째, 전반적인 고용과 관련하여, 일부 사람들이 일주일에 4일을 일하기로 결정하면 더 많은 일자리가 생기는 일이 반드시 뒤따르지 않습니다. 조금 전에 언급했듯이, 새로운 직원을 고용하는 것은 비용이 많이 듭니다. 그리고 회사들이 할 수도 있는 다른 것들이 있습니다. 그들은 그 차이를 메우기 위해 직원들에게 초과 근무를 시킬 수도 있습니다. 설상가상으로, 회사들은 그들의 직원들에 대한 기대를 높일 수 있습니다. 그들은 주 4일 근무자들이 5일 안에 하던 일을 똑같이 끝내야 한다고 말할지도 모릅니다. 만약 그들이 그렇게 한다면, 새로운 일자리가 창출되지 않을 것이고 직원들의 현재 근무 환경은 그저 악화될 것입니다.

마지막으로, 비록 주 4일 근무제가 근무자들에게 개인적인 삶에서 더 많은 자유 시간을 주지만, 그것은 또한 그들의 전반적인 삶의 질에 부정적인 영향을 미칠 수 있는 몇 가지 위험 요소도 제공합니다. 더 짧은 주 동안 일함으로써, 근무자의 직업 안정성과 경력 발전 기회가 줄어들 수 있습니다. 주 4일 근무자들은 아마도 경기 침체기에 가장 먼저 해고될 것입니다. 또한 회사는 일주일 전체에 걸쳐 믿을 만한 책임 범위와 일관된 관리를 보장하기 위해 관리직에 주 5일 근무 직원을 두는 것을 선호하기 때문에 주 4일 근무자들은 승진에서 제외될 수 있습니다.

강의에서 언급된 요점들이 어떻게 독해 지문에 제시된 특정 주장들에 대해 의문을 제기하는지 설명하면서 그 내용을 요약해 보시오.

노트테이킹

a 4-day workweek bene.	X posi.
↑ profit ↓ error = payroll	spend ↑ 　↑ train, medi. health bene. same 　↑ space, computers
↓ unemploy.	X nece open expensi. → work over complete same X created / condi. ↓
bene - employee ↑ personal time	O → nega. job stable / career ↓ let go / eco. ↓ overlooked - promo. prefer 5

모범 답안

The reading passage and the lecture both discuss whether a 4-day workweek policy would have more benefits to the economy, employees and companies. The writer states that the policy can give advantages to each of them. However, the lecturer disagrees with the argument, saying that it would not have positive effects.

First of all, the lecturer doubts the writer's point that a 4-day workweek could increase profits with fewer errors and the same payroll costs. She argues that it is not true. Although the writer agrees that 4-day workers would not overwork and thus make fewer mistakes, the speaker points out that companies should spend money on training more staff. In addition, companies should cover health benefits for their employees and the amount of that cost would be the same regardless of the work type. Plus, there should be more space and computers in order to employ more staff, which requires extra money.

Secondly, the lecturer refutes the argument of the reading passage that the rate of unemployment would be reduced thanks to a shortened workweek. She states that it does not necessarily open up more job opportunities. This is because employing new workers is expensive, so a company might expect its workers to complete the same amount of work as though they had worked for 5 days. In response to the mentioned opinion in the reading passage, the lecturer presents the contrary opinion that new positions would not be created and working conditions would be worse.

Finally, the speaker doubts the writer's argument that the option of a 4-day workweek provides more benefits to individual employees with more personal time. She contends that it is partially true. In the reading passage and the listening lecture, more personal time could improve their quality of life, but in the listening part, the lecturer says this option might have a negative impact on their lives in that they could not advance their career and lose job stability. Furthermore, the workers might be overlooked for promotion because companies prefer 5-day workers.

(338 words)

독해 지문과 강의는 모두 주 4일 근무제가 경제, 직원, 그리고 회사에 더 많은 혜택을 줄 수 있을지에 대해 논의한다. 글쓴이는 그 정책이 그들 각각에게 이점을 줄 수 있다고 말한다. 하지만, 강의 진행자는 정책이 긍정적인 영향을 미치지 않을 것이라고 말하며 그 주장에 동의하지 않는다.

우선, 강의 진행자는 주 4일 근무제가 더 적은 오류와 동일한 급여 비용으로 이익을 증가시킬 수 있다는 글쓴이의 주장에 의구심을 갖는다. 강의 진행자는 그것이 사실이 아니라고 주장한다. 비록 글쓴이는 주 4일 근무 근로자들이 과로를 하지 않기 때문에 실수를 덜 할 것이라는 것에 동의하지만, 강의 진행자는 기업들이 더 많은 직원을 교육시키는 데 돈을 써야 한다고 지적한다. 게다가, 회사들은 직원들을 위한 건강 혜택을 보장해야 하며 그 비용의 금액은 업무 유형에 상관없이 동일할 것이다. 또한, 더 많은 직원을 고용하기 위해 더 많은 공간과 컴퓨터가 있어야 하는데, 이것은 추가적인 돈을 필요로 한다.

둘째, 강의 진행자는 단축된 주당 근무일로 실업률이 낮아질 것이라는 독해 지문의 주장을 반박한다. 강의 진행자는 그것이 반드시 더 많은 일자리 기회를 열어주지는 않는다고 말한다. 이는 새로운 직원을 고용하는 데 비용이 많이 들어서, 회사는 직원들이 5일 동안 일한 것과 같은 양의 업무를 마칠 것으로 기대할지도 모르기 때문이다. 독해 지문에 언급된 의견에 대응해, 강의 진행자는 새로운 직책이 만들어지지 않고 근무 여건이 더 나빠질 것이라는 상반된 의견을 제시한다.

마지막으로, 강의 진행자는 주 4일 근무제의 선택이 개인적인 시간을 더 많이 가진 개별 직원들에게 더 많은 혜택을 제공한다는 글쓴이의 주장에 의구심을 갖는다. 강의 진행자는 그것이 부분적으로 사실이라고 주장한다. 독해 지문과 청해 강의에서는, 개인적인 시간이 많아지면 삶의 질이 향상될 수 있지만, 청해 파트에서, 강의 진행자는 이 선택 사항이 경력을 발전시키지 못하고 고용 안정성을 잃을 수 있다는 점에서 이들의 삶에 부정적인 영향을 미칠 수도 있다고 말한다. 게다가, 회사들은 주 5일 근무자를 선호하기 때문에, 주 4일 근로자들은 승진에서 제외될 수도 있다.

어휘

push for ~을 추진하다 **workweek** 주당 노동 시간(일수) **payroll** 급여 지불 총액 **prone to** ~의 경향이 있는 **workload** 업무량

medical benefit 의료 보험 **dent** 감소, 훼손 **job opening** (직장의) 빈 자리 **job stability** 고용 안정성 **let go** ~을 해고하다 **economic downturn** 경기 침체 **overlook** (일자리, 직책에 대해) 고려 대상으로 삼지 않다 **reliable** 믿을 만한, 신뢰할 수 있는 **coverage** 책임 (범위) **consistent** 변함없는 **supervision** 관리, 감독

overwork 과로하다 **cover** ~을 보장하다 **job opportunity** 일자리(취업) 기회 **partially** 부분적으로

실전문제 1 – 표적 광고

문제 해석 및 분석

교수가 마케팅 수업을 가르치고 있다. 교수의 질문에 응답하는 게시글을 작성하시오.
답변은 다음과 같이 하도록 한다.
• 본인의 의견을 표출하고 이를 뒷받침하시오.
• 본인의 말로 토론에 기여하시오.
좋은 답안은 100단어 이상으로 작성된다.

존스 교수:
기업들은 표적 광고라고 불리는 새로운 광고 전략을 개발했습니다. 일반 대중을 대상으로 광고를 만드는 대신, 기업들은 이제 일정한 특성이나 관심을 가진 소비자들에게 광고를 직접적으로 전달하고 있습니다. 아래의 질문에 대한 답변을 토론 게시판에 작성해 주세요: 표적 광고는 윤리적인가요, 아니면 개인정보 침해인가요?

저스틴:
나는 표적 광고에는 어떤 문제도 없다고 생각합니다. 만약 우리가 표적 광고를 받고 싶지 않다면, 우리는 개인정보 설정을 변경하기만 하면 됩니다. 그리고, 기업들은 서비스나 제품과 관련된 관심을 가진 사람들에게 접근함으로써 비용을 절약할 수 있습니다. 마케팅 비용을 절약함으로써, 기업들은 고객들을 위해 가격을 낮출 수 있습니다.

헤일리:
나는 저스틴과 동의하지 않습니다. 나는 표적 광고가 사람들의 개인정보를 침해한다고 생각합니다. 웹사이트는 사람들의 개인정보를 추적하고 그것을 자신들의 목적에 사용해서는 안 됩니다. 사람들의 생활을 침범하는 대신, 기업들은 대규모 대중에게 관심을 끄는 광고를 만들어야 합니다

모범 답안

Justin made a good point that targeted advertising can save companies money on marketing. In addition, they can improve the quality of their products with the money they save. However, he did not mention another important effect of the targeted marketing method. In my opinion, marketing to target specific consumers with certain traits has more benefits. This is because consumers can easily find products or services they need. For example, while I was shopping online for a gym bag, it was difficult to find one with inner compartments. Thankfully, an advertisement on Instagram showed me the model I was looking for, and I bought one right away. Therefore, targeted marketing is very advantageous to both companies and consumers.

(118 words)

저스틴은 표적 광고가 기업들에게 마케팅 비용을 절약하는 데 도움이 된다는 좋은 점을 지적했습니다. 추가적으로, 절약한 돈으로 제품의 품질을 개선할 수 있습니다. 그러나, 그는 표적 마케팅 방법의 다른 중요한 효과를 언급하지 않았습니다. 내 생각에는, 일정한 특성을 가진 특정 소비자들을 대상으로 마케팅하는 것이 더 많은 장점이 있습니다. 이는 소비자가 필요한 제품이나 서비스를 쉽게 찾을 수 있기 때문입니다. 예를 들어, 나는 운동용 가방을 온라인 쇼핑할 때 내부 구획이 있는 것을 찾기 어려웠습니다. 다행히도 인스타그램 광고에서 찾고 있던 모델을 보여주었고, 그것을 바로 구매했습니다. 그러므로, 표적 마케팅은 기업과 소비자 모두에게 매우 유리합니다.

targeted advertising 표적 광고 audience 대중, 청중, 관중 ethical 윤리적인 privacy 개인정보 violation 침해 personal information 개인정보 gym bag 운동용 가방 compartment 칸, 칸막이, 구분, 구획

실전문제 2 – 경제 성장 vs 환경 보호

문제 해석 및 분석

교수가 정치학 수업을 가르치고 있다. 교수의 질문에 응답하는 게시글을 작성하시오.
답변은 다음과 같이 하도록 한다.
• 본인의 의견을 표출하고 이를 뒷받침하시오.
• 본인의 말로 토론에 기여하시오.
좋은 답안은 100단어 이상으로 작성된다.

리드 교수:
일부 사람들은 정부가 일자리와 소비할 돈을 제공하기 때문에 경제 성장을 우선시해야 한다고 말합니다. 다른 사람들은 환경 보호가 더 긴요한 것이라고 말합니다. 나는 이 주제에 대한 여러분의 의견을 알고 싶습니다. 다음 수업 전에 다음 주제에 대해 토론해 주세요: 만약 당신이 정책 입안자라면, 경제 성장과 환경 보호 중 어느 것을 우선시하겠습니까? 그 이유는 무엇인가요?

마크:
개인적으로, 나는 경제 성장을 선택할 것입니다. 많은 사회적 문제는 경제 성장을 통해서만 해결될 수 있습니다. 가난하고 일자리가 없는 사람들이 아주 많습니다. 강한 경제는 더 많은 일자리를 창출하여, 가난을 줄이고 모두에게 더 높은 생활 수준을 제공할 수 있습니다.

켈리:
우리는 단 하나의 지구를 가지고 있습니다. 만약 우리가 그것을 돌보지 않는다면, 미래 세대가 고통을 겪을 것입니다. 경제 성장은 중요하지만, 환경에 부정적인 영향을 미치지 않아야 합니다. 우리는 친환경 에너지와 같은 친환경적인 실천에 투자해야 깨끗한 환경을 유지할 수 있을 것입니다.

모범 답안

Kelly made a good point that policy-makers should prioritize protecting the environment. In addition, they can invest in building more recycling centers to promote environmentally friendly practices. However, she did not mention another important effect of protecting the environment. In my opinion, investment in the environment has more benefits for health. This is because we can live healthier in a cleaner environment with fresh air and clean water. For example, studies show that people who live in the countryside have much healthier lungs than those of people who live in the city. Furthermore, people who live in rural areas tend to have longer lifespans. Therefore, environmental protections must be given high priority.

(112 words)

켈리는 정책 결정자들이 환경 보호를 우선시해야 한다는 좋은 점을 지적했습니다. 추가적으로, 그들은 환경 친화적인 실천을 촉진하기 위해 더 많은 재활용 센터를 건설하는데 투자할 수 있습니다. 하지만, 그는 환경 보호의 다른 중요한 효과를 언급하지 않았습니다. 내 생각에는, 환경에 대한 투자는 건강에 더 많은 혜택을 가져옵니다. 이는 우리가 공기가 신선하고 물이 깨끗한 청정한 환경에서 더 건강하게 살 수 있기 때문입니다. 예를 들어, 연구에 따르면 시골에 사는 사람들은 도시에 사는 사람들보다 훨씬 건강한 폐를 가지고 있다고 합니다. 뿐만 아니라, 시골 지역에 사는 사람들은 평균 수명이 더 길다는 경향이 있습니다. 그러므로, 환경 보호는 높은 우선순위가 주어져야 합니다.

실전문제 3 - 전공 선택 기준

문제 해석 및 분석

교수가 교육학 수업을 가르치고 있다. 교수의 질문에 응답하는 게시글을 작성하시오.
답변은 다음과 같이 하도록 한다.
- 본인의 의견을 제출하고 이를 뒷받침하시오.
- 본인의 말로 토론에 기여하시오.
좋은 답안은 100단어 이상으로 작성된다.

챠베즈 교수:
대학에 지원하는 학생들은 어떤 전공을 선택할지 결정하는 어려운 과제를 마주하게 됩니다. 이 선택은 그들의 미래 직업에 영향을 미칠 수 있기 때문에, 학생들은 많은 요소들을 신중히 고려해야 합니다. 수업에서의 토론 전에, 다음 질문에 대해 여러분의 생각을 듣고 싶습니다: 대학 전공을 선택할 때 가장 중요한 요소는 무엇이라고 생각하나요? 그 이유는 무엇인가요?

루씨:
나는 학문적인 능력을 기반으로 전공을 선택하는 것이 가장 중요하다고 생각합니다. 예를 들어, 숫자 계산에 어려움을 겪지만 창의적인 글쓰기에 능숙한 경우, 물리학 전공보다 영어 전공이 더 적합할 것입니다. 그렇지 않으면 강의를 이해하고 과제를 처리하는 데 어려움을 겪을 수 있습니다.

피터:
적성이 중요할 수 있지만, 나는 전공을 결정하는 가장 중요한 요소는 열정이어야 한다고 생각합니다. 만약 당신이 공부하는 주제에 대해 열정이 없다면, 수업이 매우 지루하게 느껴질 수 있습니다. 당신은 공부하는 전공에 흥미를 잃을 수 있고, 심지어 중퇴할 수도 있습니다!

모범 답안

Lucy and Peter gave good examples of factors that are important when deciding on a college major. Certainly, academic ability and passion should be taken into consideration. However, they did not mention another important factor. In my opinion, it is essential to consider the earning potential of a major. This is because many students have difficulty finding a job or receive a very low salary after graduation. For example, my friend followed her love for music and graduated from a renowned college for music. However, she is struggling to make a living as a musician and has a part-time job to support herself. Therefore, the projected pay of a major must be seriously considered.

(114 words)

루씨와 피터는 대학 전공을 결정할 때 중요한 요소에 대해 좋은 예시를 들었습니다. 확실히, 학업 능력과 열정은 고려해야 할 요소입니다. 하지만, 그들은 다른 중요한 요소를 언급하지 않았습니다. 내 생각에는, 전공의 수입 잠재력을 고려하는 것이 매우 중요합니다. 이는 많은 학생들이 졸업 후 취업에 어려움을 겪거나 매우 낮은 급여를 받는 경우가 많기 때문입니다. 예를 들어, 나의 친구는 음악에 대한 사랑을 쫓아 유명한 음악 대학을 졸업했습니다. 그러나 그녀는 음악가로서 생계유지에 어려움을 겪고 있으며, 생계를 위해 아르바이트를 하고 있습니다. 그러므로, 전공의 예상 수입은 진지하게 고려되어야 합니다.

어휘

workload (많은 양의) 과제 **aptitude** (잠재적인) 적성 **passionate** 열정 있는 **drop out** 중퇴하다 **renowned** 유명한 **projected** 예상되는

실전문제 4 – 우주 탐사 vs 빈곤 퇴치

문제 해석 및 분석

교수가 정치학 수업을 가르치고 있다. 교수의 질문에 응답하는 게시글을 작성하시오.
답변은 다음과 같이 하도록 한다.
- 본인의 의견을 표출하고 이를 뒷받침하시오.
- 본인의 말로 토론에 기여하시오.
좋은 답안은 100단어 이상으로 작성된다.

양 교수:
많은 국가들이 매년 우주 기관에 수십억 달러의 자금을 지원합니다. 이러한 기관들은 다른 행성에서 생명을 찾고, 새로운 은하를 발견하며, 우주를 이해하기 위해 노력합니다. 다음 주 수업 전에, 이 주제에 대해 여러분의 의견을 알고 싶습니다. 다음 질문에 대해 토론 게시판에 논의해 주세요: 정부는 우주 탐사에 돈을 써야 할까요, 아니면 그 돈을 빈곤과의 싸움에 써야 할까요?

톰:
나는 정부가 우선적으로 지구 상의 문제에 집중해야 한다고 생각합니다. 정부의 도움이 필요한 많은 사람들이 가난에 처해 있습니다. 현재 시민의 10% 이상이 빈곤선 아래에서 살고 있다고 읽었으며, 이 수치는 세계 인구에서는 훨씬 큽니다.

케이티:
나는 동의하지 않습니다. 나는 우주 프로그램이 일자리 창출을 통해 사람들에게 혜택을 줄 수 있다고 생각합니다. 우주 프로그램과 우주 연구 시설 덕분에 수천 개의 일자리가 창출되고 있습니다. 이에는 과학자, 연구원, 컴퓨터 프로그래머와 같은 전문적인 직업들이 포함됩니다. 다른 사람들은 연구 시설을 유지하는 데 고용되기도 합니다.

모범 답안

Tom made a good point that the government should invest in combating poverty. In addition, the government needs to provide aid for those who are unemployed. However, he did not mention another important reason for spending on poverty. In my opinion, working on policies to alleviate poverty will create a safer living environment. This is because poverty is associated with higher crime rates. For example, a city in Mexico was suffering from income inequality and high rates of violent crime. After the government implemented several policies to help poor neighborhoods, the number of crimes decreased, making the city much safer. Therefore, dealing with poverty must be given high priority.

(109 words)

톰은 정부가 빈곤과의 싸움에 투자해야 한다는 좋은 점을 지적했습니다. 추가적으로, 정부는 실직자들에게 지원을 제공해야 합니다. 하지만, 그는 빈곤에 대한 지출의 다른 중요한 이유를 언급하지 않았습니다. 내 생각에는, 빈곤 완화를 위한 정책 수립은 더 안전한 생활 환경을 조성할 것입니다. 이는 빈곤과 범죄율이 관련이 있기 때문입니다. 예를 들어, 멕시코의 한 도시는 소득 불평등과 고도의 폭력 범죄율로 고통받고 있었습니다. 정부가 가난한 지역을 돕기 위해 여러 정책을 시행한 후 범죄 발생 건수가 감소하여 도시가 훨씬 안전해졌습니다. 그러므로, 빈곤 문제에 대한 대응에 높은 우선순위를 주어야 합니다.

combat 싸우다 fund 자금을 지원하다 organization 기관 poverty line 빈곤선 global population 세계 인구 aid 지원, 도움
alleviate 완화하다 associated with ~과 관련이 있는 inequality 불평등 implement 시행하다

실전문제 5 – 프리랜서 vs 회사 고용

문제 해석 및 분석

교수가 경영학 수업을 가르치고 있다. 교수의 질문에 응답하는 게시글을 작성하시오.
답변은 다음과 같이 하도록 한다.
• 본인의 의견을 표출하고 이를 뒷받침하시오.
• 본인의 말로 토론에 기여하시오.
좋은 답안은 100단어 이상으로 작성된다.

싱 교수:
많은 대학 졸업생들은 졸업 후 입사 지원합니다. 그러나, 다른 사람들은 프리랜서로서 일하거나 창업하는 길을 선택합니다. 다음 수업 전에,
다음 질문에 대해 토론 게시판에 글을 작성해주시기 바랍니다: 자기 혼자서 일하는 것이 더 낫나요, 아니면 회사에 고용되는 것이 더 낫나
요?

그레이스:
프리랜서의 가장 큰 장점 중 하나는 높은 수입입니다. 제가 읽은 기사에 따르면 편집자, 과외 교사, 웹 디자이너와 같은 프리랜서 직종의 연
봉이 5만 달러가 넘는다고 하는데, 꽤 높은 수준입니다. 지금은 다른 수업을 들으러 가야 하지만, 나중에 더 많은 사례를 포스팅하겠습니다.

조셉:
나는 그레이스와 동의하지 않습니다. 프리랜서라는 것은 수입이 매달 크게 달라질 수 있다는 것을 의미합니다. 하지만, 회사에서 일하면 매달
일정한 수입을 얻습니다. 내일 일감이 들어올지 걱정하는 대신 저축과 취미 생활에 집중할 수 있습니다.

모범 답안

Grace made a good point that being self-employed has more benefits. In addition, some freelance jobs,
such as makeup artists and translators, can have high incomes. However, she did not mention another
important benefit of working for oneself. In my opinion, the main advantage of being self-employed is
having a better work and life balance. This is because instead of working at set company hours, you can
work your own hours on your own time. For example, when I was working as a freelancer doing product
design, I was able to run errands such as walking my dog or going to the bank. Therefore, it is better to
work for yourself than for a company.

(115 words)

그레이스는 자영업에 더 많은 혜택이 있다는 좋은 점을 지적했습니다. 추가적으로, 메이크업 아티스트나 번역가와 같은 일부 프리랜서 직업
은 수입이 높을 수 있습니다. 하지만, 그녀는 스스로 일하는 것의 다른 중요한 장점을 언급하지 않았습니다. 내 생각에는, 자영업의 가장 큰
장점은 일과 삶의 균형이 더 좋다는 것입니다. 이는 정해진 회사 근무 시간에 맞춰 일하는 대신 원하는 시간에 원하는 시간에 일할 수 있기
때문입니다. 예를 들어, 프리랜서로 제품 디자인을 할 때는 강아지를 산책시키거나 은행에 가는 등의 간단한 일을 볼 수 있었습니다. 그러므
로, 회사보다 자신을 위해 일하는 것이 좋습니다.

graduate 졸업생 start your own business 창업하다 income 수입 salary per year(=yearly salary) 연봉 work and life balance 워라벨(일과 삶의 균형) run errands 간단한 일을 보다, 심부름을 하다

실전문제 6 - 스마트폰

교수가 사회학 수업을 가르치고 있다. 교수의 질문에 응답하는 게시글을 작성하시오.
답변은 다음과 같이 하도록 한다.
- 본인의 의견을 표출하고 이를 뒷받침하시오.
- 본인의 말로 토론에 기여하시오.
좋은 답안은 100단어 이상으로 작성된다.

홀 교수:
대부분의 사람들이 스마트폰을 소유하거나 사용한다고 해도 과언이 아닙니다. 이처럼 스마트폰이 널리 보급된 만큼 스마트폰이 사람들의 삶에 미치는 영향에 대해 알아보는 것이 중요합니다. 하지만 먼저, 이 주제에 대해 어떻게 생각하는지 알고 싶습니다. 다음 질문에 대해 토론해 주세요: 스마트폰이 사람들의 의사소통 방식에 긍정적인 영향을 미치나요, 아니면 부정적인 영향을 미치나요?

딜런:
스마트폰은 많은 장점을 제공하는 훌륭한 기술 발전입니다. 스마트폰 덕분에 멀리 떨어져 있는 친구나 가족과 연락을 주고받을 수 있습니다. 메신저 앱과 영상 통화를 사용하여 사랑하는 사람들과 연락할 수 있습니다. 바로 어젯밤에, 스웨덴에 있는 친구와 영상 통화를 했습니다!

조이:
스마트폰은 피할 수 있었던 의사소통 오해로 이끌 수 있다고 생각합니다. 사람들은 너무 자주 문자 메시지나 소셜 미디어 플랫폼을 사용하여 의사소통을 합니다. 이러한 의사소통 방식은 편리하지만 얼굴 표정, 몸짓, 목소리 톤이 부족합니다. 따라서 메시지를 오해하기 쉽습니다.

Dylan made a good point that smartphones help people stay connected with people. In addition, people using smartphones can post pictures of their lives to share with friends and family. However, he did not mention another important effect of smartphones. In my opinion, smartphones are a great tool for communicating in the workplace. This is because we can access our emails and messages on our phones. For example, I often use my smartphone to respond to emails while I am commuting to work. I can also ask my coworkers questions and receive responses quickly thanks to instant messaging applications. Therefore, smartphones bring about a positive impact on communication between people in the workplace.

(113 words)

딜런은 스마트폰이 사람들 간 연락을 유지하는 데 도움이 된다는 좋은 점을 지적했습니다. 추가적으로, 스마트폰을 사용하는 사람들은 자신의 생활 사진을 게시하여 친구 및 가족과 공유할 수 있습니다. 하지만, 그는 스마트폰의 다른 중요한 효과를 언급하지 않았습니다. 내 생각에는, 스마트폰은 직장에서의 커뮤니케이션을 위한 훌륭한 도구입니다. 이는 스마트폰으로 이메일과 메시지에 접속할 수 있기 때문입니다. 예를 들어 나는 출퇴근 중에 스마트폰으로 이메일 답장을 보내는 경우가 많습니다. 또한 메신저 앱 덕분에 동료들에게 궁금한 점을 물어보고 빠르게 답변을 받을 수 있습니다. 그러므로, 스마트폰은 직장 내 사람들 간의 커뮤니케이션에 긍정적인 영향을 미치고 있습니다.

prevalence 널리 보급 impact 영향(을 주다) technological advancement 기술 발전 stay in touch 연락을 유지하다 miscommunication (의사소통 오류로 인한) 오해 commute 통근하다, 통학하다 instant messaging application (인터넷에서 실시간으로 메시지와 데이터를 주고받을 수 있는) 메신저 앱

실전문제 7 – 기업의 긍정적 영향

문제 해석 및 분석

교수가 경영학 수업을 가르치고 있다. 교수의 질문에 응답하는 게시글을 작성하시오.
답변은 다음과 같이 하도록 한다.
- 본인의 의견을 표출하고 이를 뒷받침하시오.
- 본인의 말로 토론에 기여하시오.
좋은 답안은 100단어 이상으로 작성된다.

프라이스 교수:
좋은 일이든 나쁜 일이든, 기업이 사회에 미치는 영향이 크다는 것은 부인할 수 없는 사실입니다. 어떤 사람들은 기업이 모두를 위해 공헌해야 할 사회적 책임이 있다고 말하기도 합니다. 이 주제에 대한 여러분의 의견을 알고 싶습니다. 다음은 학급 토론 게시판의 질문입니다: 기업이 사회에 긍정적인 영향을 미칠 수 있는 가장 효과적인 방법은 무엇이라고 생각하나요?

다이아나:
기업이 의미 있는 영향력을 발휘할 수 있는 가장 좋은 방법은 지역사회에 환원하는 것입니다. 이는 도움이 필요한 사람들에게 즉각적인 영향을 미칠 수 있습니다. 기업이 기부할 수 있는 몇 가지 방법으로는 학교에 기금을 지원하고, 노숙자 쉼터에 기부하고, 자사 제품을 무료로 제공하는 것이 있습니다. 이러한 기부는 특히 현지에서 이루어질 경우 큰 도움이 될 것입니다.

찰스:
환경 친화적인 사업 관행을 따름으로써 기업은 사회에 큰 영향을 미칠 수 있다고 생각합니다. 기업은 재생 에너지를 사용해 플라스틱 사용량을 줄이거나 생분해성 제품을 생산할 수 있습니다. 이러한 관행이 비즈니스 표준이 된다면 다른 기업들도 이를 따라 하게 되어 더 친환경적인 사회가 될 것입니다.

모범 답안

Diana and Charles gave good examples of ways companies can positively impact society. Certainly, giving back to the community and using renewable energy are meaningful ways for companies to contribute to their community. However, they did not mention another important effect. In my opinion, companies can hire more local workers. This is because doing so would bring the positive effect of revitalizing the local economy. For example, a global company in my town hired local workers, which enabled the money to circulate within the community. As a result, other local businesses also benefited through having more business. Therefore, companies should consider opening more jobs to local people to influence society positively.

(111 words)

다이애나와 찰스는 기업이 사회에 긍정적인 영향을 미칠 수 있는 좋은 예시를 들었습니다. 확실히, 지역사회에 환원하고 재생 에너지를 사용하는 것은 기업이 지역사회에 공헌할 수 있는 의미 있는 방법입니다. 하지만, 그들은 다른 중요한 효과를 언급하지 않았습니다. 내 생각에는, 기업은 현지 근로자를 더 많이 고용할 수 있습니다. 이는 그렇게 하면 지역 경제 활성화라는 긍정적인 효과를 가져올 수 있기 때문입니

다. 예를 들어, 제가 사는 마을의 한 글로벌 기업은 지역 근로자를 고용하여 지역 사회 내에서 돈이 순환할 수 있도록 했습니다. 그 결과 다른 지역 기업들도 더 많은 비즈니스를 통해 혜택을 받았습니다. 그러므로, 기업은 사회에 긍정적인 영향을 미치기 위해 지역 주민들에게 더 많은 일자리를 제공하는 것을 고려해야 합니다.

어휘

social responsibility 사회적 책임 **effective** 효과적인 **impact** 영향을 미치다 **community** 지역사회 **homeless shelter** 노숙자 쉼터 **business practice** 사업적 관행 **follow suit** (방금 남이 한대로) 따라 하다 **renewable energy** 재생 에너지 **revitalize** 활성화하다, 새로운 활력을 주다 **circulate** 순환하다, 순환시키다

실전문제 8 - 세금 부과

문제 해석 및 분석

교수가 정치학 수업을 가르치고 있다. 교수의 질문에 응답하는 게시글을 작성하시오.
답변은 다음과 같이 하도록 한다.
• 본인의 의견을 표출하고 이를 뒷받침하시오.
• 본인의 말로 토론에 기여하시오.
좋은 답안은 100단어 이상으로 작성된다.

로빈슨 교수:
정부는 종종 상품과 서비스에 세금을 부과하며, 이는 소비 시장에 영향을 미칩니다. 다음 수업에서는 건강에 해로운 제품에 대한 정부의 세금에 대해 논의할 것입니다. 이 주제에 대한 여러분의 의견을 알고 싶습니다. 수업 전에 이 질문에 답해 주세요: 건강에 해로운 제품에 세금을 부과하는 정책을 지지하겠습니까, 반대하겠습니까? 그 이유는 무엇인가요?

줄리:
나는 건강에 해로운 제품에 세금을 부과하는 것은 좋은 생각이라고 생각합니다. 단 음료와 정크 푸드를 섭취하는 것은 당뇨병과 비만을 비롯한 많은 진지한 질병의 원인이 됩니다. 정부가 이러한 제품에 세금을 부과하면 사람들이 이러한 제품을 구매하지 않게 되고 이러한 건강 문제로 고통받는 사람이 줄어들 것입니다.

폴:
나는 이러한 상품에 세금을 부과하는 것에 반대합니다. 이러한 세금은 소득이 많지 않은 가정을 불공평하게 겨냥합니다. 부유한 사람들은 영향을 받지 않지만, 이러한 제품을 신뢰할 수 있는 식량 공급원으로 만 구입할 수 있는 저소득층 가정은 돈을 절약하기 위해 더 건강에 해로운 제품을 구입할 것입니다. 따라서 이러한 제품에 세금을 부과한다고 해서 건강 문제가 해결되지는 않습니다.

모범 답안

Julie made a good point that the government should impose taxes on unhealthy products to discourage people from eating them. In addition, fewer citizens would suffer from high blood pressure and other illnesses. However, she did not mention another important effect of taxing unhealthy products. In my opinion, taxing unhealthy foods has more financial benefits. This is because people can avoid unnecessary spending on improving their health. To explain, many people spend large amounts of money on gym memberships, dietary supplements, and hospital payments. By imposing extra taxes on unhealthy products and raising the prices, people are not likely to buy them and will spend less money on these things. Therefore, government taxation on unhealthy products must be seriously considered.

(120 words)

줄리는 정부가 건강에 해로운 제품에 세금을 부과하여 사람들이 이러한 제품을 먹지 못하도록 해야 한다는 좋은 점을 지적했습니다. 추가적으로, 고혈압 및 기타 질병으로 고통받는 시민이 줄어들 것입니다. 하지만, 그는 건강에 해로운 제품에 세금을 부과하는 다른 중요한 효과를 언급하지 않았습니다. 내 생각에는, 건강에 해로운 식품에 세금을 부과하면 재정적으로 더 많은 이점이 있습니다. 이는 사람들이 건강을 개선하기 위해 불필요한 지출을 피할 수 있기 때문입니다. 예를 들어, 많은 사람들이 헬스장 회원권, 건강 보조 식품, 병원비 등에 많은 돈을 지출합니다. 건강에 해로운 제품에 추가 세금을 부과하고 가격을 인상하면 사람들은 이러한 제품을 구매하지 않을 것이고 이러한 제품에 지출하는 돈도 줄어들 것입니다. 그러므로 건강에 해로운 제품에 대한 정부의 과세는 진지하게 고려되어야 합니다.

어휘

taxation 세금 (과세) **diabetes** 당뇨병 **obesity** 비만 **affluent** 부유한 **discourage** 막다, 의욕을 꺾다 **dietary supplements** 건강 보조 식품

실전문제 9 – 동아리 활동

문제 해석 및 분석

교수가 교육학 수업을 가르치고 있다. 교수의 질문에 응답하는 게시글을 작성하시오.
답변은 다음과 같이 하도록 한다.
- 본인의 의견을 표출하고 이를 뒷받침하시오.
- 본인의 말로 토론에 기여하시오.
좋은 답안은 100단어 이상으로 작성된다.

스튜어트 교수:
대학은 주로 배움의 장소로 알려져 있지만, 학생들은 조직과 동아리를 구성하기도 합니다. 몇 가지 예로는 스포츠 팀, 학생회, 종교 단체 등이 있습니다. 다음 수업 전에 이 질문에 대해 수업 토론 게시판에 적어 주시기 바랍니다: 학생 단체와 동아리 활동이 대학생에게 유익한가요, 아니면 방해가 되는가요?

브레드:
종종, 동아리 활동이 학생들의 학업에 방해가 됩니다. 나는 학업 성취가 대학에 다니는 데 있어 가장 중요한 요소라고 굳게 믿습니다. 하지만 일부 학생 단체는 많은 시간과 헌신을 요구합니다. 이는 소중한 공부 시간을 빼앗아 성적을 낮추는 결과를 초래할 수 있습니다.

제니퍼:
나는 과외 활동은 스트레스를 해소하는 좋은 방법이라고 생각합니다. 대학생들은 수업에 대한 압박감을 많이 느끼며, 이는 불안과 우울증으로 이어질 수 있습니다. 스포츠나 예술과 같은 동아리 활동은 학업에 대한 부담을 덜어주는 데 도움이 될 수 있습니다.

모범 답안

Jennifer made a good point that student organizations and club activities benefit students. In addition, music clubs can alleviate academic stress and pressure. However, she did not mention another important effect of extracurricular activities. In my opinion, extracurricular activities enable students to enjoy their university lives. This is because these activities can help students make friends and form good memories. For example, I participated in an art club during my freshman year. All of the members quickly became friends since everyone shared a similar interest. Of all the things that happened during my first year of university, the most memorable one is collaborating on painting a large mural with my friends. Therefore, joining school clubs must be seriously considered.

(119 words)

제니퍼는 학생 조직과 동아리 활동이 학생들에게 도움이 된다는 좋은 점을 지적했습니다. 추가적으로, 음악 동아리는 학업 스트레스와 압박감을 완화할 수 있습니다. 하지만, 그녀는 과외 활동의 다른 중요한 효과를 언급하지 않았습니다. 내 생각에는, 과외 활동은 학생들이 대학 생활을 즐길 수 있게 해줍니다. 이는 이러한 활동은 학생들이 친구를 사귀고 좋은 추억을 형성하는 데 도움이 될 수 있기 때문입니다. 예를 들어, 나는 1학년 때 미술 동아리에 참여했습니다. 멤버들 모두 비슷한 관심사를 공유했기 때문에 금방 친해졌습니다. 대학 1학년 때 있었던 일 중에서 가장 기억에 남는 것은 친구들과 함께 대형 벽화를 그리는 공동 작업을 한 것입니다. 그러므로, 학교 동아리에 가입하는 것은 진지하게 고려되어야 합니다.

어휘

student government 학생회 **academic achievement** 학업 성취 **extracurricular activity** 과외 활동 **anxiety** 불안 **depression** 우울증 **pressure** 부담 **alleviate** 완화하다 **form** 형성하다, 만들다 **collaborate** 공동 작업을 하다 **mural** 벽화

실전문제 10 - 스마트폰

문제 해석 및 분석

교수가 사회학 수업을 가르치고 있다. 교수의 질문에 응답하는 게시글을 작성하시오.
답변은 다음과 같이 하도록 한다.
• 본인의 의견을 표출하고 이를 뒷받침하시오.
• 본인의 말로 토론에 기여하시오.
좋은 답안은 100단어 이상으로 작성된다.

산토스 교수:
대부분의 사람들이 스마트폰을 소유하고 있다고 해도 과언이 아닙니다. 오늘날 스마트폰은 사람들의 삶에서 중요한 위치를 차지하고 있습니다. 다음 수업 전에 이 주제에 대해 생각해 보시기 바랍니다. 수업 토론 게시판에서 다음 질문에 답해 주세요: 스마트폰 사용이 사람들에게 미치는 가장 큰 영향은 무엇이라고 생각하나요? 스마트폰이 왜 이런 영향을 미친다고 생각하나요?

캘빈:
스마트폰이 사람들을 덜 사교적으로 만들었다고 생각합니다. 사람들은 지하철, 버스, 심지어 길을 걷는 동안에도 끊임없이 휴대전화를 들여다보고 있습니다. 사람들은 실제 주변 사람들과 소통하는 대신 소셜 미디어에 접속하거나 동영상을 보는 것을 선호합니다.

제인:
나는 켈빈과 동의하지 않습니다. 나는 스마트폰은 사람들이 연락을 유지하는 데 도움이 되었습니다. 스마트폰 덕분에 다른 사람과 소통할 때 거리는 문제가 되지 않습니다. 스마트폰으로 언제 어디서나 문자 메시지를 보내고, 전화를 걸고, 이메일을 쓸 수 있습니다.

모범 답안

Calvin and Jane gave good examples of the effects smartphones have on people. Certainly, people can become antisocial or communicate effectively by using smartphones. However, they did not mention another significant effect. In my opinion, smartphones make education much more accessible. This is because there are many smartphone applications available that provide learning materials and activities for free. For example, I recently started learning French through a free application that offers basic vocabulary and grammar lessons. There are even videos available where an instructor teaches basic phrases and how to use them in context. I can track my progress and take language tests through the application. Therefore, mobile learning enables education to be more approachable.

(115 words)

캘빈과 제인은 스마트폰이 사람들에게 미치는 영향에 대해 좋은 예시를 들었습니다. 확실히, 사람들은 스마트폰을 사용함으로써 반사회적이 되거나 효과적으로 소통하지 못할 수 있습니다. 하지만 그들은 다른 중요한 효과를 언급하지 않았습니다. 내 생각에는, 스마트폰이 교육에 대한 접근성을 훨씬 더 높여준다고 생각합니다. 이는 학습 자료와 활동을 무료로 제공하는 스마트폰 애플리케이션이 많이 있기 때문입니다. 예를 들어, 나는 최근에 기본 어휘와 문법 수업을 제공하는 무료 애플리케이션을 통해 프랑스어를 배우기 시작했습니다. 강사가 기본 구문과 문맥에 맞게 사용하는 방법을 알려주는 동영상도 있습니다. 애플리케이션을 통해 진행 상황을 추적하고 언어 시험을 볼 수 있습니다. 그러므로, 모바일 학습을 통해 교육에 더 쉽게 접근할 수 있습니다.

overstatement 과언 **occupy** 차지하다 **constantly** 끊임없이 **sociable** 사교적인 **interact** 소통하다, 상호 작용하다 **antisocial** 반사회적인 **application** 애플리케이션, 앱 **vocabulary** 어휘 **grammar** 문법 **instructor** 강사 **phrase** 구문 **context** 문맥

실전문제 11 – 대학 자원 투자

문제 해석 및 분석

교수가 교육학 수업을 가르치고 있다. 교수의 질문에 응답하는 게시글을 작성하시오.
답변은 다음과 같이 하도록 한다.
• 본인의 의견을 표출하고 이를 뒷받침하시오.
• 본인의 말로 토론에 기여하시오.
좋은 답안은 100단어 이상으로 작성된다.

파텔 교수:
대학은 한정된 재정을 가지고 있기 때문에 더 많은 관심과 자원을 제공하기 위해 여러 분야에 우선순위를 정해야 합니다. 다음 수업 전에 이 주제에 대해 생각해 보시기 바랍니다. 수업 토론 게시판에서 다음 질문에 답해 주세요: 대학이 운동 프로그램과 도서관 중 어느 분야에 우선적으로 자금을 지원해야 한다고 생각하나요?

라이언:
나는 스포츠 프로그램이 도서관보다 우선시되어야 한다고 생각하지 않습니다. 대학은 사람들이 공부하고 학술 연구를 수행할 수 있는 환경을 제공하는 데 중점을 두어야 하며, 도서관은 정보를 위한 필수 자원입니다. 대학이 도서관에 더 많은 돈을 투자한다면 학생들은 더 높은 수준의 교육을 받을 수 있을 것입니다.

엠마:
나는 운동 프로그램이 더 중요하다고 생각합니다. 스포츠는 대학 커뮤니티를 하나로 묶을 수 있습니다. 학생과 교직원 모두 소속 대학의 경기에 참석하여 학교의 승리를 응원할 수 있습니다. 이런 행사에서 사귈 수 있는 친구들을 생각해 보세요! 어젯밤에 우리 대학의 농구 경기를 보러 갔는데 정말 기억에 남는 경험이었습니다!

모범 답안

Emma made a good point that funding athletic programs unites the school community, including faculty and students. In addition, participating in football games can create good memories for students. However, she did not mention another important effect of school programs related to athletics. In my opinion, participants of athletic programs can get healthy both mentally and physically. For example, my university offers group exercise programs to all students for free. When I felt depressed from studying, I joined one of the running programs. This helped me overcome my feelings of depression, and I was able to stay fit while working out. Therefore, athletic programs must be given high priority.

(109 words)

엠마는 운동 프로그램에 자금을 지원하면 교직원과 학생을 포함한 학교 공동체가 단합할 수 있다는 좋은 점을 지적했습니다. 추가적으로, 축구 경기에 참여하는 것은 학생들에게 좋은 추억을 만들어 줄 수 있습니다. 하지만 그녀는 운동과 관련된 학교 프로그램의 다른 중요한 효과를 언급하지 않았습니다. 내 생각에는, 운동 프로그램 참가자는 정신적으로나 육체적으로 건강해질 수 있습니다. 예를 들어, 우리 대학은 모든 학생들에게 단체 운동 프로그램을 무료로 제공합니다. 공부 때문에 우울한 기분이 들었을 때 나는 달리기 프로그램에 참여했습니다. 이를 통해 우울감을 극복할 수 있었고 운동하면서 건강을 유지할 수 있었습니다. 그러므로 운동 프로그램은 높은 우선순위가 주어져야 합니다.

어휘

resource 자원 athletic 체육의, 운동의 conduct research 연구하다 academic 학술적인 memorable 기억에 남는 faculty 교직원 stay fit 건강을 유지하다 work out 운동하다

실전문제 12 – 대형 슈퍼마켓 vs 지역 시장

문제 해석 및 분석

교수가 경제학 수업을 가르치고 있다. 교수의 질문에 응답하는 게시글을 작성하시오.
답변은 다음과 같이 하도록 한다.
• 본인의 의견을 표출하고 이를 뒷받침하시오.
• 본인의 말로 토론에 기여하시오.
좋은 답안은 100단어 이상으로 작성된다.

그레이 교수:
쇼핑은 지난 수십 년 동안 진화해 왔습니다. 대형 슈퍼마켓 체인의 등장으로 많은 소규모 상점들이 경쟁에 어려움을 겪고 있습니다. 수업에 오기 전에 여러분의 생각을 알고 싶습니다. 다음은 토론 게시판에서 답변할 질문입니다: 대형 슈퍼마켓에서 쇼핑하는 것이 더 좋은가요, 아니면 지역 시장에서 쇼핑하는 것이 더 좋은가요?

토마스:
사람들이 슈퍼마켓에서 쇼핑하는 이유는 편리하기 때문이라고 생각합니다. 슈퍼마켓은 한 층에 농산물, 육류, 유제품 등 다양한 섹션이 있습니다. 슈퍼마켓에서는 옷, 비누, TV와 같은 비식품 품목도 판매합니다. 쇼핑 목록에 필요한 모든 것을 한 지붕 아래에서 찾을 수 있습니다.

노라:
나는 로컬 마켓에 더 신선한 농산물이 있다는 것을 알고 있습니다. 슈퍼마켓은 상업적으로 재배하고 일찍 수확한 후 장거리 운송을 통해 매장까지 운반한 농산물을 판매합니다. 하지만 로컬 마켓에서는 지역 농부들이 재배하고 익었을 때 수확한 과일과 채소를 판매합니다. 더 신선할 뿐만 아니라 맛도 더 좋습니다.

모범 답안

Thomas made a good point that large supermarkets are convenient for shoppers. In addition, shoppers can find a wide range of products all in one place. However, he did not mention another important benefit of large supermarket chains. In my opinion, it is better to shop at supermarkets because they offer better prices. This is because supermarkets can get their supply in bulk. For example, I recently went to the local farmer's market to buy some eggs. The eggs were very expensive, so I went to the supermarket instead. In there, I was able to buy the same number of eggs for almost half the price. Therefore, a large supermarket chain is a better option than a small local market.

(120 words)

토마스는 대형 슈퍼마켓이 쇼핑객에게 편리하다는 좋은 점을 지적했습니다. 추가적으로, 쇼핑객은 다양한 제품을 한 곳에서 모두 찾을 수 있습니다. 하지만, 그는 대형 슈퍼마켓 체인의 다른 중요한 장점을 언급하지 않았습니다. 내 생각에는, 슈퍼마켓에서 쇼핑하는 것이 더 나은 가격을 제공하기 때문에 더 낫습니다. 이는 슈퍼마켓은 대량으로 공급받을 수 있기 때문입니다. 예를 들어, 나는 최근에 계란을 사기 위해 지역 농산물 시장에 갔습니다. 계란이 너무 비싸서 대신 슈퍼마켓에 갔습니다. 그곳에서는 거의 절반 가격에 같은 양의 계란을 살 수 있었습니다. 그러므로, 대형 슈퍼마켓 체인이 작은 지역 시장보다 더 나은 선택지입니다.

어휘

evolve 진화하다 **compete** 경쟁하다 **produce** 농산물 **dairy** 유제품 **under one roof** 한 지붕 아래에서 (한 곳에서) **commercially** 상업적으로 **harvest** 수확하다 **ripe** (과일이) 익은 **in bulk** 대량으로 **half the price** 반값

실전문제 13 – 삶의 질 향상 정책

문제 해석 및 분석

교수가 정치학 수업을 가르치고 있다. 교수의 질문에 응답하는 게시글을 작성하시오.
답변은 다음과 같이 하도록 한다.
• 본인의 의견을 표출하고 이를 뒷받침하시오.
• 본인의 말로 토론에 기여하시오.
좋은 답안은 100단어 이상으로 작성된다.

마이어스 교수:
앞으로 몇 주 동안 여러 지방 정부가 주민들의 삶의 질을 어떻게 개선하고 있는지 살펴볼 예정입니다. 하지만 먼저 이 주제에 대한 여러분의 생각을 알고 싶습니다. 다음 질문에 대해 토론 게시판에서 토론해 주세요: 여러분이 정책 입안자라면 지역 시민의 전반적인 삶의 질을 개선하기 위해 어떤 전략을 사용하시겠습니까?

해리:
내 생각에는, 지방 정부가 교육에 투자해야 합니다. 빈곤과 차별 등 시민들이 직면한 많은 사회 문제는 더 나은 교육으로 해결할 수 있습니다. 연구에 따르면 교육을 받은 사람들이 더 많은 돈을 벌고 사회적 인식이 더 높은 것으로 나타났습니다. 따라서 더 나은 교육에 투자하는 것은 사람들의 삶을 개선하기 위한 훌륭한 전략입니다.

루나:
더 나은 인프라를 구축하는 것은 모든 지방 정부의 우선 순위가 되어야 합니다. 여기에는 도로 보수, 교량 건설, 더 나은 대중교통 시스템 구축 등이 포함됩니다. 이러한 유형의 프로젝트는 사람들이 도시 내에서 더 쉽게 이동할 수 있도록 하여 시간을 절약하고 시민들이 더 안전하게 이동할 수 있도록 합니다.

모범 답안

Harry and Luna gave good examples of policies that the local government can carry out to improve the quality of life of its residents. Certainly, education and better infrastructure can help residents improve their lives. However, they did not mention another important factor. In my opinion, the local government should offer a social security system to people in need. This is because whether a person has an adequate amount of money for living or not is directly associated with their quality of life. To explain, those who are unemployed, retired, or disabled would be able to receive financial support from such a system and have more opportunities to improve their lives. Therefore, establishing a social security system must be given high priority.

(122 words)

해리와 루나는 지방 정부가 주민의 삶의 질을 개선하기 위해 시행할 수 있는 정책에 대한 좋은 예시를 들었습니다. 확실히, 교육과 더 나은 인프라는 주민들의 삶을 개선하는 데 도움이 될 수 있습니다. 하지만 그들은 다른 중요한 요소를 언급하지 않았습니다. 내 생각에는. 지방 정부는 도움이 필요한 사람들에게 사회 보장 시스템을 제공해야한다고 생각합니다. 이는 한 사람이 생활하기에 적절한 돈을 가지고 있는지 여부는 삶의 질과 직결되기 때문입니다. 설명하자면, 실직자, 은퇴자, 장애인은 이러한 제도를 통해 재정적 지원을 받을 수 있고 삶의 질을 향상시킬 수 있는 기회를 더 많이 가질 수 있습니다. 그러므로, 사회 보장 시스템을 구축하는 것은 놓은 우선순위가 주어져야 합니다

어휘

quality of life 삶의 질 policy-maker 정책 입안자 discrimination 차별 strategy 전략 infrastructure 인프라 public transportation system 대중교통 시스템 resident 주민 social security system 사회 보장 시스템 adequate 적절한 directly associated with ~와 직결된 disabled 장애의 establish 구축하다

실전문제 14 – 원격 근무

문제 해석 및 분석

교수가 경영학 수업을 가르치고 있다. 교수의 질문에 응답하는 게시글을 작성하시오.
답변은 다음과 같이 하도록 한다.
• 본인의 의견을 표출하고 이를 뒷받침하시오.
• 본인의 말로 토론에 기여하시오.
좋은 답안은 100단어 이상으로 작성된다.

에반스 교수:
지난 몇 년 동안 많은 기업이 원격 근무 정책을 도입했습니다. 직원들은 이제 사무실에 출근하지 않고 재택근무를 하고 있으며 다른 회사들도 같은 조치를 고려하고 있습니다. 다음 주 수업 전에 이 주제에 대한 여러분의 의견을 알고 싶습니다. 이 질문에 대한 의견을 토론 게시판에 작성해 주세요: 원격 근무에 대해 어떻게 생각하나요? 원격 근무가 유익하다고 생각하나요, 그렇지 않다고 생각하나요?

클라라:
내 생각에는, 원격 근무는 대체로 긍정적입니다. 직원들은 재택근무를 할 때 생산성이 더 높았다고 답했습니다. 회사에서는 동료와 의미 없는 대화를 나누거나 시끄러운 동료와 함께 있는 등 업무 시간을 빼앗는 방해 요소가 많기 때문일 수 있습니다.

케빈:
원격 근무에는 몇 가지 장점이 있지만, 다른 사람들과 효과적으로 소통하기가 더 어려워진다고 생각합니다. 내 경험상, 온라인 회의보다 직접 대면하는 회의가 더 생산적이었습니다. 대면 회의는 토론에 훨씬 더 집중할 수 있게 해줍니다.

Clara made a good point that working from home increases productivity. In addition, working at home does not have the distraction of workplace gossip. However, she did not mention another important effect of remote work. In my opinion, the biggest benefit of working from home is that it can save workers money. This is because they can live away from a metropolis, where housing and living costs are very high. For example, my sister used to live in London to be close to her company. Fortunately, her company implemented a remote work policy, and she was able to return to her hometown in the countryside, saving her money on transportation and housing costs. Therefore, remote work must be seriously considered.

(120 words)

클라라는 재택근무가 생산성을 높인다는 좋은 점을 지적했습니다. 추가적으로, 재택근무는 직장 내 소문으로 인한 산만함이 없습니다. 하지만 그는 원격 근무의 다른 중요한 효과를 언급하지 않았습니다. 내 생각에는, 재택근무의 가장 큰 장점은 근로자의 비용을 절감할 수 있다는 점입니다. 이는 주거비와 생활비가 매우 높은 대도시에서 멀리 떨어져 살 수 있기 때문입니다. 예를 들어, 내 여동생은 회사 근처에 살기 위해 런던에 살곤 했습니다. 다행히 회사에서 원격 근무 정책을 시행하면서 시골에 있는 고향으로 돌아올 수 있게 되어 교통비와 주거비를 절약할 수 있었습니다. 그러므로, 원격 근무는 진지하게 고려되어야 합니다.

어휘

remote work 원격 근무 productive 생산성이 높은 distraction 집중을 방해하는 것, 방해 요소 engage in conversation 대화를 나누다
face-to-face 대면 metropolis 대도시 housing 주택, 주거

실전문제 15 - 온라인 수업

문제 해석 및 분석

교수가 교육학 수업을 가르치고 있다. 교수의 질문에 응답하는 게시글을 작성하시오.
답변은 다음과 같이 하도록 한다.
• 본인의 의견을 표출하고 이를 뒷받침하시오.
• 본인의 말로 토론에 기여하시오.
좋은 답안은 100단어 이상으로 작성된다.

넬슨 교수:
최근 많은 대학에서 온라인 강의를 더 많이 시행하고 있습니다. 학생들은 이제 캠퍼스에 가지 않고 집에서 수업을 들을 수 있으며, 다른 대학들도 이러한 추세를 따르는 것을 고려하고 있습니다. 다음 주 수업 시간을 앞두고, 이 문제에 대한 여러분의 의견을 알고 싶습니다. 다음 질문에 대해 토론해 주세요: 온라인 수업이 대학에서 전반적으로 긍정적인 추세라고 생각하나요, 그렇지 않나요? 그 이유는 무엇인가요?

카렌:
나는 온라인 수업은 비용을 낮춰 교육 접근성을 높인다고 생각합니다. 과거에는 저소득층 가정의 학생들이 학비, 주거비, 통학비 때문에 어려움을 겪었습니다. 하지만, 온라인 강의를 통해 집에서 수업을 들을 수 있게 되면서, 경제적 부담이 많이 줄었습니다.

차드:
나는 카렌의 지적이 이해가 갑니다. 하지만, 나는 온라인 수업이 교육의 질을 떨어뜨린다고 생각합니다. 교수님과 같은 반 친구들이 단지 화면 속 얼굴로만 있으면, 수업 참여도가 떨어지고 집중력이 떨어지는 것은 당연한 일입니다. 또한 건설적인 소통과 협동도 어렵습니다. 나는 대학이 오프라인 수업을 다시 도입해야 한다고 생각합니다.

..

모범 답안

Karen made a good point that online classes reduce education costs. In addition, students choosing online courses do not need to worry about paying for dormitories. However, she did not mention another important effect of online lessons. In my opinion, online classes make receiving an education more convenient. This is because students can take a class almost anywhere regardless of their situation. For example, I once was sick with a high fever during the semester. However, I did not want to miss my next class because it was an important one. Thankfully, because my class was held online, I was able to join the class despite being ill at home. Therefore, online courses are a positive trend.

(117 words)

카렌은 온라인 수업이 교육 비용을 절감한다는 좋은 점을 지적했습니다. 추가적으로, 온라인 수업을 선택하는 학생들은 기숙사 비용에 대해 걱정할 필요가 없습니다. 하지만, 그녀는 온라인 수업의 다른 중요한 효과를 언급하지 않았습니다. 내 생각에는, 온라인 수업은 교육받는 것을 더 편리하게 만듭니다. 이는 학생들이 상황에 관계없이 거의 모든 곳에서 수업을 들을 수 있기 때문입니다. 예를 들어, 나는 학기 중에 고열로 아팠던 적이 있습니다. 하지만 중요한 수업이었기 때문에 다음 수업을 놓치고 싶지 않았습니다. 다행히 수업이 온라인으로 진행되었기 때문에 집에서 아팠음에도 불구하고 수업에 참여할 수 있었습니다. 그러므로, 온라인 강의는 긍정적 추세입니다.

어휘

implement 시행하다 accessible 접근성이 높은 low-income family 저소득층 가정 burden 부담 engage 참여하다 concentration 집중(력) constructively 건설적으로 offline class 오프라인 수업, 현장 수업 dormitory 기숙사

실전문제 16 – 리더십

문제 해석 및 분석

교수가 사회학 수업을 가르치고 있다. 교수의 질문에 응답하는 게시글을 작성하시오.
답변은 다음과 같이 하도록 한다.
• 본인의 의견을 표출하고 이를 뒷받침하시오.
• 본인의 말로 토론에 기여하시오.
좋은 답안은 100단어 이상으로 작성된다.

해리스 교수:
어떤 사람들은 리더를 단순히 이끄는 사람이라고 말하지만, 다른 사람들은 좋은 리더가 되기 위해서는 그 이상의 것이 필요하다고 주장합니다. 리더십을 갖춘 인재를 찾는 대학과 기업이 늘어남에 따라 다음 질문을 고려하는 것이 중요합니다: 좋은 리더의 가장 중요한 자질은 무엇이라고 생각하나요?

안나:
나는 인내심이 리더의 가장 중요한 자질이라고 생각합니다. 여러 사람과 함께 일할 때 사소한 오해, 갈등, 기타 어려움이 발생하는 것은 당연한 일입니다. 훌륭한 리더는 좌절하지 않고 인내심을 가지고 이러한 장애물을 헤쳐 나갈 수 있도록 팀을 이끌어야 합니다.

크리스토퍼:
나는 훌륭한 리더는 적극적으로 경청하는 사람이어야 한다고 생각합니다. 적극적 경청이란 말의 의미와 의도를 이해하려고 노력하는 것을 의미합니다. 이는 리더에게 특히 중요한데, 리더는 팀원들의 피드백을 경청하고 팀원들이 자신의 의견이 중요하다고 느낄 수 있어야 하기 때문입니다.

Anna and Christopher gave good examples of important qualities of a good leader. Certainly, being patient and a good listener are highly desirable characteristics. However, they did not mention another important factor of being a good leader. In my opinion, a good leader should be knowledgeable. This is because they can understand what each team member, as experts in a specific field, can contribute, and make the best decisions for the team. For example, the regional manager of the company I work for has a deep understanding of each department. Thus, she is able to coordinate collaborations between departments, such as the finance and marketing teams, for company projects. Therefore, being well-informed is an important quality in a leader.

(119 words)

안나와 크리스토퍼는 좋은 리더의 중요한 자질에 대한 좋은 예시를 들었습니다. 확실히, 인내심과 좋은 경청자는 매우 바람직한 특성입니다. 하지만 그들은 좋은 리더가 되기 위한 다른 중요한 요소를 언급하지 않았습니다. 내 생각에는, 좋은 리더는 많이 알아야 합니다. 특정 분야의 전문가로서 각 팀원이 무엇을 기여할 수 있는지 이해하고 팀을 위한 최선의 결정을 내릴 수 있기 때문입니다. 예를 들어, 내가 근무하는 회사의 지역 관리자는 각 부서에 대해 깊이 이해하고 있습니다. 따라서, 재무팀과 마케팅팀과 같은 부서 간의 협업을 조율하여 회사 프로젝트를 진행할 수 있습니다. 그러므로, 많이 아는 것은 리더의 중요한 자질입니다.

어휘

quality 자질 patience 인내 miscommunication (의사소통 오류로 인한) 오해 conflict 갈등 frustrated 좌절하는 obstacle 장애물 active listener 적극적으로 경청하는 사람 matter 중요하다 desirable 바람직한 knowledgeable 많이 아는 expert 전문가 coordinate 조율하다 well-informed 많이 아는

실전문제 17 - 도시화

문제 해석 및 분석

교수가 사회학 수업을 가르치고 있다. 교수의 질문에 응답하는 게시글을 작성하시오.
답변은 다음과 같이 하도록 한다.
• 본인의 의견을 표출하고 이를 뒷받침하시오.
• 본인의 말로 토론에 기여하시오.
좋은 답안은 100단어 이상으로 작성된다.

가르시아 교수:
앞으로 몇 주에 걸쳐 도시화의 다양한 영향을 살펴볼 예정입니다. 그 어느 때보다 더 많은 사람들이 시골을 떠나 도시에 살게 되면서 전 세계적으로 도시 인구가 증가했습니다. 다음 수업을 시작하기 전에 다음 질문을 생각해 보시기 바랍니다: 도시의 급속한 성장이 사회에 긍정적인 영향을 미칠까요, 아니면 부정적인 영향을 미칠까요?

벨라:
나는 더 많은 사람들이 도시로 이주하는 것은 좋은 일이라고 생각합니다. 도시에는 일과 교육의 기회가 더 많은 것으로 알려져 있습니다. 사람들이 도시로 오면 자녀를 더 좋은 교사가 있는 학교에 보낼 수 있습니다. 또한 도시에는 시골보다 훨씬 더 많은 일자리가 있습니다.

제이콥:
도시는 질병이 확산될 가능성이 더 높습니다. 도시는 인구 밀도가 높기 때문에 사람들은 특히 버스나 지하철과 같은 장소에서 항상 서로 가

까이 붙어 있습니다. 따라서 사람들이 밀폐된 공간에서 같은 공기를 마시기 때문에 질병이 쉽게 전염됩니다.

Jacob made a good point that the rapid growth of cities leads to more chances of spreading diseases. In addition, viruses can be transmitted rapidly in restaurants and shopping malls. However, he did not mention another disadvantage of cities. In my opinion, bigger cities will lead to higher crime rates. This is because, with a higher population, cities will have more burglaries, robberies, and murders than rural areas. For example, a family member who recently moved from the countryside to a large city had his car broken into while he was at a store. This had never happened to him in his hometown. Therefore, I think that a larger population in cities will lead to even more crime.

(118 words)

제이콥은 도시의 급속한 성장으로 인해 질병이 확산될 가능성이 높아진다는 좋은 점을 지적했습니다. 추가적으로, 식당과 쇼핑몰에서 바이러스가 빠르게 전파될 수 있습니다. 하지만, 그는 도시의 다른 단점을 언급하지 않았습니다. 내 생각에는, 더 큰 도시는 범죄율이 높아지는 것으로 이어질 것입니다. 이는 인구가 많을수록 도시는 시골 지역보다 절도, 강도, 살인이 더 많이 발생하기 때문입니다. 예를 들어, 최근 시골에서 대도시로 이사한 한 가족은 가게에 있는 동안 차가(차 안의 물건들이) 도난당했습니다. 고향에서는 이런 일이 한 번도 일어나지 않았습니다. 그러므로, 나는 도시에 인구가 많아지면 범죄가 더 많이 발생할 것이라고 생각합니다.

urbanization 도시화 job opportunity 일자리 (취업 기회) spread 퍼지다, 확산하다 densely 밀도가 높은 proximity 가까움 transmit 전염시키다 enclosed 둘러싸인, 밀폐된 burglary 절도 robbery 강도 break into 몰래 침입하다

실전문제 18 – 토론 수업 vs 강의 수업

교수가 교육학 수업을 가르치고 있다. 교수의 질문에 응답하는 게시글을 작성하시오.
답변은 다음과 같이 하도록 한다.
• 본인의 의견을 표출하고 이를 뒷받침하시오.
• 본인의 말로 토론에 기여하시오.
좋은 답안은 100단어 이상으로 작성된다.

알바레즈 교수:
교사들은 학생들에게 최고의 교육을 제공하고자 노력하기 때문에 항상 최고의 교수법이 무엇인지에 대한 논쟁이 있어 왔습니다. 앞으로 몇 주에 걸쳐 교실에서 실행되는 다양한 교수법을 살펴볼 것입니다. 수업 전에 이 질문에 대한 답을 준비해 주세요: 토론 중심 수업과 강의 중심 수업 중 어느 것을 더 선호하나요?

제임스:
개인적으로, 나는 청각적 학습자입니다. 즉, 선생님이 설명해 주실 때 정보를 더 잘 이해한다는 뜻입니다. 강의는 대개 정해진 구조가 있기 때문에 나의 속도에 맞춰 쉽게 따라가고 필기할 수 있습니다. 하지만 토론은 종종 주제를 벗어나서 따라가기 어렵다는 것을 알게 되었습니다.

릴리:
나는 토론할 기회가 많은 수업을 선호합니다. 토론을 통해 반 친구들의 다양한 관점을 들을 수 있기 때문에 나의 생각의 폭이 넓어집니다. 또한 어려운 주제에 대해 반 친구들과 이야기하면서 피드백을 받을 수 있습니다. 나는 이러한 상호작용을 소중하게 생각하며 전반적으로 더

쉽게 배우는 데 도움이 됩니다.

Lily made a good point that a discussion-oriented class broadens students' perspectives. In addition, students can learn more by debating with their classmates. However, she did not mention another important effect of class discussions. In my opinion, discussions help students learn how to socialize. This is because students can learn how to express their ideas while respecting others. For example, I used to have difficulty sharing my opinion with other people and tended to agree with everyone else. Fortunately, one of my teachers made discussion groups for the semester. Through this class, I learned how to express my thoughts respectfully. Therefore, it is better for schools to offer a discussion-oriented class than to offer a lecture-oriented class.

(117 words)

릴리는 토론 중심 수업이 학생들의 관점을 넓혀준다는 좋은 점을 지적했습니다. 또한 학생들은 반 친구들과 토론을 통해 더 많은 것을 배울 수 있습니다. 하지만, 그녀는 수업 토론의 다른 중요한 효과를 언급하지 않았습니다. 내 생각에는, 토론은 학생들이 사회화하는 방법을 배우는 데 도움이 됩니다. 이는 학생들이 다른 사람을 존중하면서 자신의 생각을 표현하는 방법을 배울 수 있기 때문입니다. 예를 들어, 나는 예전에는 다른 사람들과 의견을 나누는 데 어려움을 겪었고 다른 모든 사람의 의견에 동의하는 경향이 있었습니다. 다행히 한 선생님께서 한 학기 동안 토론 그룹을 만들어 주셨습니다. 이 수업을 통해 나는 내 생각을 정중하게 표현하는 방법을 배웠습니다. 그러므로, 학교에서는 강의 위주의 수업보다 토론 위주의 수업을 하는 것이 더 좋습니다.

debate 논쟁(하다), (토론)하다 discussion-oriented 토론 중심적인 lecture-oriented 강의 중심적인 auditory learner 청각적 학습자 perspective 관점 interaction 상호작용 broaden 넓히다 respectfully 정중하게

실전문제 19 – 현대의 건강 vs 과거의 건강

교수가 사회학 수업을 가르치고 있다. 교수의 질문에 응답하는 게시글을 작성하시오.
답변은 다음과 같이 하도록 한다.
- 본인의 의견을 표출하고 이를 뒷받침하시오.
- 본인의 말로 토론에 기여하시오.
좋은 답안은 100단어 이상으로 작성된다.

포스터 교수:
사람들은 그 어느 때보다 오래 살고 있습니다. 전 세계적으로 기대 수명이 늘어났습니다. 그러나 일부 사람들은 이것이 반드시 사람들이 더 건강해졌다는 것을 의미하지는 않는다는 의견을 표명하고 있습니다. 다음 주 수업 전에 이 주제에 대한 여러분의 의견을 알고 싶습니다. 이 질문에 대해 토론 게시판에 글을 써주세요: 지금 사람들은 과거보다 더 건강할까요?

홀리:
나는 의학 발명의 발전 덕분에 사람들이 훨씬 더 건강해졌다고 생각합니다. 예전에는 예기치 못한 질병으로 일찍 사망하는 경우가 많았죠. 하지만 지금은 엑스레이나 CT 스캔과 같은 의료 장비의 발달로 의사들이 질병을 조기에 진단하고 치료할 수 있게 되었습니다.

마이클:
나는 홀리와 동의하지 않습니다. 나는 사람들이 그 어느 때보다 스트레스를 많이 받는다고 생각합니다. 우리가 살고 있는 사회는 사람들에게 성공에 대한 많은 압박을 가합니다. 더 많은 사람들이 학업이나 직업 때문에 스트레스를 받습니다. 이러한 높은 스트레스 수준은 사람들을 스트레스 관련 질병에 더 취약하게 만들 수 있습니다.

Holly made a good point that people in the present are much healthier than people were in the past. In addition, MRIs and other modern machines help doctors treat illnesses. However, she did not mention another important factor that has led to better health. In my opinion, better education has contributed to healthier people. This is because schools educate people about how to care for themselves to keep their health in good condition. For example, my younger brother in elementary school recently learned about harmful bacteria and how important it is to wash his hands regularly. Afterwards, he always washes his hands before meals and reminds the family to do so as well. Therefore, people today are much healthier than people in the past.

(124 words)

홀리는 현재 사람들이 과거 사람들보다 훨씬 더 건강하다는 좋은 점을 지적했습니다. 추가적으로, MRI와 기타 최신 기계는 의사가 질병을 치료하는 데 도움이 됩니다. 하지만 그녀는 더 나은 건강으로 이어진 또 다른 중요한 요소를 언급하지 않았습니다. 내 생각에는, 더 나은 교육이 더 건강한 사람들을 만드는 데 기여했다고 생각합니다. 이는 학교는 사람들이 건강을 좋은 상태로 유지하기 위해 스스로를 돌보는 방법에 대해 교육하기 때문입니다. 예를 들어, 초등학교에 다니는 남동생은 최근에 해로운 박테리아에 대해 배우고 손을 자주 씻는 것이 얼마나 중요한지 배웠습니다. 그 후로 그는 식사 전에 항상 손을 씻고 가족들에게도 손을 씻도록 상기시킵니다. 그러므로, 오늘날의 사람들은 과거의 사람들보다 훨씬 건강합니다.

어휘

life expectancy 기대 수명 advancement 발전 diagnose 진단하다 pressure 압박감 vulnerable 취약한

실전문제 20 - 기대 수명 증가

문제 해석 및 분석

교수가 사회학 수업을 가르치고 있다. 교수의 질문에 응답하는 게시글을 작성하시오.
답변은 다음과 같이 하도록 한다.
• 본인의 의견을 표출하고 이를 뒷받침하시오.
• 본인의 말로 토론에 기여하시오.
좋은 답안은 100단어 이상으로 작성된다.

아담스 교수:
지난 몇 세기 동안 전 세계적으로 기대 수명이 증가했습니다. 이제 사람들은 최대 100세까지 살 것으로 예상되며, 많은 노인들이 이 한계점을 넘고 있습니다. 다음 수업이 시작되기 전에 토론 게시판에서 다음 질문에 답해 주시기 바랍니다: 기대 수명이 늘어난 가장 큰 요인은 무엇이라고 생각하나요? 왜 이런 효과가 있다고 생각하나요?

제시카:
나는 생활 수준의 향상은 사람들이 더 오래 사는 이유에 중요한 역할을 했다고 생각합니다. 예전에는 사람들이 쓰레기를 길거리에 버렸고

정화되지 않은 물로 인해 많은 질병에 걸렸습니다. 지금은 하수도 시스템이 갖춰져 있고 깨끗한 물을 쉽게 구할 수 있어 훨씬 더 위생적인 환경에서 살고 있습니다.

마이크:
의학의 발전은 기대 수명이 늘어난 가장 큰 이유입니다. 과거에는 치명적이었던 질병을 치료할 수 있게 되었습니다. 과거에는 유행병이었을 병도 이제는 간단한 백신으로 피할 수 있습니다. 또한 수술 및 기타 치료로 생명 연장하여, 수명 연장에 기여하고 있습니다.

모범 답안

Jessica and Mike gave good examples of factors that extend people's lifespans. Certainly, advancements in living standards and medicine have played a key role in making people live longer. However, they did not mention another important reason. In my opinion, people can live a long and good life thanks to better education. This is because people learn about health in school. To explain, public education was not common in the past and not every person was able to learn the basics of how to manage their health. Today, however, required schooling has enabled most people to know about nutrition, diet, and exercise, enabling them to live longer. Therefore, education helps to increase life expectancy.

(114 words)

제시카와 마이크는 사람들의 수명을 연장하는 요인에 대한 좋은 예시를 들었습니다. 확실히, 생활 수준과 의학의 발전이 사람들의 수명을 늘리는 데 중요한 역할을 해왔습니다. 하지만, 그들은 다른 중요한 이유를 언급하지 않았습니다. 내 생각에는, 사람들이 더 나은 교육 덕분에 길고 좋은 삶을 살 수 있다고 생각합니다. 이는 사람들이 학교에서 건강에 대해 배우기 때문입니다. 설명하자면, 과거에는 공교육이 일반적이지 않았기 때문에 모든 사람이 건강 관리 방법의 기본을 배울 수 없었습니다. 하지만 오늘날에는 의무적인 학교 교육을 통해 대부분의 사람들이 영양, 식단, 운동에 대해 알 수 있게 되었고, 이로 인해 더 오래 살 수 있게 되었습니다. 그러므로, 교육은 기대 수명을 늘리는 데 도움이 됩니다.

어휘

life expectancy 기대 수명 threshold 한계점 living standard 생활 수준 play a key role 중요한 역할을 하다 unpurified 정화되지 않은 sanitary 위생 sewer 하수도 fatal 치명적인 pandemic 유행병 prolong 연장하다 required 의무적인 schooling 학교 교육 nutrition 영양 diet 식단

Actual Test 1

Q1 Integrated Writing

Reading Passage	Listening Script
Several years ago, a man went to a sale at a private home in California and bought a box of envelopes filled with photographic negatives (which are images on film or glass that can be used to create photograph prints). The negatives were originally made in the 1920s and depicted some landscapes that are located in the western United States. Although they did not have any names on them, some people claim that the negatives were originally made by one of the greatest American photographers of the 20th century, Ansel Adams. There are several reasons to back up this argument.	The arguments made in the reading that the negatives in question were originally made by Ansel Adams are hardly convincing. Sure, they have some things in common with Adams' work, but all of those similarities can be easily explained.
Firstly, the landscapes captured in the negatives were the same as some of those that Ansel Adams had photographed. In one of them, a large pine tree leans downward on a cliff. A photograph that was undoubtedly taken by Adams in the 1920s shows a tree with the same unusual characteristics.	Firstly, the negative featuring the leaning pine tree, you know, this is not a tree that only Ansel Adams knew about. It's actually one of Yosemite National Park's famous landmarks. Hundreds of thousands of people visited that park in the 1920s. The particular pine tree in question was one of the park's most popular attractions. Since that tree was an icon that represented Yosemite, Ansel Adams wasn't the only photographer, there were countless others, who took pictures of it.
Secondly, the negatives had been organized in envelopes that were numbered and labeled by hand. The handwriting on those envelopes is similar to none other than Virginia Adams, who was the wife of Ansel Adams. She was known to help her husband out with his work, so the believers that the negatives were originally taken by Ansel Adams say that Virginia most likely helped Ansel organize the negatives by writing down location names of where they were taken and assigning numbers to them.	Secondly, you read that place names were written by hand on the envelopes, like the names of famous Yosemite landmarks. The thing is, some of those location names were spelled incorrectly. Yosemite is where Virginia Adams was raised. She knew Yosemite extremely well thanks to her father, who was an artist with an art studio in the park. Do you really think that she would not know how to spell the names of places that she knew well since she was a small child?
Thirdly, quite a few of the negatives showed signs of fire damage, which could have occurred during a studio fire that once destroyed or damaged almost one third of Ansel Adams' negatives. This fire damage is considered another piece of evidence that the negatives purchased at the sale did indeed belong to Ansel Adams.	In regard to the fire damage on the negatives, well... it is questionable either because photographers in the 1920s used a dangerous process to make their negatives. Some very flammable chemicals were involved in it. It was very easy for them to catch fire. Lots of professional photographers had their work damaged by fire because a fire in a photographer's studio was nothing out of the ordinary in those days.

몇 년 전, 한 남자가 캘리포니아의 한 개인 주택에서 열린 공매 행사에 가서 사진 원판(사진 인쇄물을 만드는 데 사용할 수 있는 필름이나 유리에 있는 이미지)으로 가득 찬 봉투들이 들어 있는 상자를 샀다. 그 사진 원판들은 원래 1920년대에 만들어졌고 미국 서부에 위치한 몇몇 풍경을 묘사했다. 비록 그것들이 어떤 이름도 가지고 있지 않았지만, 어떤 사람들은 그 사진 원판들이 원래 20세기의 가장 위대한 미국 사진작가 중 한 명인 앤설 아담스에 의해 만들어졌다고 주장한다. 이 주장을 뒷받침하는 몇 가지 이유가 있다.

첫째, 그 사진 원판에서 포착된 풍경들은 앤설 아담스가 찍은 풍경들 중 일부와 같았다. 그 중 하나에서는 커다란 소나무가 절벽 아래로 기울어져 있다. 의심할 여지없이 아담스가 1920년대에 찍은 한 사진이 이와 똑같이 특이한 특징을 가진 나무를 보여준다.

둘째로, 그 사진 원판들은 손으로 번호를 매기고 라벨을 붙인 봉투에 정리되어 있었다. 봉투에 적힌 필체는 다름 아닌 앤설 아담스의 아내였던 버지니아 아담스와 비슷하다. 그녀는 남편의 일을 돕는 것으로 알려져 있었기 때문에, 그 원판들이 원래 앤설 아담스에 의해 찍혔다고 믿는 사람들은 버지니아가 그것들이 찍힌 장소의 이름을 적고 그들에게 번호를 할당함으로써 앤설이 원판들을 정리하는 것을 도왔을 가능성이 높다고 말한다.

셋째, 원판 중 꽤 많은 수가 화재 손상의 징후를 보였는데, 이는 한때 앤설 아담스의 원판 중 거의 3분의 1을 파괴하거나 손상시킨 스튜디오 화재 중에 발생했을 수도 있다. 이 화재 손상은 공매 행사에서 구입한 원판들이 실제로 앤설 아담스의 것이라는 또 다른 증거로 간주된다.

문제의 원판들이 원래 앤설 아담스에 의해 만들어졌다는 독해 지문에서 나온 주장은 설득력이 거의 없습니다. 물론, 그것들은 아담스의 작품과 몇 가지 공통점이 있지만, 그 모든 유사점들은 쉽게 설명될 수 있습니다.

우선, 기울어진 소나무가 특징인 원판은, 아시다시피, 이것은 앤설 아담스만이 알고 있던 나무가 아닙니다. 그것은 사실 요세미티 국립공원의 유명한 주요 지형지물 중 하나입니다. 1920년대에 수십만 명의 사람들이 그 공원을 방문했습니다. 문제의 그 특정 소나무는 그 공원의 가장 인기 있는 명소 중 하나였습니다. 그 나무는 요세미티를 상징하는 아이콘이었기 때문에, 앤설 아담스만이 그 나무를 찍은 유일한 사진가가 아니었고, 다른 수많은 사람들이 있었습니다.

두 번째로, 여러분은 유명한 요세미티 주요 지형지물들의 이름처럼 봉투에 지명들이 손으로 쓰여져 있음을 읽었습니다. 문제는, 그 장소 이름들 중 몇 개는 철자가 틀렸다는 것입니다. 요세미티는 버지니아 아담스가 자란 곳입니다. 그녀는 요세미티 공원에 예술 스튜디오를 가지고 있는 예술가였던 그녀의 아버지 덕분에 요세미티를 매우 잘 알고 있었습니다. 당신은 정말로 그녀가 어렸을 때부터 잘 알고 있던 장소의 이름을 쓰는 법을 모를 것이라고 생각하나요?

원판들의 화재 손상과 관련하여, 음… 1920년대의 사진작가들이 원판들을 만들기 위해 위험한 과정을 이용했기 때문에 그것 또한 의심스럽습니다. 매우 인화성 있는 화학 물질들이 그 과정에 관련되어 있었습니다. 원판들에 불이 붙는 것은 매우 쉬웠습니다. 당시 사진사 스튜디오에 불이 난 것은 전혀 특이한 일이 아니었기 때문에 많은 전문 사진작가들이 화재로 인해 작품을 손상시켰습니다.

문제

강의에서 언급된 요점들이 어떻게 독해 지문에 제시된 특정 주장들에 대해 이의를 제기하는지 설명하면서 그 내용을 요약해 보시오.

노트테이킹

negatives AA?	X convin.
pine tree unusual	X X only Yosemite ↑ visit popular
envelope handwriting V A	spell incorrect raised know

fire	question.
damage	flammable chemi.
	easy fire
	X ordi.

모범 답안

The reading passage and the lecture both discuss whether photographic negatives sold in a private home in California were made by Ansel Adams, one of the greatest photographers of the 20th century. The writer states that three reasons back up the argument that the images were made by him. However, the lecturer disagrees with the argument, saying that the explanation in the reading is unconvincing.

First of all, the lecturer doubts the writer's point that a large pine tree in the negatives was the same as other landscapes taken by Ansel Adams. She argues that it is not true. Although the writer states that the photograph of the tree shows its unusual characteristics, the lecturer points out that Ansel Adams was not the only one who took a picture of the tree. This is because the leaning pine tree was a kind of icon, one of the popular attractions. In fact, countless other photographers came to Yosemite National Park and took pictures of it.

Secondly, the lecturer refutes the argument of the reading passage that numbers and labels on the envelopes with the negatives are similar to the handwriting from Adam's wife, Virginia Adams. She states that some of the spellings on the envelopes are incorrect. In response to the mentioned evidence in the reading passage, the lecturer presents contrary evidence that Virginia would have not spelled the names of those places in a wrong way. This is because she was raised in Yosemite.

Finally, the speaker doubts the writer's argument that fire damage on the negatives could be from a fire at Ansel Adam's studio. She contends that it is questionable. Since photographers in those days used flammable chemicals to make negatives, a fire at photographers' studios was normal in those days. In the reading passage, the fire damage on some negatives indicates that those belong to Ansel Adams, but in the listening part, the lecturer says many photographic works were damaged by fire.

(325 words)

독해 지문과 강의는 모두 캘리포니아의 한 개인 주택에서 판매된 사진 원판들이 20세기 가장 위대한 사진작가 중 한 명인 앤셀 아담스에 의해 만들어졌는지 여부에 대해 논의한다. 글쓴이는 그 이미지들이 그에 의해 만들어졌다는 주장을 뒷받침하는 세 가지 이유가 있나고 말한다. 하지만, 강의 진행자는 독해 지문의 설명이 납득이 가지 않는다며 이 주장에 동의하지 않는다.

먼저, 강의 진행자는 원판에 있는 큰 소나무가 앤셀 아담스가 찍은 다른 풍경과 같다는 글쓴이의 주장에 의구심을 갖는다. 강의 진행자는 그것이 사실이 아니라고 주장한다. 글쓴이는 이 나무의 사진이 특이한 특징을 보여준다고 말하지만, 강의 진행자는 이 나무의 사진을 찍은 것은 앤셀 아담스뿐만이 아니라고 지적한다. 기울어진 소나무가 인기 명소 중 하나인 아이콘의 일종이었기 때문이다. 사실, 수많은 다른 사진작가들이 요세미티 국립공원에 가서 그 나무 사진을 찍었다.

둘째, 강의 진행자는 원판들이 담긴 봉투의 숫자와 라벨이 아담스의 아내 버지니아 아담스의 필체와 유사하다는 독해 지문의 주장을 반박한다. 강의 진행자는 봉투의 철자 중 일부가 틀렸다고 말한다. 독해 지문에서 언급된 증거에 대응해, 강의 진행자는 버지니아가 그 장소들의 이름들을 잘못 쓰지 않았을 것이라는 반대 증거를 제시한다. 이는 그녀가 요세미티에서 자랐기 때문이다.

마지막으로, 화자는 그 원판들에 대한 화재 손상이 앤설 아담스의 스튜디오에서 발생한 화재로 인한 것일 수 있다는 글쓴이의 주장을 의심한다. 강의 진행자는 그것이 의심스럽다고 주장한다. 그 당시 사진작가들이 원판을 만들기 위해 인화성 화학물질을 사용했기 때문에, 그 당시에는 사진작가의 스튜디오에서 불이 나는 것이 보통이었다. 독해 지문에서, 일부 원판들의 화재 손상은 그것들이 앤설 아담스의 것임을 시사하지만, 청해 파트에서, 강의 진행자는 많은 사진 작품들이 화재로 인해 손상되었다고 말한다.

어휘

negative (네거티브 사진) 원판, 음화 **depict** ~을 표현하다, 묘사하다 **capture** ~을 …에 담다, 정확히 포착하다 **assign** ~을 배정하다, 할당하다 **in question** 문제의, 의심스러운 **attraction** 명소 **questionable** 의심스러운 **flammable** 가연성의, 불에 잘 타는 **unconvincing** 설득력이 없는, 납득하기 어려운

Q2 Writing for an Academic Discussion

문제 해석 및 분석

교수가 컴퓨터 과학 수업을 가르치고 있다. 교수의 질문에 응답하는 게시글을 작성하시오.
답변은 다음과 같이 하도록 한다.
• 본인의 의견을 표출하고 이를 뒷받침하시오.
• 본인의 말로 토론에 기여하시오.
좋은 답안은 100단어 이상으로 작성된다.

앨런 교수:
점점 더 많은 기업이 새로운 AI 기술에 투자하고 있습니다. 이러한 기술은 새로운 방식으로 더 많은 분야에 적용되고 있습니다. 앞으로 몇 주에 걸쳐 이러한 기술과 이러한 기술이 사회에 미치는 영향에 대해 다룰 예정입니다. 하지만 먼저 이 질문에 대해 생각해 보셨으면 합니다: AI는 사회에 위험할까요, 아니면 사람들의 삶을 개선할 수 있는 도구일까요?

제레미:
AI는 사회에 해를 끼칠 수 있는 위험한 기술이라고 생각합니다. 새로운 AI 기술이 개발됨에 따라 점점 더 많은 일자리가 AI에 의해 대체될 위험에 처해 있습니다. 이로 인해 많은 노동자들이 일자리를 잃고 실업률이 높아질 수 있습니다. 우리는 AI 기술의 발전이 사람들의 생계에 부정적인 영향을 미치지 않도록 주의해야 합니다.

리사:
AI는 오늘날 우리가 직면한 많은 문제를 해결할 수 있는 엄청나게 강력한 도구입니다. 인간과 달리 AI는 방대한 양의 데이터를 매우 빠르게 검토하고 근본적인 패턴을 파악할 수 있습니다. 이 기술을 잘 활용한다면 질병과 지구 온난화에 대한 잘 드러나지 않는 해결책을 제시할 수 있다고 생각해보세요!

모범 답안

Lisa made a good point that AI can solve many problems by going through enormous amounts of data and processing them quickly. In addition, this advanced technology can solve traffic congestion in cities. However, she did not mention another important effect of utilizing AI. In my opinion, AI has more benefits for safety. This is because AI enables people to protect themselves from dangerous conditions. To explain, people in the past were required to work in workplaces with poisonous chemicals and heavy machinery. They were subject to various illnesses or injuries. Fortunately, AI robots can replace human workers for these dangerous jobs. Therefore, AI can improve people's lives and make them safer.

(112 words)

리사는 AI가 방대한 양의 데이터를 빠르게 검토함으로써 많은 문제를 처리할 수 있다는 좋은 점을 지적했습니다. 추가적으로, 이 첨단 기술은 도시의 교통 혼잡을 해결할 수 있습니다. 하지만 그는 AI 활용의 다른 중요한 효과에 대해서는 언급하지 않았습니다. 내 생각에는, AI는 안전에 더 많은 이점이 있습니다. 이는 AI를 통해 사람들이 위험한 상황으로부터 스스로를 보호할 수 있기 때문입니다. 과거 사람들은 유독성 화학물질과 중장비가 있는 작업장에서 일해야 했습니다. 따라서 각종 질병이나 부상에 노출될 수 있었습니다. 다행히도 AI 로봇은 이러한 위험한 작업에서 인간 작업자를 대체할 수 있습니다. 그러므로, AI는 사람들의 삶을 개선하고 더 안전하게 만들 수 있습니다.

> **어휘**

displace(=replace) 대체하다 livelihood 생계 enormously 엄청나게 go through 검토하다, 살펴보다 underlying (겉으로) 잘 드러나지는 않은 present 제시하다 global warming 지구 온난화 utilize 활용하다 be subject to ~에 영향을 받다, ~에 노출되다

Actual Test 2

Q1 Integrated Writing

Reading Passage	Listening Script
Milk is commonly consumed in cultures around the world, but is it actually as good as we think it is? Modern science has found several reasons for us to eliminate milk from our diets entirely.	The reading does not make any convincing points, and it would not be a good idea to remove milk entirely from most people's diets.
First, according to a study in the British Medical Journal, there seems to be a correlation between drinking milk regularly and suffering bone fractures. The study followed approximately 61,400 women over a period of 20 years. Among those women, those who drank three or more glasses of milk per day were 60% more likely to develop a hip fracture, and 16% overall to fracture any bone in their body.	First, there may in fact be a correlation between milk and bone fractures. However, a substance called D-galactose is responsible for the fractures. D-galactose is a byproduct of the digestion process when humans drink fresh milk. But the risk of fractures caused by D-galactose can be avoided by just consuming fermented milk products, such as yogurt and cheese. If we consume yogurt or cheese, only a relatively small amount of the byproduct D-galactose is produced during digestion. In fact, some statistical evidence shows that consuming such fermented milk products can lower rates of bone fractures.
Second, it is a well-known fact that toxins in a woman's body can be passed on from a mother to a baby through breast milk. The same is true for milk that is obtained from cows. When a cow becomes sick and is given antibiotics by the farmers that care for it, those antibiotics can contaminate the milk from that cow. A healthy human does not need antibiotics, and consuming them causes the body to develop an immunity to them. That means that when a person does become sick, the antibiotics that would normally be used to treat their illness would be less effective, and possibly even useless.	Second, in regard to antibiotics. When a farmer's cow gets sick in the US and it is given antibiotics, the farmer is required to discard, or throw away, the milk from the sick cow. These days, companies that buy milk from farms will only accept the milk if it has little to no antibiotic residue. Government agencies perform random tests on milk to check for antibiotics. So, if unusually high levels of antibiotics are found, the government doesn't allow that milk to be sold to customers.
Third, the nutrients found in milk can easily be found in other foods. For example, fish are an excellent source of protein that is low in fat. If you are on a vegan diet, you can obtain protein from beans, nuts, or tofu. To find the B vitamins that your body needs, consume plenty of leafy green vegetables. These options would be preferable over drinking the milk of another mammal, which is not something that normally happens in nature.	Third, while people could potentially get the same nutrients as milk from other foods, those foods usually don't provide the same variety of nutrients that milk does, or the high amounts of those nutrients. For example, in order to obtain the same amount of protein, calcium, and B vitamins as in 1 cup of milk, a person would need to eat more than 50 grams of fish, approximately 150 grams of beans, and nearly 250 grams of leafy green vegetables. For most people, it would be easier to simply drink a small amount of milk. Or, of course, a milk product such as yogurt or cheese, to obtain the nutrients that their body requires.

해석

우유는 전 세계의 문화권에서 일반적으로 소비되지만, 실제로 우리가 생각하는 것만큼 좋은가? 현대 과학은 우리가 식단에서 우유를 완전히 없애야 하는 몇 가지 이유를 찾아냈다.

첫째, 영국 의학 저널의 한 연구에 따르면, 우유를 규칙적으로 마시는 일과 뼈 골절을 겪는 일 사이에는 상관 관계가 있는 것으로 보인다. 이 연구는 20년 동안 약 61,400명의 여성을 대상으로 했다. 그 여성들 중에서, 하루에 세 잔 이상의 우유를 마신 사람들은 고관절 골절이 생길 가능성이 60퍼센트 더 높았고, 전체적으로 그들의 몸에 있는 어떤 뼈도 골절될 가능성이 16퍼센트 더 높았다.

둘째, 모유를 통해 여성의 체내에 있는 독소가 엄마로부터 아기에게 전염될 수 있다는 것은 잘 알려진 사실이다. 젖소에서 얻은 우유도 마찬가지다. 소가 아프고 그것을 돌보는 농부들에 의해 항생제가 주어지면, 그 항생제는 그 소의 우유를 오염시킬 수 있다. 건강한 사람은 항생제를 필요로 하지 않으며, 항생제를 섭취하면 신체가 항생제에 대한 면역력을 발달시킨다. 이는 사람이 병에 걸렸을 때 보통 그들의 병을 치료하기 위해 사용되는 항생제가 덜 효과적이고 심지어 쓸모없을 수도 있다는 것을 의미한다.

셋째, 우유에서 발견되는 영양소는 다른 음식에서도 쉽게 찾을 수 있다. 예를 들어, 생선은 지방이 적은 훌륭한 단백질 공급원이다. 만약 당신이 채식주의 식단을 먹고 있다면, 당신은 콩, 견과류 또는 두부로부터 단백질을 얻을 수 있다. 당신의 몸이 필요로 하는 비타민 B를 찾기 위해서, 잎이 많은 녹색 채소를 많이 섭취해야 한다. 이러한 선택들은, 자연에서 일반적으로 일어나는 일이 아닌, 다른 포유동물의 우유를 마시는 것보다 더 바람직할 것이다.

이 독해 지문은 어떠한 설득력 있는 요점도 제시하지 못하는데, 대부분 사람들의 식단에서 우유를 완전히 제거하는 것은 좋은 생각이 아닐 것입니다.

첫째, 사실 우유와 뼈 골절 사이에는 상관 관계가 있을지도 모릅니다. 하지만, D-갈락토스라는 물질이 골절의 원인입니다. D-갈락토스는 인간이 신선한 우유를 마실 때 소화 과정의 부산물입니다. 하지만 D-갈락토스에 의한 골절의 위험은 요구르트나 치즈와 같은 발효유 제품을 섭취함으로써 피할 수 있습니다. 만약 우리가 요구르트나 치즈를 섭취한다면, 소화를 하는 동안 상대적으로 적은 양의 부산물 D-갈락토스가 생성됩니다. 사실, 몇몇 통계적인 증거는 그러한 발효유 제품을 섭취하는 것이 뼈 골절의 비율을 낮출 수 있다는 것을 보여줍니다.

둘째, 항생제에 관한 것입니다. 미국에서 농부의 소가 병에 걸려 항생제를 투여받으면, 농부는 아픈 소의 우유를 폐기하거나 버려야 합니다. 요즘, 농장에서 우유를 사는 회사들은 항생제 잔류물이 거의 없거나 전혀 없는 경우에만 우유를 받아들이려 합니다. 정부 기관들은 항생제를 확인하기 위해 우유에 대해 무작위 테스트를 시행합니다. 그래서, 만약 비정상적으로 높은 수준의 항생제가 발견된다면, 정부는 그 우유들이 고객들에게 팔리는 것을 허용하지 않습니다.

셋째, 사람들이 잠재적으로 다른 음식들로부터 우유와 같은 영양소를 얻을 수 있지만, 보통 그 음식들은 우유와 같이 다양한 영양소를, 또는 많은 양의 영양소를 제공하지 않습니다. 예를 들어, 우유 1컵과 같은 양의 단백질, 칼슘, 그리고 비타민 B를 얻기 위해, 사람은 50그램 이상의 생선, 약 150그램의 콩, 그리고 거의 250그램의 잎이 많은 녹색 채소를 먹어야 할 것입니다. 대부분의 사람들에게, 단순히 적은 양의 우유를 마시는 것이 더 쉬울 겁니다. 아니면, 물론, 그들의 신체가 필요로 하는 영양소를 얻기 위해서 요구르트나 치즈와 같은 유제품을요.

문제

강의에서 언급된 요점들이 어떻게 독해 지문에 제시된 특정 주장들에 대해 이의를 제기하는지 설명하면서 그 내용을 요약해 보시오.

노트테이킹

milk diet elimi. reasons	X good
bone fractures	O → X D-galactose X ← fermented - chee, yog. ↓ D-gal.

toxins antibiotics contami.	X discard / throw gov. test X sold
nut. - fish/bean protein. B	O → X same eat ↑ ↑ consume

The reading passage and the lecture both discuss whether milk should be removed from people's diet. The writer states that people should eliminate milk with three pieces of scientific evidence. However, the lecturer disagrees with the argument, saying that it is not a good idea.

First of all, the lecturer doubts the writer's point that people who drink milk regularly are more likely to suffer bone fractures. She argues that it is partially true. Although the writer and the lecturer both agree that the correlation between drinking milk and bone fractures can be seen, the speaker points out that it can be prevented by consuming fermented milk products. This is because cheese or yogurt has a relatively small amount of D-galactose, which is a by-product of consuming milk and causes bone fractures.

Secondly, the lecturer refutes the argument of the reading passage that antibiotics in milk can be passed on to people. She states that it is not true. This is because farmers should discard or throw away milk contaminated with antibiotics. In response to the mentioned evidence in the reading passage, the lecturer presents contrary evidence that the side-effect of consuming milk with cow antibiotics could not affect customers. In fact, the government conducts random tests on milk, and would not allow milk companies to buy contaminated milk from farmers.

Finally, the speaker doubts the writer's argument that people can consume nutrients found in milk from other sources. She contends that it is partially true. In the reading passage and the listening lecture, the nutrients found in milk are also found in fish or beans, but in the listening part, the lecturer says the amount of those nutrients, such as protein and B vitamin, are lower than milk. Therefore, they would be a poor replacement for milk because a person would need to consume so much additional food to get the same amount of nutrients found in milk.

(319 words)

독해 지문과 강의는 모두 사람들의 식단에서 우유를 없애야 하는지에 대해 논의한다. 글쓴이는 세 가지 과학적 증거와 함께 우유를 없애야 한다고 진술한다. 하지만, 강의 진행자는 그것이 좋은 생각이 아니라고 말하며 그 주장에 동의하지 않는다.

우선 강의 진행자는 우유를 규칙적으로 마시는 사람이 골절상을 입을 확률이 높다는 글쓴이의 지적에 의문을 제기한다. 강의 진행자는 그것이 부분적으로 사실이라고 주장한다. 우유 섭취와 뼈 골절의 상관 관계를 알 수 있다는 점에는 글쓴이와 강의 진행자 모두 공감하지만,

강의 진행자는 발효유 제품을 섭취함으로써 예방할 수 있다고 지적한다. 이는 치즈나 요구르트는 우유 섭취의 부산물로 뼈 골절을 일으키는 D-갈락토스가 상대적으로 적기 때문이다.

둘째, 강의 진행자는 우유 속 항생제가 사람에게 전해질 수 있다는 독해 지문의 주장을 반박한다. 강의 진행자는 그것이 사실이 아니라고 말한다. 이는 농부들이 항생제에 오염된 우유를 폐기하거나 버려야 하기 때문이다. 강의 진행자는 독해 지문에서 언급한 증거에 대해 우유에 소 항생제를 첨가해 섭취하는 부작용이 고객에게 영향을 미치지 않을 수 있다는 반대 증거를 제시한다. 사실, 정부는 우유에 대해 무작위로 실험을 하고, 우유 회사들이 농부들로부터 오염된 우유를 사는 것을 허락하지 않는다.

마지막으로, 강의 진행자는 사람들이 우유에서 발견되는 영양분을 다른 공급원에서 섭취할 수 있다는 글쓴이의 주장에 회의적이다. 그녀는 그것이 부분적으로 사실이라고 주장한다. 독해 지문과 청해 강의에서, 우유에서 발견되는 영양소가 생선이나 콩에서도 발견되지만, 청해 파트에서는, 강의 진행자가 단백질과 비타민 B 등 이들 영양소의 양이 우유보다 더 낮다고 말한다. 그러므로, 우유에서 발견되는 영양소의 양과 같은 양을 얻기 위해서 너무 많은 추가 음식을 섭취해야 하기 때문에, 그것들은 우유에 대한 불충분한 대체품이 될 것이다.

어휘

consume 섭취하다, 소비하다 correlation 상관 관계, 연관성 fracture 골절, 금 toxin 독소 antibiotic 항생제, 항생물질 contaminate 오염시키다 substance 물질 byproduct(=by-product) 부산물, 부작용 digestion 소화 ferment 발효되다, 발효시키다 discard 폐기하다 residue 잔여물 government agencies 정부 기관들 side-effect 부작용 poor 형편없는, 불충분한 replacement 대체품

Q2 Writing for an Academic Discussion

문제 해석 및 분석

교수가 정치학 수업을 가르치고 있다. 교수의 질문에 응답하는 게시글을 작성하시오.
답변은 다음과 같이 하도록 한다.
• 본인의 의견을 표출하고 이를 뒷받침하시오.
• 본인의 말로 토론에 기여하시오.
좋은 답안은 100단어 이상으로 작성된다.

워드 교수:
앞으로 몇 주에 걸쳐 도시화와 도시 인프라에 미치는 영향에 대해 다룰 예정입니다. 다음 수업에서는 교통 체증을 줄이기 위해 도시 정부가 시행할 수 있는 가능한 솔루션에 대해 논의할 것입니다. 하지만 그 전에 이 질문을 생각해 보시기 바랍니다: 도시 정부가 교통량을 줄이기 위해 취할 수 있는 조치에는 어떤 것이 있을까요?

캐시:
나는 정부가 더 많은 기업이 원격 근무 정책을 시행하도록 장려할 수 있다고 생각합니다. 직원들이 출퇴근할 때 자가용을 이용하거나 대중교통을 이용하기 때문에 특히 출퇴근 시간대에는 교통 체증이 심해집니다. 재택근무를 하는 직원이 늘어나면 도로에 사람이 줄어들 것입니다.

패트릭:
한 가지 방법은 개인 차량 소유자에게 세금을 부과하는 것입니다. 교통 체증과 제한된 주차 공간에도 불구하고 너무 많은 사람들이 도시에서 자동차를 소유하고 있습니다. 자가용에 세금을 부과하면 사람들이 자가용을 구입하거나 사용하지 않게 될 것입니다. 대신 사람들은 걷거나 대중교통을 이용할 것입니다.

Cathy and Patrick gave good examples of ways the city government could reduce traffic. Certainly, remote work and taxation on private vehicles can alleviate traffic congestion. However, they did not mention another important method of reducing heavy traffic. In my opinion, the city government should consider improving public transportation. This is because having easier access to buses and subway lines will lead to more people using them instead of cars. For example, I had been driving my car to campus since the nearest bus stop was a thirty-minute walk away. Thankfully, a new subway line recently opened near my house, and I am now taking the subway to campus instead. Therefore, improving public transportation must be seriously considered.

(118 words)

캐시와 패트릭은 사람들의 수명을 연장하는 요인에 대한 좋은 예시를 들었습니다. 확실히, 원격 근무와 개인 차량에 대한 과세는 교통 혼잡을 완화할 수 있습니다. 하지만, 그들은 교통 체증을 줄일 수 있는 다른 중요한 요소를 언급하지 않았습니다. 내 생각에는, 시 정부가 대중교통 개선을 고려해야 한다고 생각합니다. 이는 버스와 지하철을 더 쉽게 이용할 수 있다면 더 많은 사람들이 자가용 대신 대중교통을 이용하게 될 것이기 때문입니다. 예를 들어, 나는 가장 가까운 버스 정류장이 걸어서 30분 거리에 있기 때문에 차를 몰고 캠퍼스로 통학했습니다. 다행히 최근 집 근처에 지하철 노선이 새로 개통되어 지금은 지하철을 타고 캠퍼스로 출근하고 있습니다. 그러므로, 대중교통 개선은 진지하게 고려되어야 합니다.

urbanization 도시화 infrastructure 인프라, 사회 기반 시설 measure 조치 implement 시행하다 remote work 원격 근무 public transportation 대중 교통 rush hour 출퇴근 시간 tax 세금을 부과하다 alleviate 완화하다 traffic congestion(=traffic jam) 교통 체증